THE ECONOMETRICS OF DISEQUILIBRIUM

STUDIES IN MATHEMATICAL AND MANAGERIAL ECONOMICS

Editors

HENRI THEIL

HERBERT GLEJSER

VOLUME 26

NORTH-HOLLAND PUBLISHING COMPANY
AMSTERDAM • NEW YORK • OXFORD

THE ECONOMETRICS OF DISEQUILIBRIUM

ROGER J. BOWDEN

Professor of Applied Economics
Department of Economics
University of Western Australia

NORTH-HOLLAND PUBLISHING COMPANY
AMSTERDAM · NEW YORK · OXFORD

ISBN: 0 444 85251 4

Publishers:

NORTH-HOLLAND PUBLISHING COMPANY
AMSTERDAM • NEW YORK • OXFORD

Sole distributors for the U.S.A. and Canada:
ELSEVIER NORTH-HOLLAND, INC.
52 VANDERBILT AVENUE,
NEW YORK, N.Y. 10017

Library of Congress Cataloging in Publication Data

Bowden, Roger John.
The econometrics of disequilibrium.

(Studies in mathematical and managerial economics ; v. 26)
Includes bibliographical references and index.
1. Equilibrium (Economics) 2. Econometrics.
I. Title. II. Series.
HB145.B68 330'.01'8 78-21599
ISBN 0-444-85251-4

First edition 1978
Second printing 1981

PRINTED IN THE NETHERLANDS

INTRODUCTION TO THE SERIES

This is a series of books concerned with the quantitative approach to problems in the social and administrative sciences. The studies are in particular in the overlapping areas of mathematical economics, econometrics, operational research, and management science. Also, the mathematical and statistical techniques which belong to the apparatus of modern social and administrative sciences have their place in this series. A well-balanced mixture of pure theory and practical applications is envisaged, which ought to be useful for universities and for research workers in business and government.

The Editors hope that the volumes of this series, all of which relate to such a young and vigorous field of research activity, will contribute to the exchange of scientific information at a truly international level.

THE EDITORS

PREFACE

"Equilibrium", Keynes is reported to have said, "is blither". It is also known that he thought much the same of econometrics, so that one can be less than confident in supposing that he would have approved of a project such as this. Nevertheless it is true that disequilibrium econometrics has caught on and that much of the motivation for this research effort arises out of recent discussion in the theoretical literature of the relationship between Keynesian and neoclassical forms of thought. As difficult as some of these ideas are, it is one of the constraints that econometricians have to live with, that their empirical modelling is even more difficult. So far we can claim an adequate account of the specification and testing of only the most modest of disequilibrium representations. We may single out at least two areas in which our techniques are manifestly deficient. One is the development of an adequate rule for quantity adjustment, even in an isolated market. The other is the representation of multimarket models in which perceived constraints in one market may affect behaviour in another.

In writing this book I have accordingly had two aims in mind. In the first place, to develop a set of ideas I had been thinking about since late 1975 or early 1976 when I was on leave at the Institute for Advanced Studies in Vienna. The PAMEQ methods, as they are called in the book, are the outcome. Since I wrote this material I have come across similar or related ideas in the work of others.[1] Thus I should not want to claim priority for the basic idea itself. There seems, however to be virtue in presenting a systematic account of the representation with due attention to requirements of consistency with respect to the equilibrium case, on the one hand, and to the way in which it facilitates problems of estimation and inference, on the other.

My second aim was rather different in kind. The book format offers a freedom which journal editors cannot, the opportunity to prospect a little. One need not be wholly constrained to producing a cut and polished jewel, but one can within limits wander with the hope of picking up a few stones which may be indications of more valuable finds to come. Particularly in the latter part of the book, I have laid stress on the problems of quantity adjustment and have tried to suggest one or two possibly fruitful lines of attack, without at the same time having produced what could be regarded as a definitive treatment. Such matters of specification are what I should perceive as the once and future problems of an econometrics of disequilibrium.

Writing in an area of rapid development has its risks, and one of these is to be superseded by recent results. At the time of writing the bulk of the book, as it has gone to print, remains intact (so to speak) but there is one recent result which I ought to mention. In sections 2.3 (mixed distributions) and 5.4 (the noisy-clearing short-side model) it is asserted that the method of maximum-likelihood is not available. Very recent work[2] has shown that provided the domain of alternative parameters excludes certain "singular" points, this assertion is not true. Thus provided these singular points are recognised in advance, there need be no problem with the application of maximum-likelihood methods to such problems.

The most pleasant task in writing this preface is to say thank you. I have been greatly helped by the various people and the anonymous referees who have commented on the various papers in which some of the material was first presented. I am grateful to the editors and publishers of the *Journal of Monetary Economics*, in which much of chapter 8 first appeared, and of the *International Economic Review*, in respect of parts of chapters 3 and 5, for permission to reproduce this material. I should also like to take this opportunity of expressing my appreciation to the Institute for Advanced Studies in Vienna for their hospitality from September 1975 to May 1976. At the University of Western Australia, Darrell Turkington was always helpful on general questions of asymptotic theory. Ms. Dawn Lorimer drew the final versions of the diagrams. The manuscript was typed by Mrs. Marie Green in a virtuoso exhibition of speed, accuracy and beauty of presentation. Finally I should like to thank my wife, for putting up with it all.

Perth, Western Australia.

Footnotes to Preface

[1]For example a study of mortgage rationing by D.M. Jaffee (1972) and a study of U.K. wages and prices by J.D. Sargan ("Wages and Prices in the United Kingdom: A Study in Econometric Methodology" in *Econometric Models for National Economic Planning* (ed) P.E. Hart, G. Mills and J.K. Whittaker, Butterworths, London 1964).

[2]References: N.M. Kiefer "Discrete Parameter Variation: Efficient Estimation of a Switching Regression Model", *Econometrica* Vol. 46 No. 2 (March 1978) and R.J. Bowden "The Consistent Root of the Likelihood Equations as Maximum: A Postscript to the Theory of Parametric Identification", University of Western Australia, August 1978. In terms of the discriminant function $H_1(\theta;\theta_0)$ of chapter 2, there are singular points (θ) at which $H_1(\theta;\theta_0)$ fails to exist.

TABLE OF CONTENTS

CHAPTER ONE

A GENERAL PREVIEW

Econometrics, we like to think, is the fusion of statistical practice with economic theory, with the object of identifying structural relationships or regularities. Like most scientific enquiry, the progress of positive economics has been characterised by an interaction between theorising and observations of the real world. The immediate stimulus to theorising is often a matter of personal or informal observations and the establishment of what have been called "stylised facts". J.M. Keynes' *General Theory* is perhaps of this character. Or the stimulus may arise from a systematic and detailed study of empirical series with little or no attempt at formal model building. The monetary history by M. Friedman and A. Schwartz [1963] is a good example. However what distinguishes the proudest achievements of econometrics is that they attempt to identify, test and further develop existing theoretical constructs of genuine informational content. In this respect the interpretation by J. Hicks [1937] of the elements of Keynes' *General Theory* could be regarded as a powerful intellectual stimulus for the development of econometric model building as we know it today. The paradigm involved is that of a linear simultaneous and stochastic set of equations. The specification and estimation theory for this paradigm was begun with the work of J. Tinbergen [e.g. 1939], T. Haavelmo [1943] and developed further in the work of T.C. Koopmans and others [see e.g. Koopmans [1950]]. The discovery in the fifties of computationally tractable methods of repeated least squares, associated with the names of H. Theil and R.L. Basmann, enabled development and estimation of the formidable macroeconometric models of the late fifties and sixties.

Just as the Keynes/Hicks structural system lead to the econometric theory of linear simultaneous stochastic models, so too have recent "reinterpretations" of Keynes suggested a need for new empirical paradigms. The idea that markets may not "clear" that is, may persist in a state of disequilibrium, has recently been viewed as central to the reconciliation of Keynesian macroeconomics with individual choice theory and general equilibrium analysis. The new respectability of such ideas has lead to diffusion of interest from this specific context to others, microeconomic as well as macroeconomic. This has called forth econometric interest in specifications and estimation techniques for models of markets in disequilibrium.

To be sure, there are those who do not believe that there is in fact any tendency for markets to persist out of equilibrium, provided the latter is properly specified; or that if there is, such markets are not to be counted among those of policy interest. The proper resolution of these debates is simply to recognise that "equilibrium" should be regarded as a testable hypothesis. Any specification or estimation techniques developed for models of markets in disequilibrium should therefore allow the facility of testing whether the system is in fact an equilibrium one. In this respect, such methods might be of greater generality than existing equilibrium approaches, which do not allow the possibility of testing whether the system is in fact a disequilibrium one. In summary we should make it clear that we do not regard it as an article of faith that markets at large, or any particular market, are characterised by persistent states of disequilibrium. But we do think the profession should endeavour to develop paradigms which will at least treat such statements as testable propositions.

That economic variables may adjust only slowly to new equilibrium levels is hardly a new idea in econometrics - a wide and popular variety of partial adjustment mechanisms attests to the contrary. It is interesting to note, however, that this kind of specification has never been developed to the point of modelling an entire system. A theory behind such paradigms is developed in the present study in chapter three. However, even if partial adjustment can be applied to prices, it does not in general follow that we can at the same time countenance a similar mechanism for quantities. The need to construct paradigms for quantity adjustment in disequilibrium remains one of the most pressing burdens of any econometrics of disequilibrium. Any realistic specification, it seems, may have to be highly nonlinear, as in the "short-side" models of chapter six. The burden on techniques of estimation and inference is therefore the greater. It is not too much to say that the bulk of formal development in econometrics is concerned with processes which are either stationary or semi-stationary. For instance, the recent development of methods of regression based on the frequency domain ("Hannan estimators") assumes both harmonizable processes for the error terms and exogenous variables, and a linear ARMA-type mechanism relating these to the endogenous variables. That nonlinear and nonstationary estimation theory is relatively underdeveloped is a matter not only of its inherent difficulty but of the lack of sufficiently general or representative paradigms. The establishment of such representations for quantities in disequilibrium therefore involves close interest in nonlinear estimation theory. For this reason chapter two of the present study is explicitly devoted to general matters of nonlinear estimation.

The rest of the present chapter will be devoted to amplifying some of the foregoing considerations. Some preliminary remarks are in order. Throughout the present study we shall make intensive use of the Marshallian supply/demand apparatus, the "two blades of the scissors" closing on the resulting equilibrium price. We do not use this apparatus out of an intrinsic belief that it represents the best possible way to approach any problem of disequilibrium. Instead we view it pragmatically as the most general and robust framework available for a whole class of problems. In speaking of this very basic model, we shall speak of one axis as "price" and the other as "quantity". Obviously, with appropriate limitations specific to the problem actually being discussed, the same model is applicable to situations where the axes are labelled differently - "wage rate" for "price" and "employment" for "quantity", to take an obvious example. Moreover the emphasis, not only in this chapter but throughout the entire study, is on developing estimable specifications. In this respect, theoreticians are a privileged caste. They need only specify some monotonic transformation of excess demand as prices, or some general exchange rule governing the distribution of endowments in a non-tatonnement dynamics, in order to establish the existence of some equilibrium or construct a Liapounov function and prove stability. Econometricians have to be more specific, to specify the precise functional form of the demand or supply functions, or the price adjustment rule or the determination of quantities. To the theorist, then, the models of the kind discussed in this book must have an air of *dèja-vu*. That is the privilege of the arm-chair.

1.1 Price Adjustment

The classical textbook view of the operations of markets is one in which prices react freely and quickly to discrepancies between demand and supply. The Walrasian auctioneer is the most celebrated rationalisation of such an adjustment process. According to this formalisation, things are ordered as if there were an auctioneer balancing up offers to buy or sell at each price he calls. If there is an excess of offers to buy over offers to sell he tries another, higher price. The bidding is closed when offers are balanced, and only at this point do transactions take place. Unquestionably there are real-world markets in which something at least approximating this process occurs. One need think only of the stock exchange or commodity exchange. In any market where (a) information about available goods and their prices is freely available and (b) there are no institutional or organised barriers to price adjustment or to offers to buy or sell, the Walrasian auctioneer may properly be said to exist in shadow, if not in substance.

The question is whether there exist markets in which the above two conditions ((a) and (b)) are not met. Such markets patently do exist and are moreover of substantial economic importance. Let us consider first the violation of condition (a). Sellers may not be aware of the asking prices of other sellers. For this and other reasons, a range of such asking prices may come to exist. Buyers may therefore have to spend time and money in searching the market to discover a suitable seller. Thus if for any reason the supply curve shifts to the right (higher supply price), it may take time for buyers to realise that the shift is general. During this time an inventory of unsold goods may build up, so that we could say that the market is in a state of temporary disequilibrium.

There has in recent times been a great volume of work in what has become known as the economics of information. Much of this literature has been devoted explicitly to the way in which markets go about the "clearing" process. (For a survey see M. Rothschild [1973], and for applications to the labour market the volume edited by E. Phelps [1970]). We have noted above that imperfect information may lead to temporary disequilibrium. Just how "temporary" is a topic of some debate, one which has a bearing on the very different views of the world of neoclassical economists on the one hand and Keynesians, on the other.

As mentioned above (condition (b)) there may also be institutional barriers to effective offers to buy or sell on the part of individual agents. This categorisation may overlap with that based on imperfect information. Take for example the pricing practice, widespread in concentrated industries, known as "normal" or "target" pricing.[1] Price is set by sellers to achieve a desired rate of return expressed as a markup on either full costs or more usually costs evaluated at some "normal" level of output (say three-quarter capacity). Such pricing mechanisms may be viewed as a response to the lack of information about either the demand curve for the product in the coming period or else about the reaction of competitors. In respect of the latter it may well be that a uniform pricing code represents a tacit agreement among oligopolistic competitors. According to this, common cost increases (such as those stemming from an externally imposed wage award) may be passed on into prices with little risk to the stability of the industry concerned.

In some cases, the unfettered operations of free markets have, in their instability, been viewed as deleterious to the long-term interests of producers. Of growing importance in many countries is the control of supply by the creation of producer boards, often with power to compulsorily acquire all the output for sale. Very often such boards set prices and in doing so may not necessarily aim to clear the market in any one period or sale. They may set prices in response to underlying cost pressures, perhaps with a genuflection to the current state of demand. If the market does not clear, unsold goods are stockpiled by the authority or if perishable may be redirected to less profitable uses.[2] It will be noted that such pricing behaviour is rather similar to that described earlier for many concentrated industries. We shall refer to it in general form as the "administered pricing hypothesis".

The labour market is important enough to warrant special treatment so far as category (b) imperfections are concerned. The relevant agents here are labour unions and employers and the institutional setting is the machinery for settling wage and related disputes. The downward rigidity of money wages, and increasingly of real wages, has been widely blamed for the growth in unemployment in recent times. It is apposite here to note several different views of the relationship between unemployment and wage rates. According to one view, characteristic of more extreme proponents of neoclassical doctrines, declines in employment are temporary phenomena. Faced with falls in the demand for their product, firms lower wage rates. These lowered rates are viewed by their workers as atypical of ruling wage rates. They then quit to seek a better deal elsewhere. As the realisation sinks in that such rates are now general, the workers are eventually forced to seek employment at the new lower rate. Employment therefore rises again. The disequilibrium phenomenon of layoffs has no part to play in this theory, which indeed rings oddly to those of us accustomed to militant unionism. A consequence of the latter is the inability of any worker to seek employment at a lower wage rate. It is worth remarking, however, that the downward inflexibility of wages is not necessarily the creation of union pressure. Whatever the explanation, this downward rigidity of wages is a common fact of experience in most western economies. We take it as creating a *prima facie* case for the existence at certain times of disequilibrium in the labour market.

We have seen that for several different reasons, prices may not adjust freely to equate the forces of supply and demand. The functional relationship between price adjustment and excess demand will evidently depend on the context and causes of the inflexibility. For instance, partial adjustment mechanisms, which are used extensively in this study, may not be appropriate for labour markets unless they are suitably qualified with the introduction of a discontinuity in the adjustment parameter in referring to excess demand or excess supply. With no such formal institutional barriers, on the other hand, prices may adjust equally freely in both directions. The latter supposition is beyond question easier to handle from the statistical point of view, but we shall pay some attention (chapter 6.1) to the more difficult case where adjustment speeds are asymmetric in the manner described.

1.2 Quantities: Single Market

We have seen that prices may not move instantaneously to establish equality between demand and supply. If this is the case, transacted quantities will not be equal to the equilibrium quantity. The specification of disequilibrium quantities is the subject of this section. Even in the simplest case of a single market, considered in this section, quantity dynamics must be considered along with price determination.

1.2.1 Short-side Models. Perhaps the simplest dynamics is the following: price is determined by a Walrasian[3] adjustment mechanism (in continuous time):

$$\dot{p} = g(D(p) - S(p)) \ . \quad (1)$$

Here D(p) and S(p) are the demand and supply schedules and as usual a dot denotes the time derivative. The monotonic function g is continuous but may not be differentiable at zero. Given p at any point in time, quantities actually transacted are determined by the short-side of the market:

$$Q = \min(D,S) \ . \quad (2)$$

Figure 1.1 illustrates.

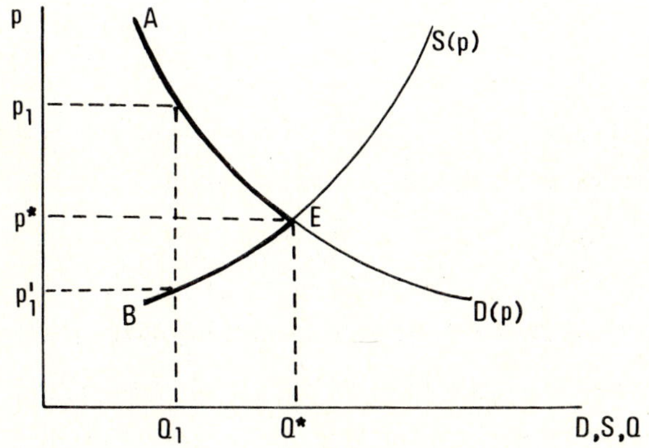

Figure 1.1

The equilibrium point E is denoted (p^*, Q^*). If price is currently p_1, the quantity Q_1 is the resulting transacted quantity, determined by the quantity people wish to buy at this high price rather than the larger quantity producers wish to sell. The dark-shaded locus AEB is the "short-side" of the market, the locus of transacted quantities corresponding to the range of prices. Unlike the demand and supply correspondences, the inverse mapping from Q to p is not single-valued; Q_1 for instance may be associated with either p_1 or p_1' in figure 1.1. The estimation difficulties this causes are discussed very extensively in chapter 5 and part of chapter 6.

The basic idea behind this model is that consumers cannot be sold more than they want, and that not more can be sold than is produced. Although these seem unexceptional as guiding principles, the particular form in which they are incorporated (namely (1) and (2)) may be questioned on several grounds:

(i) There is first the meaning of D(p) and S(p). To write them, as we have done, as functions only of p indicates that they are to be regarded as stable schedules which are in particular unaffected by the past history of the system. But are the consequences of a history of either excess demand or excess supply to be dismissed so lightly? Consider, for instance, excess supply in any one period, and suppose that the good in question is durable. The existence of unsold balances (or as they now are, inventories) of these goods may be expected to affect the supply of goods coming on to the market in the following period. Even if the good is not durable, having to dispose of unsold balances is a traumatic event which may be expected to enter current supply decisions. The general point is that the absence of a Walrasian auctioneer makes great demands on our ability to specify the way in which the consequences of disequilibrium become manifest in the behavioural schedules of economic agents.[4] Some of the difficulties involved are discussed at length in chapter 8.

(ii) The informational requirements of the clearing rule (2) are rather extreme. The strict short side model implies that at the equilibrium point E, all that is offered is sold. This implies that all buyers must have the facility of making successful contact with sellers in the period considered. Similar remarks hold for other prices; if $p < p^*$, all sellers are successfully sought out by buyers and if $p > p^*$, all buyers are successfully located by sellers. But if information of this quality is available to buyers and sellers, it is not at all apparent why the market should persist in a state of disequilibrium, for this is what is implied by the price adjustment equation (1), with $g' < \infty$. Evidently the strict short-side model is best suited to situations where the imperfection, if one can call it that, is not a result of deficiencies in information. The administered pricing model is such a possibility. In the absence of such gross imperfections, however, there is a manifest case for trying to generalise the short-side model so that in the region of equilibrium, at least, not all that is offered is sold.

(iii) Equations (1) and (2) involve a certain asymmetry with regard to the treatment of prices and quantities. If it is true that demand and supply are stable functions only of current prices, then it follows from (1) that the history of prices is entirely separable from that of transacted quantities. If this indeed adequately describes the process such a separable dynamics is very convenient. In many applications, the determination of market quantities is not at all transparent. Rather than risk specification error in this respect, one may be quite happy to restrict the scope of analysis to the reduced-form, as it were, for price determination. Such a procedure is often followed in empirical work. We have formalised a basic version in chapter 3, where it is called the "excess demand problem". On the other hand, even for this class of problem, the identification of demand and supply schedules on the basis only of price information is not usually possible. Comparative static analysis cannot be carried out with the fitted model. Even for separable models it will therefore be desirable to specify some form of quantity adjustment.

Some of the most interesting questions relate to models in which the dynamic analysis of price cannot be separated from that of quantity. A model of this kind is analysed in chapter 8, and is implicit in the empirical analysis of chapter 7. By and large, however, general specifications or paradigms for non-separable systems remain as outstanding issues.

1.2.2 Imperfect Clearing. Following on from the discussion of §1.2.1 (in particular of point (ii)) we might consider relaxing the quantity determination (2) to allow for more imperfect information on the part of economic agents. Instead of the "bang-bang" locus of figure 1.1 we suppose that the locus of observed prices and transactions is the smooth curve shown dark-shaded in figure 1.2. We shall refer to this locus as the "clearing path". The implication is that even at equilibrium prices the market is not completely "cleared".

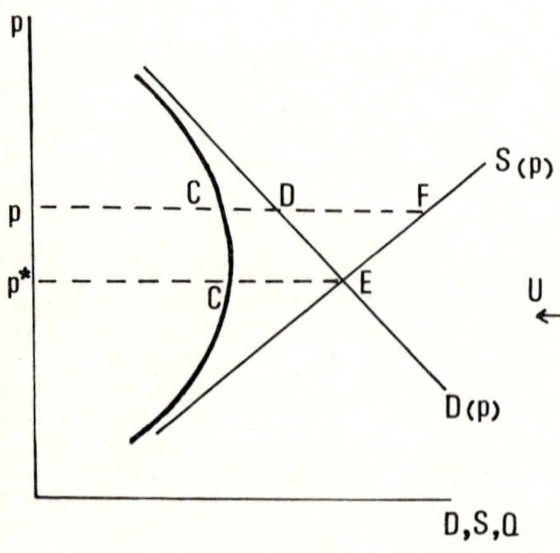

Figure 1.2

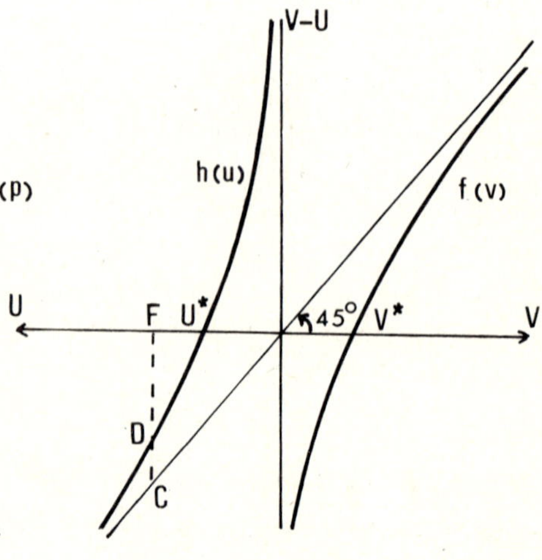

Figure 1.3

Such ideas are perhaps best known from the labour market. Even when the supply and demand for labour is in balance there may still exist a "frictional" level of unemployment, associated with an equilibrium rate of quitting and replacement. This is shown as the distance GE in figure 1.2 and denoted U^*. Denote by U the horizontal distance between the clearing path and the supply schedule (e.g. CF) and by V the corresponding distance in respect of the demand schedule (e.g. CD). An alternative representation of figure 1.2 was constructed by A. Hines [1971] and is shown as figure 1.3. Here V is shown along the R.H. horizontal axis and U is shown along the L.H. horizontal axis. Excess demand for labour is shown along the vertical axis, as V-U. Considering for instance the left-hand branch the lettering is shown to correspond with figure 1.2. The distance CF is equal to U. The distance CD is V and the difference V-U = DF. Still considering the left-hand side we could write the left-hand clearing branch as

(3) $$V-U = h(U)\ , \qquad h(U^*) = 0\ .$$

If we are to preserve the correspondence of figure 1.3 with figure 1.2, the R.H. branch must simply mirror the L.H. branch of the clearing curve of figure 1.3. That is, we must have $f(V) = h(U)$, i.e. f must be such that $f(U + h(U)) = h(U)$. Note however that such consistency is not a necessary feature of the problem, and an arbitrary f and h could be designed. This procedure could be thought of as a relaxation of the simple path of figure 1.2.

We note that the dynamic adjustment (1) may also be generalised. In a market such as that for labour, characterised by imperfect information, the difficulty firms have in locating suitable employees may not be functions only of excess demand (here, V-U). A situation where excess demand is falling may imply a different attitude to hiring and firing or job acceptance from one where it is rising. Hence we could write

(4) $\dot{W} = \phi(V-U, \dot{V-U})$.

In the general context, the rate of price change depends not only upon excess demand but also upon the rate of change of excess demand. Adjustment mechanisms of this type are discussed in chapter 3.4.1 (where they are called "acceleration modes") and are employed in the Phillips curve analysis of chapter 6.2.1.

1.3 Multiple Market Systems

As suggested earlier, much of the interest in the study of disequilibrium economics derives from current theories in macroeconomics, where statistical aggregates referring to an interplay of several or many markets are involved. It is worth remarking, however, that disequilibrium manifests itself also in microeconomic situations; indeed such applications predate the macroeconomic insights of the last few years. A conspicuous example is the effect of the rationing of credit on financial decisions. This has always been seen as one reason for the firm's V-shaped cost of credit curve, at least among those who regard the firm's cost of capital as dependent upon the leverage structure of its liabilities. A formal theory of such rationing was developed (much later) by D.M. Jaffee and F. Modigliani[5] [1969] (see also D.M. Jaffee [1971]), who distinguished "equilibrium" from "disequilibrium" rationing. The first concept refers to the fact that because common interest rates may be set over a class of borrowers with differing risk characteristics, some of the riskier borrowers will be unsatisfied with their allocation of credit and must presumably seek accommodation at a higher rate. The second ("disequilibrium") kind of rationing refers to the sort of circumstance we have discussed in section 1.2, where rates of interest may not adjust instantaneously to equalise the total force of demand and supply.

One particular kind of credit rationing is of special interest, both because of its widespread occurrence at certain times and because of the policy importance of the market concerned. Expansionary times in the market for new or used homes are usually accompanied by increases in the demand for mortgage accommodation at existing rates of interest. Since mortgage rates are often sticky, indeed are sometimes of the character of administered prices, the

the consequent rationing of the available mortgage funds has been viewed as an important ingredient in housing-market dynamics. If prospective house purchasers cannot obtain all the finance they desire, their demand for houses (*in toto*) will diminish. But the housing market is not the only one affected by such a contingency. Faced with the finance constraint, the individual may elect to increase his own equity in a prospective purchase. Devotion of more of his financial wealth (rather than human wealth) to this purpose will adversely affect his demand for other durable goods, such as motor cars. Thus a constraint on the individual's actions in one market may affect his demand or supply decisions in respect of other markets. The specification and identification of "spillover effects" constitutes a major task for the econometrics of disequilibrium. Attention is devoted to this problem in sections 6.3.1, 6.4.1 and 7.2.1 of the present study.

Discussion of financial constraints serves to introduce the macroeconomics of recent "reinterpretations" of Keynes associated particularly with the names of D. Patinkin ([1965], Ch.13), R. Clower [1965] and A. Leijonhufvud [1968]. In this case, the ultimate financial constraint is the medium of exchange, money. Individual offers to purchase may be made only in terms of money. And money may be obtained only through successful offers of sale - of goods, assets or labour services. If the individual is constrained in his offer to sell, the money constraint on his purchases will become binding. To use the established terminology, his effective or active decisions will therefore differ from his notional or target attempts, which do not involve the money constraint.

All this does not make the econometrician's task any easier, or the more guided by the precepts of economic theory. Suppose that it were possible to define aggregate schedules, in the time-honoured way of simply projecting onto the giant screen the decisions of a representative individual. Is it meaningful in any sense to make these the notional schedules, and if so will they ever be observable? At the aggregate level, the econometrician has available the economy's state-vector, incorporating prices and aggregate quantities. The latter are quantities actually transacted, which suggests that it would be more appropriate to attempt to identify some schedule of aggregate effective demands. But what laws of aggregation apply to such demands, are such aggregated schedules ever stable functions of the aggregates, and what guide if any might such aggregated schedules give to comparative static propositions? These are genuine worries, but they have not prevented us using aggregate effective schedules. As Clower [1965] pointed out the "Keynesian" consumption function, which related consumption to income (in the sense that the latter figures in National Income statistics), is of this character. Income realised by the household incorporates the constraint of how much labour it can sell. However, even if we decide that aggregation of effective schedules is possible and meaningful, there are further problems. Are dynamic adjustment mechanisms to be specified in terms of notional or effective schedules? If the former, how can we ever identify the sources of demand and supply pressure? Some of these very difficult matters are discussed further in chapters 4 and 6.

1.4 Disequilibrium and Macro-econometric Models

Most macro-econometric models (that is to say, stochastic models governing the behaviour of aggregates such as national income, the money supply, the rate of interest and so on) are equilibrium structures. On occasion this is explicitly recognised. Consider, for example the neoclassical investment analysis associated particularly with the work of D.W. Jorgensen [e.g. [1965]] which has found wide application as a basis for the investment function. One implication is that the firm can sell all the output it wishes at going product and input prices. This implies that the industry can never be in a state of excess supply. Likewise, the decision to invest is presumed unaffected by financing possibilities, a proposition typically associated with perfect capital markets. The equilibrium character of these assumptions has been recognised and attempts[6] have been made to modify the theory to allow for more inflexible output prices. The necessity to do so is apparent from a consideration of models in which, while the investment function is neoclassical, the pricing equation (usually located in another module) is based on administered modes.

More often, however, the equilibrium character of macro-econometric models is not recognised. Indeed there may be some terminological confusion involved. Consider the following Hicks/Hansen/Samuelson multiplier-accelerator model.[7] We shall suppose that Y, C, I refer to real (rather than nominal) income, consumption and investment.

(5)(a) $Y_t = C_t + I_t$

(b) $C_t = \beta_0 + \beta_1 Y_{t-1}$

(c) $I_t = \alpha_0 + \alpha_1 (Y_{t-1} - Y_{t-2})$.

This model has a long-run stationary point, namely $\bar{Y} = \frac{\alpha_0 + \beta_0}{1 - \beta_1}$. The stationary point is sometimes referred to as an "equilibrium" and deviations from this stationary point are taken as indicating a state of "disequilibrium". This terminology is misleading[8] for the model above is an equilibrium one. It may be written in full as:

$$(6)(a) \quad Y_t^d = C_t^d + I_t^d$$

$$(b) \quad Y_t = C_t + I_t$$

$$(c) \quad C_t^d = \beta_0 + \beta_1 Y_{t-1}$$

$$(d) \quad I_t^d = \alpha_0 + \alpha_1 (Y_{t-1} - Y_{t-2})$$

$$(e) \quad C_t = C_t^d$$

$$(f) \quad Y_t = Y_t^d \,.$$

Here the superscript d indicates the appropriate quantity demanded. There are six equations in the six unknowns $Y_t, C_t, I_t, Y_t^d, C_t^d, I_t^d$. The two last equations are of special significance. The last, in particular is a specification of genuine informational content; the total supply of goods (Y) is always equal to the total demand (Y^d).

If we did not impose this equation the system would be incomplete and we would have to seek alternatives for the determination of actual income in the resulting state of disequilibrium. In other words we need a theory of the supply of goods. However this is done,[9] a theory must also be constructed as to the division of this actual output into actual consumption and actual saving. Suppose, for instance that $C^d + I^d > Y$. Either consumers or producers will be left unsatisfied, and the model should specify who suffers the shortfall. If consumers, equation (6)(c) may no longer be taken as a stable relationship between actual consumption and income. If producers, a similar conclusion holds in respect of equation (6)(d). Suppose on the other hand that $Y^d < Y$. In this case actual investment will incorporate unwanted inventory accumulation. Realistic inventory equations should incorporate the "bang-bang" behaviour involving a switch to unwarranted stocks in times of deficient demand.

Recent years have seen increasing use of partial adjustment mechanisms of various kinds. Models which incorporate such adjustment mechanisms do very often involve true disequilibrium elements. A stimulating example is the model of disequilibrium neoclassical growth in continuous time constructed by A.R. Bergstrom and C.R. Wymer [1976] and fitted to the postwar U.K. economy. This has its intellectual origin in the earlier growth models of A.R. Bergstrom [1962] and A.W. Phillips [1961]. The Bergstrom/Wymer econometric model consists in 13 equations, of which 3 are identities. For our present purposes, it will be convenient to consider only the equations relating directly to the product market. Following the original notation, these equations are:

(7)(a) $$\frac{DC}{C} = \gamma_1 \log\left(\frac{\beta_1 Y}{C}\right)$$

(b) $$Dk = \gamma_3\left[\gamma_4\left\{\beta_3\left(\frac{Y}{K}\right)^{1+\beta_4} - r + \frac{Dp}{p}\right\} + \beta_5 - k\right]$$

(c) $$DY = \gamma_5\{(1-\beta_6)(C + DK + E) - Y\} + \gamma_6\{\beta_7(C + DK + E) - S\}$$

(d) $$\frac{Dp}{p} = \gamma_{10} \log\left[\frac{\beta_{10}\beta_2 w e^{-\lambda_1 t}\left\{1 - \beta_3\left(\frac{Y}{K}\right)^{\beta_4}\right\}^{-\left(\frac{1+\beta_4}{\beta_4}\right)}}{p}\right]$$

(e) $$DS = Y + I - C - DK - E$$

Here: C,Y are real consumption and income

k = proportional rate of increase of fixed capital

p = price index for gross national expenditure and exports

r = interest rate

S = stocks (real terms)

I = real imports (<u>not</u> investment, in this context)

E = real exports.

Note that E, I, r are themselves endogenous, being determined elsewhere in the system. Disturbances are omitted here.

We shall not justify these equations in detail, referring the reader to the original sources. The productive relationships are based on a CES production function with a trend term to allow for Harrod-Neutral technological progress. A feature is the use of partial adjustment mechanisms. The general character of these equations may be illustrated by reference to the price equation (d). The numerator of the RHS incorporates marginal cost $w\frac{\partial L}{\partial Y}$ evaluated at given levels of capital stock and output. This is multiplied by a constant β_{10} which allows for the possibility of imperfect competition ($\beta_{10} = \frac{e}{e+1} \geq 1$, where e is the own-price elasticity of demand for the representative firm's product). According to (d), price adjusts upward if the value of marginal product is greater than the existing price p, and the speed of adjustment parameter is the constant γ_{10}. This is therefore a Marshallian (rather than Walrasian) dynamics; for a given level of output Y, the value of labour's marginal product corresponds to the supply price and p to the demand price. Other equations have also a partial adjustment interpretation. In (7)(a) for instance, consumption adjusts to the proportional difference between $\beta_1 Y$ and current consumption C. These partial adjustments refer to representative individual behaviour. The "equilibrium" involved is not market equilibrium but a "personal" equilibrium, in which all variables other than the object of study are assumed to be fixed. In this respect, the adjustment schemes are not the same as the PAMEQ scheme considered at length in the present study. Finally we note that equation 7(c) refers to the independent supply determination whose necessity in a disequilibrium context was mooted in our discussion of the Hicks-Hansen model.

Let us now consider the implications for the study of disequilibrium of these product market relationships. Equations (a) and (b) refer to actual or observed amounts of consumption and fixed net investment. There are two polar interpretations of these equations, based on what are held to constitute the active or effective demands for consumers and producers (in respect of capital equipment).

(i) Suppose that $C^d = \beta_1 Y$ denotes the active demand function for consumer goods. That for capital goods may be derived from

$$(Dk)^d = \gamma_4\{\beta_3\left(\frac{Y}{K}\right)^{1+\beta_4} - r + \frac{Dp}{p}\} + \beta_5 \qquad \text{(see (7)(b)).}$$

Suppose that the implied active demands are greater than supply, i.e.[10] $C^d + (DK)^d > Y + I + S$. Consumers and investors (in the physical capital sense) cannot obtain all they want. This is consistent with prices adjusting upwards according to equation (d) with a finite speed of adjustment. The partial adjustment nature of equations (a) and (b) might then represent allocational rules determining the limited instantaneous available supply of goods into consumption and investment. If this is the case, however, there must be implied constraints upon the adjustment parameter γ_1 and γ_3 which cannot either be constant or arbitrary. Moreover in periods of general excess supply, consumers and investors will be subject to no supply limitations and will be able to adjust instantaneously to their desired positions. The partial adjustment mechanisms in (a) and (b) would have to switch to full adjustment in such regimes. Finally in conditions of excess demand, as described above, equation (e) would have to be adjusted to reflect the zero floor to stocks.

(ii) Suppose, on the other hand, that the active demands in (7)(a) and (b) can be interpreted as the entire RHS of these equations. For instance, we may write $C^d = \gamma_1 \log\left(\frac{\beta_1 Y}{C}\right)$. The natural interpretation of such models is in terms of persistence models, a framework into which the empirical time-series version of M. Friedman's permanent-income hypothesis also falls. Likewise the RHS of (7)(b) may exhibit adjustment with planning and procurement lags, to a desired stock of capital. According to this interpretation, unlike (i), active consumption or investment desires are always realised. For given I, however, this implies that stocks are always sufficient to allow this. It is, indeed, quite possible that because of its exponential equilibrium growth path in the model (see Bergstrom and Wymer) the stocks variable is never zero. But there is nevertheless a snag. If consumption and investment plans are always met, there can be no excess demand. Price adjustment must be infinite in the upward direction. This is certainly incompatible with the linear price adjustment mechanism (d). It seems also to be incompatible with economic history.

Whatever the interpretation of the partial adjustment mechanisms incorporated in the product-market specifications, inconsistencies therefore appear. The Bergstrom/Wymer model is an interesting attempt and is praiseworthy in its explicit recognition of the persistence of disequilibrium states. But even in this more sophisticated model, the same difficulties appear that we have noted already in connection with a disequilibrium version of the Hicks-Hansen model, namely the stability of demand and supply schedules and the behaviour of inventories.

The Southampton model (see e.g. D.F. Heathfield and I.F. Pearce [1975]) is an example of a larger model which contains explicit references to the problem of disequilibrium. The model is disaggregated into different production sectors. In each section, if appropriate, the output equation contains terms in time, profits (actually separate positive or negative excess profits), and the discrepancy between optimum and actual capital usage. It contains also separate contributions from positive $\left(\alpha_{10}\ \Delta I^{u+}_{it-1}\right)$ and negative $\left(\alpha_8\ \Delta I^{u-}_{it-1}\right)$ unplanned inventory changes in the previous period. The price equations contain the same variables. While these price equations are worthy of comment in their own right, the inclusion in both price and product equations of unplanned inventory changes goes some way towards meeting our earlier objections as to the mutual consistency of the pricing, output and inventory equations. Viewed purely from the viewpoint of disequilibrium analysis, the Southampton model is at its weakest in the empirical identification of unplanned inventory changes. Planned inventory changes are specified as related to actual output, the assumption being that planned and actual output are one and the same. There is also a trend turn to allow for the progress of inventory management techniques. However unplanned inventory changes are then simply identified with the residual from this equation. This is plainly unsatisfactory (as the authors themselves observe). Unplanned inventories must be more closely related to actual expenditure decisions.

In summary, an adequate and economical representation of quantity adjustment processes, which will deal in consistent fashion with production, demand, pricing, inventories and unfilled orders, is one of the pressing tasks for any econometrics of disequilibrium. We shall touch at different points in the present study on various facets of the quantity adjustment problem, but we lay no claim to have provided such a representation.

1.5 General Plan

We have now raised most of the problem areas for attention in the remainder of this study. The next chapter, chapter 2, is a preliminary and general discussion and development of the nonlinear estimation theory used at various points thereafter. In chapter 3 we consider the excess demand problem, which does not involve explicit consideration of nonlinear quantity adjustment. The PAMEQ specification is introduced. This is applied in chapter 4 to the estimation of the demand for money function. In chapter 5 we encounter, in the form of the simple "short-side" model, some of the awkward problems of quantity adjustment. The probabilistic structure of this model, in its various manifestations, is examined in detail, and various estimation procedures explored. In chapter 6 we investigate possible relaxations and extensions of some of the rather extreme features of the short-side model, posing the problem as one of devising an economical and robust representation of quantity clearing in conditions of imperfect information. We consider also some applications. Because of the importance of disequilibrium in housing market dynamics, the whole of chapter 7 is devoted to the empirical investigation of important facets of this market. In the last chapter, chapter 8, we leave estimation and inference as such, and turn to consider some of the extremely difficult questions of specification for any realistic process of quantity adjustment, questions as to representation and model building which must precede any attempt at estimation. In summary, our progress is from the easier to the very difficult material, proceeding from questions of price adjustment alone to the representation of a simultaneous price and quantity dynamics. Some concluding remarks end the book.

Footnotes to Chapter 1

[1]See for example studies by A.D.N. Kaplan, J.B. Dirlam and R.F. Lanzilotti [1958], O. Eckstein and G. Fromm [1968].

[2]Egg marketing boards dispose of unsold prime eggs by making powder. Often this is a cheap and apparently virtuous form of overseas aid.

[3]We may contrast this with the dynamic Marshallian apparatus: Given Q define $p^d(Q)$ as the "demand price" and $p^s(Q)$ as the "supply price". Quantity then adjusts according to $\dot{Q} = g(p^d(Q) - p^s(Q))$. Most of the development of this study will carry over, *mutatis mutandis* to Marshallian dynamics. Although this brand of dynamics may superficially seem attractive from the viewpoint of the "Keynesian reinterpretation" there are interpretive difficulties. Out of equilibrium, it is not at all clear how the functions $p^d(Q)$ and $p^s(Q)$ are to be defined. For an example, however, see the discussion of the Bergstrom/Wymer model in section 1.4.

[4]A closely related point has been made by H.I. Grossman [1974]. Suppose that the market is in a state of excess demand so that buyers are not able to obtain the quantity they desire. They might think of dissimulating their preferences to increase their apparent chances of getting more. Similar effects might hold in respect of sellers in conditions of excess supply. Write "revealed" demands and supplies as d, s respectively.

Thus (i)(a) $d = D$ if $D < S$

$= D + \beta_d(D - S)$ if $D > S$, β_d a positive parameter.

(i)(b) $s = S + \beta_s(D - S)$ if $D < S$, $\beta_s < 0$

$= S$ otherwise

(ii) $\dot{p} = \lambda(d - s)$, λ an increasing function.

Note, however that this alternative specification is in a sense simply a transformation of the basic system (1) and (2). In respect of the price dynamics we have

$$\dot{p} = \lambda((1 - \beta_s)(D - S)) \quad \text{if } D < S$$

$$= \lambda((1 + \beta_d)(D - S)) \quad \text{if } D \geq S .$$

Even though the "notional" schedules D, S are not revealed in the market place, the pricing rule (2) is nevertheless still appropriate. Moreover $Q = \min(D,S)$ still.

[5]F. Modigliani's co-authorship of a paper developing a theory of "equilibrium" rationing sits a little oddly alongside his share in the famous Modigliani-Miller proposition 1, which asserts the independence of the firm's cost of capital from its financing decisions. There appear to be some interesting finance-theoretic implications of the Jaffee-Modigliani credit-rationing theory, which are unfortunately outside the scope of the present study.

[6]Thus H.I. Grossman [1972] argued that the Keynesian investment accelerator could arise from a neoclassical production function in the presence of a demand constraint. R.J. Bowden [1974] showed that the resulting investment path could be considered as a mixture of the unconstrained neoclassical and constrained modes.

[7]For an exposition of its properties and stability requirements a good source is R.G.D. Allen [1967], Ch. 17.7.

[8]As an example, the book by J. Van Doorn entitled "Disequilibrium Economics" [1975] is almost entirely about equilibrium models, in the sense used in this study.

[9]See later discussion of the Bergstrom/Wymer model. A perceptive discussion - on the aggregate level - of some of the difficulties caused by disequilibrium is to be found in J. Stein [1971].

[10]We have here mixed stock and flow dimensions; the correct statement should be $C^d\,dt + (DK)^d\,dt > Y\,dt + I\,dt + S$. Note also that no account is taken of depreciation of the stock of capital.

CHAPTER TWO

SOME BACKGROUND THEORY OF NONLINEAR ESTIMATION

As indicated in chapter one, we can expect nonlinearity as the rule rather than the exception in modelling disequilibrium structures. There is a mild kind of nonlinearity of fairly common occurrence in the econometrics of simultaneous systems in which, while nonlinear functions of the endogenous variables may appear together with the natural variables, the unknown parameters appear linearly. This is the "linear in parameters" specification. The identification and estimation theory of such models can sometimes be handled by means of reasonably straightforward extensions of linear theory. Unfortunately it is a feature of disequilibrium models, at least those characterised by "short-side" dynamics, that the non-linearities encountered are not of this mild order.

Indeed, the essential nature of the nonlinearities involved in these models has forced a closer examination, if not a reappraisal, of some well-established general techniques and habits of mind. The most outstanding example has been the realisation that the method of maximum-likelihood cannot be viewed as a panacea for all problems of estimation, whose applicability has hitherto been limited only by the computational capacity of existing computers and the limits of currently available techniques of numerical optimisation. In his classic paper, A. Wald [1943] imposed a set of regularity conditions on the underlying distribution generating the observations. Where such conditions are not met, nonsensical results can be generated by application of the maximum-likelihood technique. In the econometrics literature, S.M. Goldfeld and R.E. Quandt [1975] showed that a suitable choice of parameter values could result in an unbounded likelihood function. We show in chapter five that this model has the same probabilistic structure as a leading disequilibrium specification. These models share a fatal flaw - from the point of view of likelihood estimation - with the class of models known in the statistical literature as "mixtures of distributions", whose nonregularity is now well recognised.

Linear models satisfy a wide class of regularity conditions for a variety of estimation techniques. The robustness of linearity creates, in a sense, a false sense of security which has on occasion led some authors (including this one) astray in the extension to nonlinear models. It is therefore useful to present a short review of some of the general methods of nonlinear estimation which will be employed or suggested in later chapters. One of our aims in doing so is to stress the errors which can arise from the unthinking application of methods acquired in the study of linear models. Apart from such catechisms, however, our primary purpose is to achieve a useful integration of identification and estimation theory to yield a compact and self-contained statement of some of the techniques we have found useful.

2.1 Identification and Classical Maximum-Likelihood Theory

2.1.1 Identification.[1] We shall start with a review of the problem of identification. This concept, as is well known, relates to the possibility of devising any method of estimation which will yield uniquely the parameters of interest. Stated in this way, there is an absence both of rigour and of a relationship with any particular method of estimation. To investigate these problems we shall start with a rather abstract approach to the identification problem. Let us denote by θ a vector of parameters of interest. With regard to the system being studied, we write θ_o as the true value of the parameter. Although this is not available to observers - indeed it is the object of investigation - we assume that the system is deterministic to the point where such a "true" value does indeed underpin the available observations.

Denote by y an observable point (vector[2]) in a Euclidean space of some finite dimension. We assume the usual distinction between a model and the set of structures which it comprises. In the abstract, we shall mean by a model a probability distribution $F(y;\cdot)$ and by a structure that distribution for a given parameter θ. So as not to impede the discussion with mathematical detail we shall assume that F is absolutely continuous[3] in y, i.e. has a density function $f(y;\theta)$.

As well as the true value θ_o, there will exist other possible values θ, forming a subspace Θ of all possible parameters. It will be convenient, even if a little restrictive at times, to assume that Θ is compact which in the case of Euclidean space is equivalent to saying that it is closed and bounded. We shall say that the parameter vector θ_o is identified in Θ if there is no other $\theta \in \Theta$ such that, with probability one, $f(y;\theta) = f(y;\theta_o)$, where the measure is taken with respect to θ_o. On the other hand, a parameter vector θ_1 is observationally equivalent to θ_o if, with probability one, $f(y;\theta_1) = f(y;\theta_o)$. In the latter case, the true parameter point θ_o is not identified.

According to the above definition, if θ_1 is observationally equivalent to θ_o, all data points have exactly the same probability under either "hypothesis" $\theta = \theta_o$ or $\theta = \theta_1$. There is therefore no way in which θ_o and θ_1 can be distinguished on the basis of observable data. A couple of points are in order at this stage. First, we have made no reference to *a-priori* restrictions. These are supposed already incorporated in the specification of F or f, so that we are discussing at this point the amount of information contributed by the data alone. Our second point concerns the treatment of "exogenous" variables (denoted by x, say, in addition to purely endogenous variables). We may if we choose rewrite the probability density in question as $f(y,x;\theta,\alpha)$, where y now refers to the "endogenous" variables. Here θ incorporates parameters of basic interest and α represents a vector of parameters, perhaps the mean or covariance matrix of the variables in x, of only marginal interest. The above definitions, and subsequent development, will be applicable to the restriction of the parameter set to those in θ. That is we need consider only the behaviour of $f(y,x;\theta,\alpha_o)$ as a function of θ, holding α at the true value α_o. For notational convenience we shall henceforth include this case by writing as before simply $f(y;\theta)$, where y may include exogenous variables and θ may include incidental parameters. The specification of x implied is that of "stochastic" exogenous variables, which are not fixed in repeated random drawings of the endogenous variables. This has to be distinguished from the view of the exogenous variables as fixed numbers. The latter specification, perhaps the more common in econometrics, calls for special treatment and will be considered in due course.

Denote by E^o the expectation of any function of y given that the true value θ_o is holding. We define a function

(1) $$H(\theta;\theta_o) = E^o \log\left[\frac{f(y;\theta)}{f(y;\theta_o)}\right]$$

$$= \int_{-\infty}^{\infty} \log\left[\frac{f(y;\theta)}{f(y;\theta_o)}\right] f(y;\theta_o)dy \ ,$$

presuming y to have the stated range. In defining this function, we have assumed that $f(y;\theta)$ and $f(y;\theta_o)$ are absolutely continuous relative to one another, so that we cannot have $f(y;\theta_o) = 0$ without $f(y;\theta) = 0$ also, in which case the quotient is presumed to have value zero. It follows from the definitions of identification given above that the parameter θ_o is identified in Θ if and only if the equation

(2) $$H(\theta;\theta_o) = 0$$

has as solution in Θ only $\theta = \theta_o$. Note that identification may be "local" if there is some small neighbourhood of θ_o in which the solution to (2) is unique.

The relationship with maximisation theory is of central interest. For this purpose, consider the related function

(3) $$H_1(\theta;\theta_o) = E^o \log f(y;\theta) \ .$$

If θ_o is identified then $H_1(\theta;\theta_o)$ has its maximum at $\theta = \theta_o$, local or global according to whether θ is locally or globally identified. For suppose that θ and θ_o are not observationally equivalent. Then

$$H(\theta;\theta_o) = E^o \log\left[\frac{f(y;\theta)}{f(y;\theta_o)}\right]$$

$$< \log E^o\left[\frac{f(y;\theta)}{f(y;\theta_o)}\right] \qquad \text{(Jensen's inequality)}$$

$$= \log \int_{-\infty}^{\infty} \frac{f(y;\theta)}{f(y;\theta_o)} f(y;\theta_o)dy$$

$$= \log 1$$

$$= 0 \ .$$

Hence for $\theta \neq \theta_o$,

$$E^o \log f(y;\theta) < E^o \log f(y;\theta_o) ,$$

from which $H_1(\theta;\theta_o) < H_1(\theta_o;\theta_o)$, as stated. If θ_o is not identified, the maximum at $\theta = \theta_o$ will not be unique.

We have seen that θ_o is identified if and only if it corresponds to a unique maximum of the function $H_1(\theta;\theta_o)$ or equivalently of the original function $H(\theta;\theta_o)$. It is therefore natural to investigate the derivatives with respect to the elements of θ of this function. Suppose that $H(\theta;\theta_o)$ is twice differentiable at θ_o. It then follows from the maximal properties of H_1 or H that:

$$H'(\theta_o;\theta_o) = \underset{\sim}{0} ,$$

where H' indicates the vector of first-order partial derivatives of H, and $\underset{\sim}{0}$ is the zero vector. One can show of the matrix (Hessian) of second-order derivatives that:

$$\text{(4)} \qquad H''(\theta_o;\theta_o) = E^o\left(\left(\frac{\partial}{\partial\theta_i\partial\theta_j} \log f(y;\theta_o)\right)\right)$$

$$= -E^o\left(\left(\frac{\partial}{\partial\theta_i} \log f(y;\theta_o) \frac{\partial}{\partial\theta_j} \log f(y;\theta_o)\right)\right) .$$

Note that H" and H_1'' are the same, and will be used interchangeably. With the above assumptions, the negative definiteness of this Hessian matrix is necessary and sufficient for the identification of θ_o. It will be observed from (4) that the Hessian matrix $H''(\theta_o;\theta_o)$ is minus the covariance matrix of the gradient vector $\left(\frac{\partial}{\partial\theta_i} \log f(y;\theta)\right)$, evaluated at $\theta = \theta_o$. Equations (4) define R.A. Fisher's classic "information matrix". The function $H(\theta;\theta_o)$ was described by S. Kullback [1959] as the information integral for discriminating $f(x;\theta_o)$ against $f(x;\theta_1)$ per observation from $f(x;\theta_o)$.

As well as providing a theoretical underpinning for the concept itself, the above development can be utilised to find out if the parameter θ_o is identified. The most convenient ways of doing this are either by direct inspection of the function H , or else by verifying that the only solution to the equation $H'(\theta;\theta_o) = \underset{\sim}{0}$ is $\theta = \theta_o$. Alternatively it may be that θ_o is not identified. In this case the subspace of observationally-equivalent parameters θ may be obtained as the solutions to $H'(\theta;\theta_o) = \underset{\sim}{0}$.

2.1.2 Classical Maximum-Likelihood. Let us now discuss the relationship between the identification of θ_o and its estimation by means of the maximum-likelihood method. The method discussed in this section presupposes that an independent sample of T observations on the data point (vector) y has been drawn. The likelihood function is formed in the usual way as the product of independent probability elements, one for each t=1...T . The estimator is chosen as that parameter vector $\hat{\theta}_T$ which maximises the likelihood function. It will be convenient to state the principal results formally:

Theorem 2.1

Assume that Θ is a compact subset of Euclidean space of finite dimension and that θ_o is identified. Assume also that for all $\theta \in \Theta$, $H(\theta;\theta_o)$ exists and that $E^o \log^2 f(y;\theta) < \infty$.

Then the maximum-likelihood estimator $\hat{\theta}_T \to \theta_o$ almost everywhere[4] as $T \to \infty$.

The proof of this theorem is quite standard and will not be reproduced here in detail. It is based on the demonstration that if L denotes the likelihood function,

$$\frac{1}{T}\log L(\theta) = \frac{1}{T}\Sigma \log f(y_t;\theta) \longrightarrow E^o \log f(y;\theta) = H_1(\theta;\theta_o) ,$$

almost everywhere as $T \to \infty$. By assumption H_1 has a unique maximum from the identification of θ_o . It is shown that the sequence of maxima for finite T of the likelihood functions $\frac{1}{T}\log L(\theta)$ tend to the maximum of the limiting function. In short, the identification criterion $H_1(\theta;\theta_o)$ can be viewed as incorporating the limiting behaviour of the likelihood function.

Our next result, also standard, gives conditions under which the resulting estimate is asymptotically Normal.

Theorem 2.2

In addition to the assumptions of Theorem 2.1, suppose that the matrix $H''(\theta;\theta_o)$ exists for all $\theta \in \Theta$. Then the statistic $\sqrt{T}(\hat{\theta}_T - \theta_o)$ has asymptotically the $N(\underset{\sim}{0}, -H''_1(\theta_o;\theta_o)^{-1})$ distribution.

The proof is not produced here since the classical case is not of primary interest for this study. It may however be constructed by following through the proof of theorem 2.4 below. In the present case we can make use of convergence and central limit theorems for identically distributed random variables, which involve weaker assumptions. As given above, the condition $H''(\theta;\theta_o) < \infty$ is weaker than most presentations, which usually require that $E^o\left|\frac{\partial^3}{\partial\theta_i^3}\log f(y;\theta)\right|$ exists for the representative parameter i.

We note that the covariance matrix involved can be estimated either as

$$-\left(\left(\frac{1}{T}\frac{\partial^2}{\partial\theta_i\partial\theta_j}\log\hat{L}\right)\right)^{-1},$$

or as the matrix

$$\left[\frac{1}{T}\frac{\partial}{\partial\theta}\log\hat{L}\,.\,\frac{\partial}{\partial\theta}\log\hat{L}'\right]^{-1},$$

where in both cases $\log\hat{L}$ denotes evaluation at the maximum-likelihood solution. These estimates are convergent almost everywhere to $-H''_1(\theta_o;\theta_o)^{-1}$.

The various desirable properties of classical maximum-likelihood estimators are well-known. Thus if the distribution f admits of a sufficient statistic, the estimator is sufficient. It is also invariant to continuous transformations, so that if $\hat{\theta}_T$ is the M.L. estimate of θ_o, $g(\hat{\theta}_T)$ is the M.L. estimate of $g(\theta_o)$. For further details we refer the reader to standard texts (e.g. H. Theil [1971], P.J. Dhrymes [1970]).

2.2 Non-Classical Maximum-Likelihood: Regularity

2.2.1 Exogenous Variables. In the previous section we assumed that the exogenous variables x_t could be regarded as independent drawings from a well-defined marginal probability distribution. As mentioned, this assumption is not the usual one in econometrics, where more often the "variables" x_t are viewed as a sequence of constants, fixed in repeated realisations of the system. Only the endogenous variables, which we shall now distinguish as y_t, can be regarded as true random variables. In order to demonstrate general propositions it has been usual to impose some elementary regularity properties on the sequence of vectors x_t. Two such specifications are:

(a) $$M_{xx} = \lim_{T\to\infty} \frac{1}{T} \sum_t x_t x_t'$$

exists, as a matrix of finite constants.

(b) The x_t sequence behaves as though it were a sequence of independent drawings from a probability distribution. Accordingly let us define an empirical frequency function

$$F_T(x) = \frac{k}{T} ,$$

where k is the number of points $x_1 \ldots x_T$ less than or equal to x. The specification (b) is then that the sequence of distribution functions converge completely as $T \to \infty$ to a proper distribution function F(x).

The two specifications (a) and (b) are not of course exclusive, indeed the combination of (a) - in the form of a boundedness condition on the sequence x_t - and (b) are sometimes imposed. In the present section we shall impose (a), but not (b) as a general requirement. On the other hand this latter specification is very useful in applications of the criteria to be presented.

With the view of the x_t as a sequence of fixed numbers, expressions like E log $f(y_t;\theta)$ are now explicitly dependent upon the value of the given constant x_t. To emphasize this dependence we shall write f as $f_t(y_t;\theta)$ or as $f(y_t;x_t,\theta)$. Functions like H or H_1, as they appeared in section 2.1 are now specific to a particular time point t. Assertions about the convergence or asymptotic distribution of the likelihood estimators cannot therefore be made on the basis of the classical theorems 2.1 and 2.2. This is indeed a point which has frequently been simply fudged in the econometrics literature. Fortunately in the case of independent drawings of the endogenous variables (y) it is reasonably straightforward to extend the classical regularity conditions to this non-classical situation.

Where appropriate, the assumptions of section 2.1 continue to hold when applied to each time point t. We assume that

$$H_{1t}(\theta;\theta_o) = E^o \log f(y_t;x_t,\theta)$$

exists and is uniformly bounded in t and θ. The first and second derivatives of this function are also supposed to exist. We shall extend the classical discussion of section 2.1 with two theorems generalising the corresponding classical results.

<u>Theorem 2.3</u>

Suppose that

(i) $\lim_{T\to\infty} \frac{1}{T} \Sigma H_{1t}(\theta;\theta_o) = H_1(\theta;\theta_o)$ uniformly in θ,

and that $H_1(\theta;\theta_o)$ is uniquely maximised at $\theta = \theta_o$

(ii) $E^o \log^2 f(y_t;x_t,\theta)$ is uniformly bounded in t and θ.

Then the M.L. estimate $\hat{\theta}_T \to \theta_o$ almost everywhere, as $T\to\infty$.

The proof is straightforward. We may write

$$\frac{1}{T}\log L(\theta) = \frac{1}{T}\Sigma \log f(y_t;x_t,\theta)$$
$$= \frac{1}{T}\Sigma E^o \log f(y_t;x_t,\theta) + \frac{1}{T}\Sigma \varepsilon_t(\theta),$$

where $\varepsilon_t(\theta) = \log f(y_t;x_t,\theta) - E^o \log f(y_t;x_t,\theta)$. Because of the sampling procedure employed, $E(\varepsilon_t/\varepsilon_{t-1},\varepsilon_{t-2}\ldots) = 0$. In view of (ii), $E\,\varepsilon_t^2$ is uniformly bounded in t and θ. It follows from the strong law of large numbers for non i.i.d. random variables that

$$\frac{1}{T}\,\Sigma\,\varepsilon_t(\theta) \longrightarrow 0\,, \text{ almost everywhere.}$$

Thus $\frac{1}{T}\log L(\theta) \xrightarrow{a.e.} H(\theta;\theta_o)$, uniformly in θ.

Now for all t, $H_{1t}(\theta;\theta_o)$ is maximised for $\theta = \theta_o$ and from (i) this maximum is unique at $\theta = \theta_o$. The rest of the proof is an application of Lemma[5] 3 of Amemiya [1973].

Condition (i) of this theorem is the generalisation to the non-classical case of the identification criterion of section 2.1. Indeed, if we make use of the empirical distribution function specification (b) above for the exogenous variables, we may regard $H_1(\theta;\theta_o)$ as defined by condition (i) of Theorem 2.3 as formally identical to the same function as defined in the classical treatment of section 2.1. With this specification then, the identification theory of the classical and non-classical cases are one and the same.

The next theorem concerns the asymptotic distribution of the non-classical likelihood estimator.

<u>Theorem 2.4</u>

In addition to the assumptions of Theorem 2.3, suppose that (iii) for some $\zeta > 0$

$$\max_h E^o\left|\frac{\partial}{\partial\theta_i}\log f(y_t;x_t,\theta_o)\right|^{2+\zeta} < M\,, \text{ a constant, uniformly}$$

in t.

(iv) the first and second moments of the random variables $\frac{\partial^2}{\partial\theta_i\partial\theta_j}\log f(y_t;x_t,\theta)$ exist and are uniformly bounded in t and θ.

Then $\sqrt{T}(\hat{\theta}_T - \theta_o)$ is asymptotically $N(\underset{\sim}{0}, -H_1''(\theta_o;\theta_o)^{-1})$, where H_1 is defined in Theorem 2.3.

Proof: In view of the definition of $H_1(\theta;\theta_o)$ in Theorem 2.3 and assumption (iv) it follows that the series $\frac{1}{T}\Sigma H''_{1t}(\theta;\theta_o)$ converges uniformly in θ to the function $H''_1(\theta;\theta_o)$. From the discussion of section 2.1, $H''_1(\theta_o;\theta_o)$ is negative definite.

By a Taylor expansion about θ_o (or law of the mean theorem),

$$\left.\frac{\partial \log L}{\partial \theta}\right|_{\theta=\hat{\theta}_T} = \frac{\partial \log L}{\partial \theta_o} + \left[\frac{\partial^2 \log L}{\partial \theta_* \partial \theta_*'}\right](\hat{\theta}_T - \theta_o) ,$$

where $\theta*$ lies between θ_o and $\hat{\theta}_T$ on the line joining these points. We can therefore write

$$\text{(5)} \qquad \sqrt{T}(\hat{\theta}_T - \theta_o) = -\left[\frac{1}{T}\frac{\partial^2 \log L}{\partial \theta_* \partial \theta_*'}\right]^{-1} \frac{1}{\sqrt{T}}\frac{\partial \log L}{\partial \theta_o} .$$

Since $\hat{\theta}_T \xrightarrow{a.e.} \theta_o$ (Theorem 2.3), it follows that $\theta* \xrightarrow{a.e.} \theta_o$.

From assumption (iv) and Lemma[6] 4 of Amemiya [1973] it follows that

$$\text{(6)} \qquad \left[\frac{1}{T}\frac{\partial^2 \log L}{\partial \theta* \partial \theta*'}\right]^{-1} \xrightarrow{a.e.} \left[H''_1(\theta_o;\theta_o)\right]^{-1} , \quad \text{as } T \to \infty$$

Let us now consider the random vector

$$\frac{1}{\sqrt{T}}\frac{\partial \log L}{\partial \theta_o} = \frac{1}{T}\Sigma \frac{\partial}{\partial \theta} \log f(y_t;x_t,\theta_o) .$$

From the definition of $H'_{1t}(\theta_o;\theta_o)$,

$$E^o \frac{1}{\sqrt{T}}\frac{\partial \log L}{\partial \theta_o} = 0 .$$

Consider now any linear combination

$$\zeta_T = \underset{\sim}{\ell}' \cdot \frac{1}{\sqrt{T}}\frac{\partial \log L}{\partial \theta_o} ,$$

where the vector $\underset{\sim}{\ell}$ is arbitrary. In view of the independent sampling assumption, we have

$$\begin{aligned} \text{Var } \zeta_T &= \underset{\sim}{\ell}' \cdot \frac{1}{T}\left[\sum_{t=1}^{T} E^o \frac{\partial \log f}{\partial \theta_o} \cdot \frac{\partial \log f}{\partial \theta_o'}\right]\underset{\sim}{\ell} \\ &= -\underset{\sim}{\ell}' \frac{1}{T}\Sigma H''_{1t}(\theta_o;\theta_o)\underset{\sim}{\ell} . \end{aligned}$$

Thus $\lim_{T\to\infty} \text{Var}\ \zeta_T = -\underset{\sim}{\ell}'\ H_1''(\theta_o;\theta_o)\underset{\sim}{\ell} > 0$.

Now from condition (iii) it can be shown (e.g. R. Basmann [1960] pp.103-4) that the Lindeberg condition for the central limit problem is satisfied (see M. Loève [1955] §6.21.2). Thus ζ_T tends in distribution to a $N(0, -\underset{\sim}{\ell}'\ H_1''(\theta_o;\theta_o)\underset{\sim}{\ell})$ variate, from which the desired result follows by utilising equations (5) and (6).

Condition (iii) above is on the distribution of the gradient vector $\frac{\partial}{\partial\theta} \log f(y_t;x_t,\theta)$. It would usually be demonstrated that the absolute third-order moment $E^o\left|\frac{\partial}{\partial\theta_i} \log f(y_t;x_t,\theta)\right|^3$ is bounded in the manner required. We note also that the required covariance matrix $-H_1''(\theta_o;\theta_o)^{-1}$ will be consistently estimated by $-\left(\left(\frac{1}{T}\frac{\partial}{\partial\theta_i\partial\theta_j} \log \hat{L}\right)\right)^{-1}$ or by $\left[\frac{1}{T}\frac{\partial}{\partial\theta} \log \hat{L}\ \frac{\partial}{\partial\theta} \log \hat{L}'\right]^{-1}$, depending upon computational considerations.

It will be useful for purposes of illustration to introduce an example at this point.

Example (Probit Analysis)

Although the identification and likelihood-estimation properties of the technique known as Probit analysis are well-known, it will be convenient not only for present illustrative purposes, but for the purposes of later referral, to introduce this technique. Let E_t be an index which is a linear function $\underset{\sim}{X}_t'\underset{\sim}{\beta}$ of bounded variables $\underset{\sim}{X}_t$, assumed fixed in repeated realisations.

Let E_t^* be a N(0,1) variable, and let

$$y_t = \begin{cases} 1 & \text{if}\quad E_t \geq E_t^* \\ 0 & \text{otherwise}\ . \end{cases}$$

In applications, the E_t^* may represent critical values of the index E_t . Thus if the object of study is car ownership, and E is an index incorporating income or wealth, E* could be thought of as a critical or threshold value, specific to a family. If E > E* the family will own a car. Now suppose that E* is distributed as N(0,1) over different families. The probability that a family (number t in the sample) chosen at random will own a car is:

$$\text{Prob}(y_t = 1/E_t) = \text{Prob}(E_t^* \le E_t) = F(E_t) ,$$

where F indicates the distribution function of E^*. Likewise, the probability that they do not own a car is

$$\text{Prob}(y_t = 0/E_t) = 1 - F(E_t) .$$

The problem is, given a series of zero-one observations for t=1...T [owning or not owning], to estimate β. The likelihood function consists in a series of terms $F(\underset{\sim}{X}_t' \underset{\sim}{\beta})$, corresponding to those t for which $y_t = 1$, and terms $1 - F(E_t)$, corresponding to the complementary event.

We can analyse the regularity of this likelihood situation using Theorems 2.3 and 2.4 and the analysis of section 2.1. Thus we write β_o as the true value of β. Fixing on an arbitrary β we may write $g(y_t, \underset{\sim}{X}_t; \underset{\sim}{\beta})$ as the density of a variable y_t with just two values (1 and 0). Accordingly,

$$\begin{aligned} g(y_t, \underset{\sim}{X}_t; \underset{\sim}{\beta}) &= F(\underset{\sim}{X}_t' \underset{\sim}{\beta}) && \text{with probability } F(\underset{\sim}{X}_t' \underset{\sim}{\beta}_o) \\ &= 1 - F(\underset{\sim}{X}_t' \underset{\sim}{\beta}) && \text{with probability } [1 - F(\underset{\sim}{X}_t' \underset{\sim}{\beta}_o)] . \end{aligned}$$

It follows that

$$\begin{aligned} H_t(\underset{\sim}{\beta}; \underset{\sim}{\beta}_o) &= E^o \log \left[\frac{g(y_t, \underset{\sim}{X}_t; \underset{\sim}{\beta})}{g(y_t, \underset{\sim}{X}_t; \underset{\sim}{\beta}_o)} \right] \\ &= \log \left[\frac{F(\underset{\sim}{X}_t' \underset{\sim}{\beta})}{F(\underset{\sim}{X}_t' \underset{\sim}{\beta}_o)} \right] . F(\underset{\sim}{X}_t' \underset{\sim}{\beta}_o) + \log \left[\frac{1 - F(\underset{\sim}{X}_t' \underset{\sim}{\beta})}{1 - F(\underset{\sim}{X}_t' \underset{\sim}{\beta}_o)} \right] [1 - F(\underset{\sim}{X}_t' \underset{\sim}{\beta}_o)] . \end{aligned}$$

It is convenient for identification purposes to draw on the empirical distribution function specification for the exogenous variables $\underset{\sim}{X}_t$. Thus we imagine that these can be regarded as independent drawings from a distribution function $\Phi(\underset{\sim}{X})$, say. We may therefore write the limiting sum $\frac{1}{T} \Sigma H_t$ as $T \to \infty$ as:

(7) $$H(\underset{\sim}{\beta};\underset{\sim}{\beta}_o) = \int_{-\infty}^{\infty}\!\!\!\cdots\!\!\int \left[\log\left[\frac{F(\underset{\sim}{X}'\underset{\sim}{\beta})}{F(\underset{\sim}{X}'\underset{\sim}{\beta}_o)}\right] F(\underset{\sim}{X}'\underset{\sim}{\beta}_o) + \log\left[\frac{1-F(\underset{\sim}{X}'\underset{\sim}{\beta})}{1-F(\underset{\sim}{X}'\underset{\sim}{\beta}_o)}\right](1-F(\underset{\sim}{X}'\underset{\sim}{\beta}_o))\right] d\phi(\underset{\sim}{X}) \; .$$

We know from the theory of section 2.1 that the integrands are ≤ 0. Suppose then that $H(\underset{\sim}{\beta};\underset{\sim}{\beta}_o) = 0$ for $\underset{\sim}{\beta} \neq \underset{\sim}{\beta}_o$. It must follow that the set of $\underset{\sim}{X}$ for which

(8) $$\log\left[\frac{F(\underset{\sim}{X}'\underset{\sim}{\beta})}{F(\underset{\sim}{X}'\underset{\sim}{\beta}_o)}\right] F(\underset{\sim}{X}'\underset{\sim}{\beta}_o) + \log\left[\frac{1-F(\underset{\sim}{X}'\underset{\sim}{\beta})}{1-F(\underset{\sim}{X}'\underset{\sim}{\beta}_o)}\right](1-F(\underset{\sim}{X}'\underset{\sim}{\beta}_o)) = 0$$

has measure 1.

Let us consider the expression on the LHS of (8) for an arbitrary $\underset{\sim}{X}$. Writing $a = F(\underset{\sim}{X}'\underset{\sim}{\beta})$, $b = F(\underset{\sim}{X}'\underset{\sim}{\beta}_o)$, equation (8) is equivalent to

$$a^b(1-a)^{1-b} = b^b(1-b)^{1-b} \, , \qquad \text{with} \quad 0 < a,\, b < 1 \, .$$

Considering the graph of the function $x^b(1-x)^{1-b}$, we note that this has a unique maximum between 0 and 1, namely $b^b(1-b)^{1-b}$ at the point $x = b$. It follows immediately from equation (9) that $a = b$, i.e. $F(\underset{\sim}{X}'\underset{\sim}{\beta}) = F(\underset{\sim}{X}'\underset{\sim}{\beta}_o)$. That is to say,

$$\underset{\sim}{X}'(\underset{\sim}{\beta} - \underset{\sim}{\beta}_o) = 0 \, .$$

Only if the empirical distribution of $\underset{\sim}{X}$ is such that all values, apart from a set of measure zero, lie on the above hyperplane, can the vector $\underset{\sim}{\beta}$ be observationally equivalent to the true value $\underset{\sim}{\beta}_o$. In particular if the empirical distribution of $\underset{\sim}{X}$ is of full rank, $\underset{\sim}{\beta}_o$ will be globally identified.

It is now a straightforward matter to verify that the hypotheses of Theorems 2.3 and 2.4 hold in respect of the Probit model. For instance we observe directly from the definition of g given earlier and the boundedness of the $\underset{\sim}{X}_t$ sequence that $E^o \log^2 g(y_t,\underset{\sim}{X}_t;\underset{\sim}{\beta})$ and $E^o\left|\frac{\partial}{\partial\beta_h}\log g(y_t,\underset{\sim}{X}_t;\underset{\sim}{\beta})\right|^3$ are both uniformly bounded in β and t. Probit estimators are therefore strongly consistent and have asymptotically a $N(\beta_o, -H''(\underset{\sim}{\beta}_o;\underset{\sim}{\beta}_o)^{-1})$ distribution, where $H''(\beta_o;\beta_o)$ is obtained as the Hessian matrix of second-order partial derivates of the function $H(\beta;\beta_o)$ defined by equation (7).

2.2.2 Autoregressive Schemes. Models in which the value of the endogenous variable at time t (y_t) is dependent upon its value in previous periods ($y_{t-1}, y_{t-2}\ldots$) are of widespread occurrence in econometrics at large, and no less so in the particular context of disequilibrium econometrics. It would be useful to extend the general regularity ideas of §2.2.1 to encompass this situation. At first sight this may not appear feasible, since the assumption of independent drawings of successive y_t is plainly no longer met. However, where the values of y_t can be regarded as generated by innovations ε_t which are independently distributed temporally, it is possible to extend at least part of our regularity theory in reasonable straightforward fashion.

To fix ideas, we suppose that, given y_{t-1}, observations on y_t are generated by the implicit structural form:

(9) $$\Phi(y_t, y_{t-1}, \varepsilon_t, x_t, \theta_o) = 0 ,$$

where as usual y_t, ε_t and x_t are vectors. The ε_t are white-noise disturbances, serially independent. We shall specify that (9) has a reduced form, i.e. an explicit solution for y_t of the form

(10) $$y_t = \phi(y_{t-1}, x_t, \varepsilon_t, \theta_o) .$$

Finally we shall assume that the model is asymptotically stochastically stable. In particular limits of sample moments like $\frac{1}{T}\Sigma y_t y_t'$ or $\frac{1}{T}\Sigma y_t y_{t-1}'$ exist almost everywhere and are independent of the initial conditions.

Let $f(y_t; y_{t-1}, x_t, \theta_o)$ indicate the conditional density function of y_t given y_{t-1}. We shall be interested in a class of models such that the formal likelihood function, i.e. the probability attached to the sample $y_1 \ldots y_T$, admits of the decomposition

(11) $$L(y_1 \ldots y_T; y_o, \theta_o) = \prod_{t=1}^{T} f(y_t; y_{t-1}, x_t, \theta_o) ,$$

where the initial value y_o is regarded as a given number. The likelihood function can then be decomposed into the product of the conditional density functions for individual periods. This decomposition arises in a variety of cases out of the Jacobian relating the innovations ε_t to y_t. A leading case is the class of models with additive error term:

(12) $$y_t = \phi(y_{t-1}, x_t, \theta_o) + \varepsilon_t .$$

In this case, the Jacobian relating y_t to ε_t, $t=1\ldots T$, is lower triangular, with unity down the diagonal. Its determinant is therefore unity. Hence

$$L(y_1 \ldots y_T; y_o) = \prod_{t=1}^{T} g(\varepsilon_t^*) ,$$

where g is the density of the ε_t and $\varepsilon_t^* = y_t - \phi(y_{t-1}, x_t, \theta_o)$.

Let us return, then to the general form (11), in terms of the one-period conditional distributions, f_t. It would be useful to be able to generalise theorems 2.3 and 2.4 by considering these one-period conditional distributions in the same light as the elementary distributions $f(y_t, x_t, \theta)$. This is only partly successful. We have, first:

Theorem 2.5

Consider the random variable $\log(y_t, y_{t-1}, x_t, \theta)$. Denote by $H_{1t}(\theta; \theta_o, y_{t-1})$ and $V_t(\theta; \theta_o, y_{t-1})$ its mean and variance conditional upon y_{t-1}, both assumed to exist. Suppose that

(i) $\frac{1}{T} \Sigma H_{1t}(\theta; \theta_o, y_{t-1}) \longrightarrow H_1(\theta; \theta_o)$ almost everywhere, uniformly in θ, and $H_1(\theta; \theta_o)$ is uniquely maximised at $\theta = \theta_o$.

(ii) The one-period conditional densities are such that $E^o_{y_{t-1}} V_t(\theta; \theta_o, y_{t-1})$ is bounded, uniformly in t and θ.

Then the maximum-likelihood estimator tends almost everywhere to the true value θ_o.

Proof. Write $\log f(y_t;y_{t-1},x_t,\theta) = H_{1t}(\theta;\theta_o,y_{t-1}) + \xi_t$, where $E\xi_t/y_{t-1} = 0$. The recursive relationship (10) together with the independence of successive ε_t, may then be used to show that the sequence ξ_t obeys the strong law of large numbers. The required result follows as for theorem 2.3.

However it is no longer possible to prove the analogue of theorem 2.4 (in respect of the asymptotic distribution of the resulting estimate) by considering the individual conditional probability densities f_t. Demonstration of the asymptotic normality of the M.L. estimate must be carried through afresh for every model considered. In many instances it will turn out that the resulting asymptotic covariance matrix will be equal to $-H_1''(\theta_o;\theta_o)^{-1}$ where the function H is defined by theorem 2.5 above. As a generic term, we shall refer to such situations as regular.

Example. At this point an example may help to make the foregoing theory a little more concrete. Consider the linear model:

$$By_t = C_1y_{t-1} + C_2x_t + u_t ,$$

where u_t is a serially uncorrelated disturbance vector. The vector y has order G. This model has a (full-rank) reduced form

$$y_t = \Pi_1y_{t-1} + \Pi_2x_t + e_t ,$$

where $e_t = B^{-1}u_t$ and $\Omega = E\,e_te_t'$. We assume that the characteristic roots of Π_1 are less than one in absolute value. As usual denote by (o) the true values of the parameters. Write

$$\varepsilon_t = y_t - \Pi_1^o y_{t-1} - \Pi_2^o x_t .$$

Note that $e_t - \varepsilon_t = (\Pi_1^o - \Pi_1)y_{t-1} + (\Pi_2^o - \Pi_2)x_t$. Now

$$\log f(y_t;y_{t-1},x_t,\theta) = -\tfrac{1}{2}\log \Pi - \tfrac{1}{2}\log(\det \Omega) - \tfrac{1}{2}e_t'\Omega^{-1}e_t .$$

The term $e_t'\Omega^{-1}e_t = \varepsilon_t'\Omega^{-1}\varepsilon_t + 2\varepsilon_t'\Omega^{-1}(e_t - \varepsilon_t) + (e_t - \varepsilon_t)'\Omega^{-1}(e_t - \varepsilon_t)$.

Hence

$$\log f(y_t;y_{t-1},x_t,\theta) = -\frac{G}{2}\log \Pi - \tfrac{1}{2}\log(\det \Omega) - \tfrac{1}{2}(\varepsilon_t'\Omega^{-1}\varepsilon_t)$$
$$- \varepsilon_t'\Omega^{-1}\Big[(\Pi_1^o - \Pi_1)y_{t-1} + (\Pi_2^o - \Pi_2)x_t\Big]$$
$$- \tfrac{1}{2}\Big[(\Pi_1^o - \Pi_1)y_{t-1} + (\Pi_2^o - \Pi_2)x_t\Big]'\Omega^{-1}\Big[(\Pi_1^o - \Pi_1)y_{t-1} + (\Pi_2^o - \Pi_2)x_t\Big] \quad (13)$$

Taking expectations with respect to the true parameters θ_o,

$$E^o \log f(y_t;y_{t-1},x_t,\theta) = -\frac{G}{2}\log \Pi - \tfrac{1}{2}\log(\det \Omega) - \tfrac{1}{2}\,\text{trace}(\Omega^{-1}\Omega_o)$$
$$- \tfrac{1}{2}\,\text{trace}(\Pi_1^o - \Pi_1)\Omega^{-1}(\Pi_1^o - \Pi_1)y_{t-1}y_{t-1}'$$
$$- \text{trace}(\Pi_2^o - \Pi_2)\Omega^{-1}(\Pi_1^o - \Pi_1)y_{t-1}x_t' - \text{trace}(\Pi_2^o - \Pi_2)\Omega^{-1}(\Pi_2^o - \Pi_2)x_t x_t' . \quad (14)$$

Under our stability assumptions, $\frac{1}{T}\Sigma\, y_{t-1}y_{t-1}'$, $\frac{1}{T}\Sigma\, y_{t-1}x_t'$ and $\frac{1}{T}\Sigma\, x_t x_t'$ tend almost everywhere to corresponding "population" moment matrices, which will depend upon Π_1^o, Π_2^o and Ω^o. Thus the sum $\frac{1}{T}\Sigma\, H_{1t}(\theta;\theta_o,y_{t-1})$ tends almost everywhere to a function $H_1(\theta;\theta_o)$ independent of the initial conditions. This function will be maximised with respect to Π_1 and Π_2 by minimising

$$E\begin{bmatrix} y_{t-1}' & x_t' \end{bmatrix}\begin{bmatrix} (\Pi_1^o - \Pi_1)'\Omega^{-1}(\Pi_1^o - \Pi_1) & (\Pi_1^o - \Pi_1)'\Omega^{-1}(\Pi_2^o - \Pi_2) \\ (\Pi_2^o - \Pi_2)'\Omega^{-1}(\Pi_1^o - \Pi_1) & (\Pi_2^o - \Pi_2)'\Omega^{-1}(\Pi_2^o - \Pi_2) \end{bmatrix}\begin{bmatrix} y_{t-1} \\ x_t \end{bmatrix} .$$

The unique choice $\Pi_1 = \Pi_1^o$, $\Pi_2 = \Pi_2^o$ results. The reduced-form of the autoregressive model is therefore identified. The standard rank and order conditions in terms of the elements of B and C are applicable, and we suppose that these are satisfied.

Assume that the 4th-order moments of ε_t exist. From equation (13), the conditional second moments of $\log f_t$ exist and in view of our compactness assumption on θ are uniformly bounded. Moreover $\frac{\partial}{\partial\theta}\log f(y_t;y_{t-1},x_t,\theta_o)$ depends only upon the elements of ε_t and is therefore serially uncorrelated. The maximum-likelihood estimators of B, C_1, C_2 are therefore strongly consistent. One can also show by arguments similar to those of theorem 2.4 that the resulting estimates are asymptotically Normal, with covariance matrix equal to $-H_1''(\theta_o;\theta_o)^{-1}$, where the limiting function $H_1(\theta;\theta_o)$ is defined above.

We may now summarise the development of sections 2.1 and 2.2. This has been directed towards setting up certain classes of problems which we may recognise as regular in the sense (a) that the resulting likelihood estimators are consistent and (b) the estimators are asymptotically Normal, with a standard asymptotic covariance matrix. This covariance matrix may be recognised as minus the inverse of the information matrix. The latter matrix has in some cases to be established by a limiting process, rather than being a characteristic of any actual probability distribution. Nevertheless there is a strong generic similarity between the different versions of this information matrix, emphasised in our survey by writing it as $H_1''(\theta_o;\theta_o)$ in each case. In short, by a regular estimation situation we shall in this book mean a model which satisfies conditions (a) and (b) above.

2.3 Non-regular Likelihood: Mixed Distributions

We should not assume from the foregoing sections that only regular likelihood situations are to be met with in econometrics. A well-known example where this is not so is in the "errors-in-variables" model, where the number of parameters (the unobservable or "permanent" components) tends to infinity with the sample size. A more important example for our purposes because of its relationship with the "short-side" models of chapter 5, concerns the problem known in the statistical literature as "mixed distributions". To consider it in its simplest form, let us specify a variable y subject to the density:

$$f(y;\theta) = c_1 f_1(y;\theta_1) + c_2 f_2(y;\theta_2) \quad , \tag{15}$$

where $\theta = (\theta_1, \theta_2)$, the f_i are proper densities and $c_1 + c_2 = 1$ with $c_i > 0$. This model can be generalised to $i > 2$ and indeed to a continuous weighting or density function c. The identifiability of densities of this form has been considered by, among others, H. Teicher [1961], [1963] and S.J. Yakowitz and J.D. Spragin [1968]. In the example (15) above, provided that $c_1^o \neq c_2^o$ there are no identification problems if the f_i are normal and θ refers to the mean vectors and covariance matrices.

Consider, however, the problem of estimating θ by the method of maximum-likelihood. To fix ideas, we take the following example (Kiefer and Wolfowitz [1956]):

$$\begin{aligned} f(y;\mu,\sigma^2) &= {}^3/_4 \frac{1}{(2\Pi)^{\frac{1}{2}}} \exp(-\tfrac{1}{2}(y-\mu)^2) + \tfrac{1}{4} \frac{1}{(2\Pi)^{\frac{1}{2}}\sigma} \exp\left[-\tfrac{1}{2} \frac{(y-\mu)^2}{\sigma^2}\right] \\ &= {}^3/_4\, n_1(y;\mu,1) + \tfrac{1}{4}\, n_2(y;\mu,\sigma^2) \quad , \end{aligned} \tag{16}$$

in an obvious notation. This is a mixture of two normal densities with variances 1 and σ^2. Given as independent sample $y_1 \ldots y_T$, let us try $\hat{\mu} = y_1$ and consider what happens as we let $\sigma^2 \to \infty$.

Now

(17) $$\log L(\mu,\sigma^2) = \sum_t \log f(y_t;\mu,\sigma^2) .$$

With $\hat{\mu} = y_1$,

$$\log f(y_1;\hat{\mu},\sigma^2) = \log\left[\tfrac{3}{4}\frac{1}{(2\Pi)^{\frac{1}{2}}} + \tfrac{1}{4}\frac{1}{(2\Pi)^{\frac{1}{2}}\sigma}\right]$$

which we can make as high as we please by letting $\hat{\sigma} \to 0$.

Let us see what happens to the next term in the sum (17), namely

$$\log f(y_2;\hat{\mu},\sigma^2) = \log\left(\tfrac{3}{4}\, n_1(y_2;y_1,1) + \tfrac{1}{4}\, n_2(y_2;y_1,\sigma^2)\right) .$$

As $\sigma^2 \to \infty$, the second term in the RHS (n_2) tends to zero. But the first term (n_1) remains fixed, independently of the behaviour of σ^2 . Hence $\log f(y_2;\hat{\mu},\sigma^2)$ remains bounded below with our choice for $\hat{\mu}$ and σ^2 . Similarly for the remaining elements of the sum (17). There is, in other words, no countervailing force to the dominating unboundedness of the first element $\log f(y_1;\hat{\mu},\sigma^2)$ as $\sigma^2 \to \infty$. Our choice of $\hat{\mu} = y_1$, $\sigma^2 \to \infty$ has therefore resulted in an unbounded likelihood function.

The problem is evidently of greater generality than this particular example. In regular situations, any choice which makes one or more elements of the likelihood function infinite will automatically render others zero. With the mixed distribution case, this no longer happens. It follows that maximum-likelihood estimators are not consistent. D.W. Hosmer Jr. [1973] has confirmed this finding on the basis of a simulation study of a mixture of two normal distributions. Even in moderately large samples he found that the likelihood method performed very poorly. In general, further *a-priori* information is usually necessary to ensure regularity in mixed distribution work. We might, for instance, require of the mixture of $n_1(y;\mu_1,\sigma_1^2)$ and $n_2(y;\mu_2,\sigma_2^2)$ that $\sigma_1^2 = k\,\sigma_2^2$, with $k > 0$, known. This will ensure that the unboundness referred to cannot arise.

2.4 Computational Considerations and Linearised M.L. Estimators

In this section we review briefly some computational considerations associated with finding the maximum of the likelihood function $\log L(\theta)$ in a regular estimation situation. This will serve to motivate a short discussion of the "linearised" maximum-likelihood estimator, suggested later in the book as a useful approach to some disequilibrium problems. For a more detailed review of computational matters as such, we refer the reader to S.M. Goldfeld and R.E. Quandt [1972] and for general surveys to books such as J. Kowalik and M.R. Osborne [1968] and L.C.W. Dixon [1972].

Given a function $f(\theta)$ to be maximised with respect to θ, denote by g the gradient vector $\frac{\partial f}{\partial \theta}$ and by G the Hessian matrix $\left(\left(\frac{\partial^2}{\partial\theta_i \partial\theta_j} f(\theta)\right)\right)$ of second-order partial derivatives. The gradient vector g represents the direction of maximal increase of the function $f(\theta)$. Given a direction $\underset{\sim}{v}$ in θ-space, we say that this is <u>uphill</u> if it forms an acute angle with the gradient, i.e. if $v'g > 0$. The method of <u>steepest ascent</u> consists in choosing θ_{k+1} along the gradient vector from the point θ_k reached after the kth iteration. Although this is directly uphill, so to speak, its properties are in general rather poor. The iteration may become "caged" and cycle in a 2-dimensional subspace with very little improvement in the objective function $f(\theta)$ at each iteration.

Instead, the approaches most commonly used in econometrics have been variants of the Newton-Raphson technique. We may write a Taylor expansion:

$$(18) \qquad f(\theta) = f(\theta_k) + g_k'(\theta-\theta_k) + \tfrac{1}{2}(\theta-\theta_k)'G_k(\theta-\theta_k) + O(\theta_i-\theta_{ik})^3 ,$$

where $g_k = g(\theta_k)$ and $G_k = G(\theta_k)$. If we ignore the third-order terms, which amounts to a local quadratic approximation for f, the maximum value θ_{k+1} is given by

(19) $$\theta_{k+1} = \theta_k - G_k^{-1} g_k ,$$

which suggests the next value of θ. This is the basic Newton-Raphson technique. Unfortunately this method also suffers from a number of defects. Perhaps the most striking is that there is no guarantee that the stationary point found from (18) is indeed a maximum, i.e. that the Hessian G_k is negative definite at each stage. If not, the step involved in (19) will not even be uphill, according to the definition given above.

It is, however, possible to ensure that the matrix to be inverted in the scheme (19) is negative definite by imposing a constraint upon the step length $(\theta_{k+1} - \theta_k)$. To do this, we might consider maximising $f(\theta)$ as in (18) subject to the constraint $(\theta - \theta_k)'(\theta - \theta_k) = k^2$, an arbitrary constant. Form the Lagrangean

(20) $$L(\theta,\lambda) = f(\theta_k) + g_k'(\theta - \theta_k) + \tfrac{1}{2}(\theta - \theta_k)'G_k(\theta - \theta_k) - \lambda((\theta - \theta_k)'(\theta - \theta_k) - k^2) ,$$

where λ is a Lagrange multiplier. The stationary point occurs where

(21) $$\theta_{k+1} = \theta_k - (G_k - \lambda I)^{-1} g_k .$$

Since k is arbitrary, λ may be allotted any desired value. Thus even if G_k has positive characteristic roots, the matrix $(G_k - \lambda I)^{-1}$ can still be negative definite if $\lambda > 0$ is chosen larger than the maximal root of G_k. The uphill step is therefore preserved. On the other hand, there is no guarantee that $f(\theta_{k+1}) > f(\theta_k)$ at each step. If this turns out not to be the case, either the existing step length can be reduced, or else by using a larger value of λ a new direction can be tried.

The above method is due to S.M. Goldfeld, R.E. Quandt and Trotter [1966]. It will be observed that the maximisation involved in equation (20) is the problem of finding the maximal value of $f(\theta)$ - or its quadratic approximation - on a sphere of given radius k^2. Altering the value of λ, as suggested above, corresponds to altering the radius of the circle in which the maximum is to be sought. In a later contribution [1968], Goldfeld, Quandt and Trotter proposed a modification in which the sphere is replaced by an ellipsoid:

$$(\theta - \theta_k)'A(\theta - \theta_k) = k^2 .$$

The arbitrary positive-definite matrix A is updated during the iteration. The advantage of this variant is that if it has become apparent that there is a ridge in $f(\theta)$, the major axis of the ellipse can be aligned along the direction of the ridge, allowing a longer step length. G.Q.T. and Goldfeld and Quandt [1972] report some good results with this method in a variety of nonlinear situations.

Even for relatively small problems, the process of obtaining the Hessian of a likelihood function may be tedious and prone to be human error. As a computing matter, storage requirements may become heavy for a problem of moderate size. There are several possible ways of tackling these difficulties. One approach is to use a variant of the conjugate gradient idea. In what is perhaps the most widely used such variant, the method of Davidon, Fletcher and Powell [1959], [1963], the required inverse is in effect built up sequentially employing a sequence of orthogonal vectors. The storage problem is especially economical with the method of Fletcher and Reeves [1964]. Conjugate gradient methods have been used by R.P. Byron [1977] to handle the heavy storage problems involved in the generalised least squares analysis of consumer expenditure systems. An alternative general approach to the necessity of explicitly obtaining the Hessian of the likelihood function is to use the result that, when evaluated at the true value, the matrices

$$(22) \qquad -\left(\left(\frac{1}{T}\frac{\partial}{\partial\theta_i\partial\theta_j}\log\hat{L}\right)\right)$$

and the sample covariance matrix of the gradient vector

$$(23) \qquad \frac{1}{T}\frac{\partial}{\partial\theta}\log\hat{L}\,\frac{\partial}{\partial\theta}\log\hat{L}'$$

are asymptotically the same for a regular estimation problem. This suggests that at each step we replace the Hessian (G_k) of the likelihood function by the estimated covariance matrix (23), evaluated at the current iteration θ_k. The latter matrix can be constructed using only first-order partial derivatives.

We have now reached a convenient point to introduce the method sometimes known as "linearised" maximum-likelihood. Perhaps the first explicit statement of this result in the econometrics literature is by T. Rothenburg and C.T. Leenders [1964], although they point out that the method appears to be of earlier genesis in the statistical literature.

Theorem 2.6

Suppose that in a regular estimation problem we have available some consistent estimate $\tilde{\theta}$ of θ_o, with sampling variance of order $\frac{1}{T}$. Denote by $\hat{\theta}$ the true maximum-likelihood estimator. Then the "linearised" M.L. estimator defined by

$$(24) \qquad \theta^L = \tilde{\theta} - \left(\left(\frac{1}{T}\frac{\partial^2}{\partial\theta_i\partial\theta_j}\log L(\tilde{\theta})\right)\right)^{-1}\left[\frac{1}{T}\frac{\partial}{\partial\theta}\log L(\tilde{\theta})\right]$$

has the same asymptotic distribution as $\hat{\theta}$. The Hessian in (24) may be replaced by the sample covariance matrix (23) of the gradient vector.

A rationalisation, though not a formal proof, of this procedure follows from the discussion of sections 2.1, 2.2 and the Newton-Raphson algorithm outlined earlier in the present section.

We know from the presumed identification of θ_o that $H''_1(\theta_o;\theta_o)$ is negative definite. Thus the limiting likelihood function is always concave in some neighbourhood of the true value θ_o. Given a consistent estimate $\hat{\theta}$, this ultimately belongs to this neighbourhood with a probability approaching unity. The Newton-Raphson step in (19), using $\tilde{\theta}$ as the initial stage will achieve the maximum of the likelihood function in a number of steps which approaches unity as the consistent estimate $\tilde{\theta}$ approaches θ_o. The linearised M.L. estimator is thus asymptotically equivalent to the full maximisation procedure.

On the other hand, the asymptotic concavity of the log-likelihood function may be cold comfort so far as finite samples are concerned. As pointed out in connection with the Newton-Raphson method, the Hessian as evaluated in (24) may not be negative definite if $\tilde{\theta}_T$ is some distance removed from θ_o for a finite sample T. The resulting step implied by (24) may well be <u>downhill</u> from the initial estimate $\tilde{\theta}$. Although this does not preclude the resulting value from being closer to the true value θ_o than the implied value $\tilde{\theta}$, one is nevertheless entitled to feel a little uncomfortable at such a contingency. It is interesting to speculate on a general procedure based on the substitution of $\tilde{\theta}$ for stage k in the G.Q.T. formula (21). To ensure consistency one would have to arrange for the factor λ to be a random variable tending in probability to zero as the sample size $T \to \infty$. Apart from this interesting possibility, the small-sample properties of the linearised maximum-likelihood estimator have not been investigated. Of course if one can show that the likelihood function is globally concave, whatever the value of θ, every step represented by (24) will then be uphill. In these circumstances, one would expect the linearised M.L. estimator to have favourable small-sample properties.

2.5 Two-Stage Least Squares Methods[7]

As we saw in the previous section, it is advantageous to have available for the purposes of a likelihood estimation an initial consistant estimate of the desired parameter. In other cases, the use of the method of maximum-likelihood may be thought inappropriate. Apart from the computational difficulties already referred to, one may lack confidence as to the accuracy of specification of some of the equations in the system under study. This translates into the employment of full-information maximum-likelihood, for it is known that the performance of this method in estimating one equation will be adversely affected by specification errors in another. For several different reasons, therefore, it is advantageous to have available a limited-information method with convenient computational properties. The method of two-stage least squares and associated techniques have shown promise in disequilibrium situations involving simultaneous nonlinear equations. In this and the following section we shall review the theory of nonlinear two-stage least squares and develop some new results necessary for later chapters.

It will be useful first to outline the calculations for the 2SLS method as applied to linear models. For a more detailed account we refer the reader to chapter 9 of H. Theil [1971], one of the originators of the method. Without loss of generality, the first equation of a system of G linear equations may be written in data-matrix form as

$$(25) \qquad \underset{\sim}{y}_1 = Y_1 \underset{\sim}{\beta}_1 + X_1 \underset{\sim}{\gamma}_1 + \underset{\sim}{u}_1 \ .$$

Here Y_1 and X_1 are $T\times G_1$ and $T\times K_1$ data-matrices for the endogenous and exogenous variables actually included in the first equation. As usual u_{1t} is the disturbance term, and $\underset{\sim}{u}_1$ the vector of realisations.

The 2SLS computational procedure is as follows:

Stage 1: Regress Y_1 on all the exogenous variables X, obtaining fitted values $\hat{Y}_1$.

Stage 2: Returning to equation (25), regress $\underset{\sim}{y}_1$ on $\hat{Y}_1$ and X_1 to obtain the 2SLS estimates $\hat{\underset{\sim}{\beta}}_1$ and $\hat{\underset{\sim}{\gamma}}_1$.

Perhaps the most widely-used justification of this procedure is based on an instrumental variables argument. There are in turn two steps to this argument: (i) that $\hat{Y}_1$ is an acceptable instrument for Y_1, i.e. is correlated with the latter and asymptotically uncorrelated with the disturbance vector $\underset{\sim}{u}_1$ and (ii) that the resulting instrumental variables estimate is equivalent to simply replacing Y_1 by the instrument $\hat{Y}_1$ in (25). With this as background, we may now turn to consider nonlinear systems.

The following representation of a system of G nonlinear equations will be general enough to encompass most of the points of interest in the ensuing discussion:

$$(26) \qquad y_{it} = \underset{\sim}{\beta}_i' \underset{\sim}{g}_i(\underset{\sim}{y}_t^i, \underset{\sim}{x}_t^i, \underset{\sim}{\alpha}_i) + \underset{\sim}{\gamma}_i' \underset{\sim}{x}_t^i + u_{it} \; ; \quad i=1...G \, .$$

Here the following notational conventions are employed:

$\underset{\sim}{g}_i$ indicates a vector of nonlinear functions occurring in the ith equation.

$\underset{\sim}{y}_t^i$ indicates the endogenous variables occurring in the above vector. Where no danger of confusion occurs we shall often drop the superscript i. The included exogenous variables are similarly denoted.

$\underset{\sim}{\alpha}_i$ is a vector of parameters occurring nonlinearly in the ith equation.

$\underset{\sim}{\beta}_i$, $\underset{\sim}{\gamma}_i$ are vectors of parameters occurring linearly.

u_{it} is the ith disturbance term. We suppose such disturbance terms to be serially uncorrelated.

An important special case of (26) is the "linear in parameters" (LIP) specification:

(27) $$y_{it} = \underset{\sim}{\beta}_i' \, \underset{\approx}{g}_i(\underset{\sim}{y}_t^i, \underset{\sim}{x}_t^i) + \underset{\sim}{\gamma}_i' \, \underset{\sim}{x}_t^i + u_{it} \; ; \quad i=1\ldots G \; .$$

Here the internal parameters α_i of equation (26) do not appear. In either (26) or (27) we shall suppose, as an elementary completeness requirement, that the endogenous variables y_{it} can in principle be expressed (or solved) in terms of the exogenous variables and the disturbance terms. This is not to say, however, that such solutions can be found analytically. We note that the exogenous variables may for the purposes of subsequent discussion include lagged values of the endogenous variables, so that we shall henceforth speak of x_t as incorporating the predetermined variables. Finally we assume that the parameters to be estimated are in fact identified.[8]

Let us turn then to the 2SLS estimation of the nonlinear systems (26) and (27). In the remainder of the present section we shall consider problems that arise in employing this technique in the context of LIP models such as (27). Let us investigate first the following procedures. We first regress the included RHS endogenous variables on all the predetermined variables, obtaining fitted values $\hat{\underset{\sim}{y}}_t^i$. Let us consider two possible variants:

(a) $g_i(\hat{\underset{\sim}{y}}_t^i, \underset{\sim}{x}_t^i)$ is used as a vector of instruments for the corresponding $g_i(\underset{\sim}{y}_t^i, \underset{\sim}{x}_t^i)$ in the instrumental-variables estimation of equation (27). (I.V.)

(b) $g_i(\hat{\underset{\sim}{y}}_t^i, \underset{\sim}{x}_t^i)$ replaces $g_i(\underset{\sim}{y}_t^i, \underset{\sim}{x}_t^i)$ in the ordinary least squares estimation of (27). (2.S.L.S.)

As a general matter, it appears that the I.V. technique (a) is consistent, but that the strict 2SLS method is not. To illustrate the distinctions involved, it will be helpful to consider a simple model

(28) $$y_{1t} = \beta_1 \, g(y_t, x_t) + \gamma_1 x_t + u_{1t}$$

where y_t is a single scalar endogenous variable and x_t a scalar predetermined variable which we shall assume strictly exogenous, obeying standard regularity conditions. From the stage one regression we may write $\hat{\underset{\sim}{y}} = P_X \underset{\sim}{y}$, where $P_X = X(X'X)^{-1}X'$ is the least-squares projection matrix in the regression of y_t on all the exogenous variables. Let $E\, y_t/X_t = f(X_t)$ denote the expectation of y_t conditional on the predetermined variables (denoted here X_t) . That is to say,

(30) $$y_t = f(X_t) + \varepsilon_t ,$$

where $E\,\varepsilon_t/X_t = 0$. Now write $\underset{\sim}{e}_t$ as the tth column of $I_{T\times T}$, the identity matrix of order T . Then

$$\hat{y}_t = \underset{\sim}{e}_t' P_X \underset{\sim}{y} = \underset{\sim}{e}_t' P_X \underset{\sim}{f} + \underset{\sim}{e}_t' P_X \underset{\sim}{\varepsilon} .$$

Expanding g_t in Taylor series to terms of second order we have approximately:

(31) $$g(\hat{y}_t, x_t) = g_{xt} + (\underset{\sim}{e}_t' P_X \underset{\sim}{\varepsilon}) g_{xt}' + \tfrac{1}{2}(\underset{\sim}{e}_t' P_X \underset{\sim}{\varepsilon})^2 g_{xt}'' ,$$

where $g_{xt} = g(\underset{\sim}{e}_t' P_X \underset{\sim}{f}, x_t)$.

Let us consider the asymptotic relationship between the disturbance u_{1t} and the suggested instrument. We have

(32) $$\frac{1}{T}\Sigma\, g(\hat{y}_t, x_t) u_{1t} \simeq \frac{1}{T}\Sigma\, g_{xt}\, u_{1t} + \frac{1}{T}\Sigma\, (\underset{\sim}{e}_t' P_X \underset{\sim}{\varepsilon}) g_{xt}'\, u_{1t} + \frac{1}{2T}\Sigma\, (\underset{\sim}{e}_t' P_X \underset{\sim}{\varepsilon})^2 g_{xt}''\, u_{1t} .$$

It is easy to show that the first two terms on the RHS tend in probability to zero. The quadratic term can be written, apart from the factor ½, as

$$\left(\frac{\varepsilon' X}{T}\right)\left(\frac{X'X}{T}\right)^{-1}\left(\frac{1}{T}\Sigma\, X' e_t e_t' X\, \bar{\bar{u}}_{1t}\right)\left(\frac{X'X}{T}\right)^{-1}\left(\frac{X'\varepsilon}{T}\right) ,$$

where $\bar{\bar{u}}_{1t} = g_{xt}''\, u_{1t}$ is now a sequence of non-identically distributed but independent random variables (as are also the ε_t) . The typical term in the inner matrix is

$$\frac{1}{T}\sum_t x_{1t}\, x_{jt}\, \bar{\bar{u}}_t ,$$

which from the strong law of large numbers can be shown to tend in probability to zero. The vector $\frac{X'\varepsilon}{T}$ has a similar limit. Thus the entire term tends in probability to zero. Hence for models in which g_t is a quadratic in y_t, the term $g(\hat{y}_t, x_t)$ is asymptotically uncorrelated with the disturbance term u_{1t}, suggesting that the I.V. method is consistent.

However we can say a little more than this. Assume that the function $g(y_t, x_t)$ has a (bounded) variance for each t , and that when evaluated at the point $\underset{\sim}{e}_t' P_X \underset{\sim}{f}$, the derivatives of all orders of $g(\cdot, x_t)$ exist and are bounded. The first term of equation (32) above can be written $\frac{1}{\sqrt{T}}\left(\frac{1}{\sqrt{T}}\Sigma\, g_{xt}\, u_{1t}\right)$. The term inside the brackets tends in distribution to a random variable with finite variance. The entire term is therefore of order $T^{-\frac{1}{2}}$. The second term can be written as

$$\frac{1}{T}\left(\Sigma \frac{\underset{\sim}{X}_{t\cdot}'\, g_{xt}'\, u_{1t}}{\sqrt{T}}\right)\left(\frac{X'X}{T}\right)^{-1}\left(\frac{X'\underset{\sim}{\varepsilon}}{\sqrt{T}}\right) , \quad \text{where } \underset{\sim}{X}_{t\cdot}' = \underset{\sim}{e}_t' X .$$

The first and third bracketed terms tend in distribution to random variables while the second tends[9] to a matrix of constants. The term is therefore of order T^{-1}. Finally, the third-order term may be expressed as:

$$\frac{1}{T^{3/2}}\left(\frac{\underset{\sim}{\varepsilon}'X}{\sqrt{T}}\right)\left(\frac{X'X}{T}\right)^{-1}\left(\left(\frac{1}{\sqrt{T}}\sum_t x_{1t}\, x_{jt}\, \bar{\bar{u}}_t\right)\right)\left(\frac{X'X}{T}\right)^{-1}\left(\frac{X'\underset{\sim}{\varepsilon}}{\sqrt{T}}\right) ,$$

which is of order $T^{-3/2}$. Evidently all the terms of the infinite Taylor expansion (32) decrease in powers of $T^{-\frac{1}{2}}$. An intuitive (but not rigorous) explanation for this lies in the ascending powers of $(\underset{\sim}{e}_t' P_X \underset{\sim}{\varepsilon})$ which is itself of order $T^{-\frac{1}{2}}$.

Now since the terms in the Taylor expansion decrease in powers of $T^{-\frac{1}{2}}$ we may truncate the expansion after the term of order T^{-1}. It follows from our preliminary analysis above that the instrument $g(\hat{y}_t, x_t)$ and the disturbance term u_{1t} are asymptotically uncorrelated. This argument is due to R.J. Bowden and D.W. Turkington [1978]. They show, by means of the same Taylor expansion, that the sum

$$\frac{1}{T} \sum_t g(\hat{y}_t, x_t) g(y_t, x_t)$$

tends in probability to a finite constant. From these remarks, it follows that $g(\hat{y}_t, x_t)$ is an acceptable instrument for $g(y_t, x_t)$ in the estimation of equation (28). In other words, the I.V. estimator is consistent, is asymptotically Normally distributed, and its asymptotic covariance matrix can be obtained as the standard instrumental variables limiting expression.

Let us consider, on the other hand, the strict 2SLS method. We may write:

$$(33) \qquad y_{1t} = \beta_1 \, g(\hat{y}_t, x_t) + \gamma_1 \, x_t + v_t \, ,$$

where the new disturbance term

$$(34) \qquad v_t = \beta_1 (g(y_t, x_t) - g(\hat{y}_t, x_t)) + u_{1t} \, .$$

Now least squares applied to equation (33) will be consistent if

$$\text{plim} \frac{1}{T} \sum g(\hat{y}_t, x_t) \left[(g(y_t, x_t) - g(\hat{y}_t, x_t)) + u_{1t} \right] = 0 \, .$$

Instrumental variables requires only the limit involving u_{1t} to be zero. We see that the consistency requirements of the strict 2SLS technique are more demanding. For a nonlinear function the expression

$$(35) \qquad \text{plim} \frac{1}{T} \sum g(\hat{y}_t, x_t) \left[g(y_t, x_t) - g(\hat{y}_t, x_t) \right]$$

does not, in general tend to zero in probability. In the linear case, terms like $\sum_t \hat{y}_t (y_t - \hat{y}_t)$ are exactly zero, for any finite sample size, as an elementary least squares orthogonality property. This orthogonality property is not preserved by the nonlinear function g , as can quickly be seen in the present case by employing the expansions (30) and (31). Nor is it even true in a limiting sense as $T \to \infty$.

The sum (35) will be zero if the variables to be projected upon the range space of exogenous variables are not the basic variables y_t , but the entire functions g . Since there is no reason to expect these functions to be even approximately linear functions of X , a better procedure is to project in stage one the functions g on a polynomial in the elements of X . This procedure was suggested by H. Kelejian [1971]. The asymptotic properties of this strict 2SLS technique have been investigated by T. Amemiya [1974], who showed that the asymptotic covariance matrix is obtained by analogy with linear 2SLS with the function g interpreted as a new variable.

One consideration to be observed is that if two or more functions (g_1 and g_2 say) of the endogenous variables appear in the equation under consideration, the order of the approximating polynomial must be the same for each. For suppose on the contrary that we employed two different approximating polynomials, of order N_1 and N_2 . Write $\hat{g}_i = P_{N_i} g_i$, i=1,2, where $P_N = N(N'N)^{-1}N'$ is the least squares projection matrix for a polynomial in the elements of X . Write also

$$\underset{\sim}{g}_i = \underset{\sim}{\hat{g}}_i + \underset{\sim}{v}_i , \quad \text{where } v_i = (I - P_N) g_i , \quad i=1,2 .$$

In other words, $\underset{\sim}{v}_1$ indicates the residual vector in the regression of function g on the polynomial in the elements of X . Likewise for $\underset{\sim}{v}_2$. Set up the stage two regression as:

$$\underset{\sim}{y}_1 = \beta_1 \underset{\sim}{\hat{g}}_1 + \beta_2 \underset{\sim}{\hat{g}}_2 + \gamma_1 \underset{\sim}{x}_1 + \underset{\sim}{\xi}_1 ,$$

where $\underset{\sim}{\xi}_1 = \underset{\sim}{u}_1 + \beta_1 \underset{\sim}{v}_1 + \beta_2 \underset{\sim}{v}_2$. We then have, for instance,

$$\text{plim}\ \frac{1}{T}\ \hat{g}_1'\ \xi_1 = \text{plim}\ \frac{1}{T}\ g_1'\ P_{N_1}\ u_1 + \beta_1\ \text{plim}\ \frac{1}{T}\ g_1'\ P_{N_1}(I - P_{N_1})\ g_1$$

$$+ \beta_2\ \text{plim}\ \frac{1}{T}\ g_1'\ P_{N_1}(I - P_{N_2})\ g_2\ .$$

The first two terms are zero. But if the polynomial indicated by N_1 is not the same as that indexed by N_2, the product $P_{N_1}(I - P_{N_2}) \neq 0$, and inconsistency will result.

Our original discussion of the instrumental variables technique employed as an instrument for $g(y_t, x_t)$ the value $g(\hat{y}_t, x_t)$, where $\hat{y}_t$ represented a projection of y_t on all the exogenous variables (X). We note that a more efficient instrument might result from regressing y_t in stage one upon a polynomial in the exogenous variables, as suggested already for the strict 2SLS technique.

We have reviewed two different approaches to the two-stage least squares problem; the first based on instrumental variables with values fitted from stage one substituted inside the nonlinear functions, the second a strict 2SLS technique in which the entire nonlinear function is treated as a new variable. The question as to which general approach is more efficient may be examined by recalling that the strict 2SLS technique can itself be interpreted as instrumental variable estimation, with $\hat{g}_t$ serving as an instrument for g_t. In terms of standard efficiency comparisons for IV techniques, we then have to ask which instrument is more closely correlated with g_t; $\hat{g}_t$ (strict 2SLS) or $g(\hat{y}_t, x_t)$ (the mooted IV technique)? In its full generality this is a difficult question to answer, but one special case is worthy of consideration.

Reconsidering equation (28), it may be that the RHS endogenous y_t has a reduced form which is linear in the exogenous variables. This circumstance is characteristic of an important class of disequilibrium models discussed at length in chapter 5. Suppose in addition (i) that the function g is badly nonlinear over its likely range, (ii) that the variation in the exogenous variables is large compared with that among the structural residuals. In such circumstances $g(\hat{y}_t, x_t)$ will mirror fairly faithfully the variation in the functions $g(y_t, x_t)$. On the other hand, a high-order approximating polynomial may be necessary for the strict 2SLS technique. If this is impracticable for operational and other reasons (including the effective degrees of freedom), the I.V. technique will be superior to the strict 2SLS calculation. Bowden and Turkington [1978] have confirmed this finding with simulation studies. They find that the performance of the strict 2SLS technique is crucially dependent upon the order of the approximating polynomial. If this is too low, the I.V. technique performs better. This was true even for models where the reduced form was not linear in the exogenous variables. Provided that the variation in the exogenous variables was large relative to the disturbance variation, the I.V. technique offered operational convenience together with reasonable efficiency.

Turkington and Bowden did not compare their results with the "naive 2SLS" technique (option (b) above where $g(\hat{y}_t, x_t)$ simply replaces $g(y_t, x_t)$ in the ordinary least squares calculation of equation (27)). An earlier study by S.M. Goldfeld and R.E. Quandt [1968] claimed very poor results for this technique, but it was subsequently pointed out by Edgerton [1972] that the equation they employed was not in fact estimable by this or any other technique. Our own simulation results reported in chapter 5.6.3 for a disequilibrium model indicated quite good M.S.E. results for this technique. Since naive 2SLS is known to be inconsistent (see above) this indicates that favourable variance properties may counterbalance the presumed inconsistency.

2.6 Conditional Expectations and Two-Stage Least Squares

Let us return to the general model of section 2.5, which encompasses both LIP and non-LIP specifications:

$$y_{it} = \underset{\sim}{\beta}_i' \underset{\sim}{g}_i(\underset{\sim}{y}_t^i, \underset{\sim}{x}_t^i, \underset{\sim}{\alpha}_i) + \underset{\sim}{\gamma}_i' \underset{\sim}{x}_t^i + u_{it} \; ; \qquad i=1\ldots G \; . \tag{26}$$

Suppose that we could write

$$\underset{\sim}{g}_i(\underset{\sim}{y}_t^i, \underset{\sim}{x}_t^i, \alpha_i) = \underset{\sim}{h}_i(X_t;\theta) + \varepsilon_t \; , \tag{36}$$

where $\underset{\sim}{h}_i(X_t;\theta)$ indicates the expectation of the vector function g_i, conditional upon the values of all the predetermined variables (X_t) of the model. As H. Kelejian [1971] has pointed out, the conditional expectations $h_i(X_t;\theta)$ can in many respects be regarded as "ideal" instruments for the functions g_i. As functions only of the predetermined variables, they are uncorrelated with the disturbance terms u_{it}. Moreover we might expect them to mirror any pronounced nonlinearities of the g_i, so that the correlation between the instrument and the variable should be good. Indeed we observe that the use of conditional expectations leads to the Kalman/Bucy theory of optimal prediction for state-space models. Such results do not automatically extend to the essentially nonlinear models discussed here. They might, however, be considered to offer a qualified degree of support for the view of the conditional expectations $h_i(X;\theta)$ as optimal instruments for the nonlinear functions g_i.

There are however some obvious difficulties in the disposition of this instrument. In the first place, it may be impossible to obtain a closed-form expression for the functions h_i. And even if this were possible, $h_i(X_t,\theta)$ will almost always depend upon basic parameters (such as $\underset{\sim}{\beta}_i$, $\underset{\sim}{\gamma}_i$ and the parameters of the disturbance process) which are unknown - and whose determination is indeed the object of the exercise. Remarkably enough however, both these difficulties can be overcome in certain disequilibrium contexts. The functions h_i can be explicitly solved. And though we may not know the parameters θ, it may be possible to devise procedures to consistently estimate this vector. This is not to imply that we have available consistent estimates of the basic parameters (β_i, α_i or γ_i), but only of those compound parameters, functions of these basic parameters and limited in number, which go to make up θ.

It will be useful to state the estimation results for model (26) formally:

Theorem 2.7

Assume that the functions h_i as defined in equation (36) exist, are of bounded variation, and are continuous in θ. Their first derivatives with respect to θ are bounded. Assume also that the residuals ε_t defined by (36) have bounded second moments. Finally suppose that a consistent estimate $\hat{\theta}_T$ of θ is available. Then:

(i) The functions $\hat{h}_i = h_i(X_t, \hat{\theta}_T)$ are acceptable instruments for the functions $g_i(\underset{\sim}{y}_t^i, \underset{\sim}{x}_t^i, \underset{\sim}{\alpha}_i)$.

(ii) The strict 2SLS calculation, in which the $\hat{h}_i$ simply replaces the g_i in an ordinary least squares regression, yields consistent estimates.

Proof. It will suffice to consider the simple model employed in section 2.5, namely

$$(37) \qquad y_{1t} = \beta_1 g(y_t, x_t) + \gamma_1 x_t + u_{1t} ,$$

where y_t and x_t are arbitrary scalar endogenous and predetermined variables. Although (37) is a LIP model, the same argument will apply to non-LIP models (26) in respect of those parameters $\underset{\sim}{\beta}_i$ and $\underset{\sim}{\gamma}_i$ which enter linearly. We write $E g(y_t, x_t)/x_t = h(X_t, \theta) = h_t(\theta)$ where X_t indicates all the predetermined variables.

(i) We have formally:

$$\text{plim}\,\frac{1}{T}\sum_t h_t(\hat{\theta}_T)u_{1t} = \text{plim}\,\frac{1}{T}\sum_t h_t(\theta)u_{1t}$$
$$+ \text{plim}\,\frac{1}{T}\Sigma(h_t(\hat{\theta}_T) - h_t(\theta))u_{1t} \;.$$

The first term on the RHS is zero. With regard to the second,

$$\left|\frac{1}{T}\Sigma(h_t(\hat{\theta}_T) - h_t(\theta)u_{1t}\right| \le \max_{t\le T}\left|h_t(\hat{\theta}_T) - h_t(\theta)\right| \cdot \frac{1}{T}\sum_t \left|u_{1t}\right| \;.$$

It follows from Slutsky's theorem applied to the continuous function max(·) that the RHS of this inequality approaches zero in probability at $T \to \infty$. Result (i) follows.

(ii) We shall prove this part by showing that the I.V. normal equations for stage 2 are asymptotically the same as the OLS equations for this stage. We start by writing the second stage calculation based on (37) as:

(38) $$y_{1t} = \beta_1 h_t(\hat{\theta}_T) + \gamma_1 x_t + v_t \;,$$

where $v_t = \beta_1 \varepsilon_t - \beta_1(h_t(\hat{\theta}_T) - h_t(\theta)) + u_{1t}$

and $\varepsilon_t = g_t - h_t(\theta)$.

The Normal equations for instrumental variables are:

(39) $$\begin{bmatrix} \frac{1}{T}\Sigma h_t(\hat{\theta}_T)g_t & \frac{1}{T}\Sigma h_t(\hat{\theta}_T)x_t \\ \frac{1}{T}\Sigma g_t x_t & \frac{1}{T}\Sigma x_t^2 \end{bmatrix} \begin{bmatrix} \hat{\beta}_1 \\ \hat{\gamma}_1 \end{bmatrix} = \begin{bmatrix} \frac{1}{T}\Sigma h_t(\hat{\theta}_T)y_{1t} \\ \frac{1}{T}\Sigma x_t y_{1t} \end{bmatrix}$$

The Normal equations for strict 2SLS are:

(40)
$$\begin{bmatrix} \frac{1}{T}\Sigma h_t(\hat{\theta}_T)^2 & \frac{1}{T}\Sigma h_t(\hat{\theta}_T)x_t \\ \frac{1}{T}\Sigma h_t(\hat{\theta}_T)x_t & \frac{1}{T}\Sigma x_t^2 \end{bmatrix} \begin{bmatrix} \hat{\hat{\beta}}_1 \\ \hat{\hat{\gamma}}_1 \end{bmatrix} = \begin{bmatrix} \frac{1}{T}\Sigma h_t(\hat{\theta}_T)y_{1t} \\ \frac{1}{T}\Sigma x_t y_{1t} \end{bmatrix}$$

It will be convenient for later purposes to take what may appear an unnecessarily circuitous route to the proof of the asymptotic equivalence of (39) and (40). Subtract (39) from (40) to obtain:

(41)
$$\begin{bmatrix} \frac{1}{T}\Sigma h_t(\hat{\theta}_T)^2 & \frac{1}{T}\Sigma h_t(\hat{\theta}_T)x_t \\ \frac{1}{T}\Sigma h_t(\hat{\theta}_T)x_t & \frac{1}{T}\Sigma x_t^2 \end{bmatrix} \begin{bmatrix} \hat{\beta}_1 - \hat{\hat{\beta}}_1 \\ \hat{\gamma}_1 - \hat{\hat{\gamma}}_1 \end{bmatrix} = -\hat{\beta}_1 \begin{bmatrix} \frac{1}{T}\Sigma h_t(\hat{\theta}_T)(g_t - h_t(\hat{\theta}_T)) \\ \frac{1}{T}\Sigma x_t(g_t - h_t(\hat{\theta}_T)) \end{bmatrix}$$

Consider first the matrix on the LHS of equation (41). Since $\hat{\theta}_T$ is by assumption consistent, it is easy to show that this tends in probability to a nonsingular matrix of constants. Turning to the RHS, we know that $\hat{\beta}_1 \xrightarrow{p} \beta_1$ from the consistency of IV (part (i)). The term

(42)
$$\frac{1}{T}\Sigma h_t(\hat{\theta}_T)(g_t - h_t(\hat{\theta}_T)) = \frac{1}{T}\Sigma h_t(\hat{\theta}_T)\varepsilon_t - \frac{1}{T}\Sigma h_t(\hat{\theta}_T)(h_t(\hat{\theta}_T) - h_t(\theta)) ,$$

where ε_t is defined by equations (38) above. In turn, we may write the first term of this sum as

$$\frac{1}{T}\Sigma h_t(\hat{\theta}_T)\varepsilon_t = \frac{1}{T}\Sigma h_t(\theta)\varepsilon_t + \frac{1}{T}(h_t(\hat{\theta}_T) - h_t(\theta))\varepsilon_t .$$

From the strong law of large numbers for non-identical but independent random variables, the first term on the RHS tends to zero in probability.

The second term can be shown to tend to zero by an argument used in part (i). Returning to (42), we may expand $\hat{h}_t$ in Taylor series about the true value to obtain:

$$h_t(\hat{\theta}_T) = h_t(\theta) + (\theta_T - \theta)h_t(\theta_*) ,$$

where θ_* lies between θ and θ_T and consequently $\xrightarrow{p} \theta$ as $T \to \infty$. The second term on the RHS of (42) may therefore be written $(\hat{\theta}_T - \theta) \frac{1}{T} \Sigma h_t(\hat{\theta}_T)h_t(\theta_*)$. It follows from the consistency of $\hat{\theta}_T$ that this expression $\xrightarrow{p} 0$. Hence the entire expression defined by equation (42) has zero as its probability limit. By similar arguments, the other term on the RHS of (41) shares this limit. It follows that

$$\text{plim}\begin{bmatrix}\hat{\hat{\beta}}_1 \\ \\ \hat{\hat{\gamma}}_1\end{bmatrix} = \text{plim}\begin{bmatrix}\hat{\beta}_1 \\ \\ \hat{\gamma}_1\end{bmatrix} = \begin{bmatrix}\beta_1 \\ \\ \gamma_1\end{bmatrix} ,$$

as required.

Two comments are in order concerning the results of this theorem:

(a) Although the proof as given for part (ii) presupposes a LIP model, there is nothing to prevent its applicability to the estimation of $\underset{\sim}{\beta}_i$ and $\underset{\sim}{\gamma}_i$ in the more general non-LIP model (26). We note that part (i) and the methods of the previous section are applicable only to LIP models. Consequently the use of the conditional expectation in the manner suggested by part (ii) of this theorem may be the only general approach available for non-LIP models.

(b) We have as yet said nothing concerning the asymptotic covariance matrices of the two estimators. The ACM of the instrumental variables estimators can be obtained according to the usual formula. In the case of our simple model, this is:

$$\sigma_1^2 \text{ plim} \begin{bmatrix} \frac{1}{T}\Sigma h_t(\hat{\theta}_T)g_t & \frac{1}{T}\Sigma h_t(\hat{\theta}_T)x_t \\ \frac{1}{T}\Sigma g_t x_t & \frac{1}{T}\Sigma x_t^2 \end{bmatrix}^{-1} \begin{bmatrix} \frac{1}{T}\Sigma h_t^2(\hat{\theta}_T) & \frac{1}{T}\Sigma h_t(\hat{\theta}_T)x_t \\ \frac{1}{T}\Sigma h_t(\hat{\theta}_T)x_t & \frac{1}{T}\Sigma x_t^2 \end{bmatrix}$$

$$\cdot \begin{bmatrix} \frac{1}{T}\Sigma h_t(\hat{\theta}_T)g_t & \frac{1}{T}\Sigma h(\hat{\theta}_T)x_t \\ \frac{1}{T}\Sigma g_t x_t & \frac{1}{T}\Sigma x_t^2 \end{bmatrix}^{-1} .$$

This can be shown by arguments outlined in the course of the proof of theorem 2.7 to be the same as:

(43)
$$\sigma_1^2 \begin{bmatrix} \lim \frac{1}{T}\Sigma h_t^2(\theta) & \lim \frac{1}{T}\Sigma h_t(\theta)x_t \\ \lim \frac{1}{T}\Sigma h_t(\theta)x_t & \lim \frac{1}{T}\Sigma x_t^2 \end{bmatrix}^{-1} .$$

This has the same form as the limiting covariance matrix which would be obtained by mechanically applying the usual OLS formula to stage 2 of the strict 2SLS calculation.

However it does not follow from this that in fact the asymptotic covariance matrix of the strict 2SLS procedure is given by (43). Let us refer back to equation (41). The inverse matrix on the LHS has the limit (43) above. Premultiply both sides of (41) by this matrix. Apart from the inverse (43) as a limiting multiplicative factor, the vector $\sqrt{T} \begin{bmatrix} \hat{\beta}_1 - \hat{\hat{\beta}}_1 \\ \hat{\gamma}_1 - \hat{\hat{\gamma}}_1 \end{bmatrix}$ has the same limiting distribution as

$$-\hat{\beta}_1 \begin{bmatrix} \frac{1}{\sqrt{T}} h_t(\hat{\theta}_T)(g_t - h_t(\hat{\theta}_T)) \\ \\ \frac{1}{\sqrt{T}} \Sigma x_t(g_t - h_t(\hat{\theta}_T)) \end{bmatrix},$$

which in general is not available. For our present purposes we note that $\sqrt{T} \begin{bmatrix} \hat{\hat{\beta}}_1 \\ \hat{\hat{\gamma}}_1 \end{bmatrix}$ has not the same limiting distribution as $\sqrt{T} \begin{bmatrix} \hat{\beta}_1 \\ \hat{\gamma}_1 \end{bmatrix}$.

It follows that the limiting covariance matrix of the strict 2SLS procedure is not the same as (43). No general formula appears to exist.

We have now concluded our survey and development of non-linear estimation techniques. As a survey it has been slanted towards the particular exigencies of work on disequilibrium models. One or two general techniques not covered here, such as nonlinear least squares, will later turn up, but we find it convenient to discuss their properties at the point of application. Nor have we explictly concerned ourselves with efficiency aspects of nonlinear estimation. A theory of efficient instrumental variables exists for linear systems (J.M. Brundy and D.W. Jorgenson [1971]). However no general criteria exist for nonlinear models, though the matter has received some recent discussion (e.g. D.W. Jorgenson and J-J. Laffont [1974]). Where efficiency considerations are raised in the present study, the level of discussion is therefore rather intuitive.

Footnotes to Chapter 2

[1]This section is based on R.J. Bowden [1973], but much of the raw material is due to A. Wald [1943].

[2]We shall adopt special notation to distinguish vectors ($\underset{\sim}{y}$ rather than y) only when there is danger of confusion with scalars. The order of these vectors may be any finite number, but we have no need as yet to specify any particular order.

[3]The distributions of chapter 5 do not obey this assumption. However their irregularity does not appear to be specifically due to this failure. As pointed out in Bowden [1973], the continuity assumption is not necessary for the definitions that follow.

[4]The terms "with probability one", "almost certainly", "strongly consistent" are synonymous with "almost everywhere". Use of this mode of convergence is becoming more widespread in econometrics. It refers to the simultaneous behaviour of θ_t for t greater than some given value T. Thus if

$$\text{Prob}\left[|\theta_t - \theta_o| < \varepsilon \text{ ; for all } t > T\right] \longrightarrow 1 \text{ as } T \to \infty$$

we say that θ_T tends almost certainly to θ_o. This "tail condition" is stronger than convergence in probability. An easy to understand distinction is in P. Whittle [1970]. As a notational convention, we write $\theta_T \xrightarrow{a.c.} \theta_o$ or $\theta_T \xrightarrow{a.e.} \theta_o$, while $\theta_T \xrightarrow{p} \theta_o$ denotes convergence in probability.

[5]Let $Q_T(w,\theta)$ be a measurable function on a measurable space Ω and for each w in Ω a continuous function of θ in a compact set Θ. Then there exists a measurable function $\hat{\theta}_T(w)$ such that

$$Q_T(w,\hat{\theta}_T(w)) = \sup_{\theta\in\Theta}.\ Q_T(w,\theta) \ , \qquad w \in \Omega \ .$$

If $Q_T(w,\theta) \xrightarrow{a.e.} Q(\theta)$ uniformly for all θ in Θ, then $\hat{\theta}_T(w)$ converges to θ_o almost everywhere, where θ_o is the unique maximum of $Q(\theta)$.

[6]Let $f_T(w,\theta)$ be a measurable function on a measurable space Ω, and for each $w \in \Omega$ a continuous function for θ in a compact set Θ. If $f_T(w;\theta)$ converges to $f(\theta)$ a.e. uniformly in θ and if $\hat{\theta}_T(w) \xrightarrow{a.e.} \theta_o$, then $f_T(w,\hat{\theta}_T(w) \xrightarrow{a.e.} f(\theta_o)$.

[7]I am grateful to Darrell Turkington for specific help with this section.

[8]The identification theory of LIP models has received a general treatment by F.M. Fisher [1966]. Fisher defines identification in this context as the absence of functional transformations of the disturbance terms u_{it} which yield a system of the same functional form as the original system, and compatible with the *a-priori* restrictions on the elements of β_i and γ_i. For nonlinear models, this appears to be a different concept from the classical definition incorporated in §2.1, where identification is viewed as a property of the implied probability distribution function of the endogenous variables. From this point of view Fisher's results are necessary for the identification of β_i and γ_i, but it is not apparent that they are sufficient.

[9]Strictly speaking, we should recognise the possibility that X contains lagged endogenous variables and speak of the limit in probability of $\frac{X'X}{T}$.

CHAPTER THREE

THE PAMEQ SPECIFICATION AND THE EXCESS-DEMAND PROBLEM

In this chapter, we consider the paradigm referred to in chapter 1 as the "excess-demand" problem. As we have suggested, complete approaches to disequilibrium analysis might attempt to model both price and quantity determination. In this way, estimates of the underlying demand and supply curves, "notional" or "effective" as the case may be, may be derived. However the specification requirements for complete models of this kind are rather demanding, and in some cases the extra information from considering quantity dynamics may not be important. In other situations the nature of the demand and supply schedules may be such that they can be identified from consideration of the excess-demand functions alone. The development of chapter 4 is an example. There is therefore ample motivation for considering in detail the estimation of excess-demand functions, relating price changes to imbalances in demand and supply.

We shall point out that existing econometric treatments of this problem involve what can be regarded as a defect from the statistical viewpoint. This is that equilibrium is not a testable proposition in the chosen framework. The present chapter is therefore a convenient point at which to introduce the specification of adjustment processes in terms of a partial adjustment to an imputed moving equilibrium (the PAMEQ specification). This consists in a transformation of existing adjustment mechanisms, according to which it is possible to test that the model is always in equilibrium by simply setting a certain "friction" parameter equal to zero. The benefits of this specification are not confined to problems of inference. We shall see that it allows a natural decomposition of the history of a time series into disequilibrium fluctuations superimposed on longer-run equilibrium movements. The equilibrium values themselves can be regarded as estimable, and the PAMEQ specification permits a straightforward approach to this problem.

3.1 The Excess-Demand Problem in Existing Treatments

We start by considering non-stochastic demand and supply schedules for a single good. In continuous-time we might write:

$$\text{(1) (a)} \quad D(t) = a_1 p(t) + \underset{\sim}{X}_1(t)'\underset{\sim}{b}_1 \quad , \qquad a_1 \leq 0$$

$$\text{(b)} \quad S(t) = a_2 p(t) + \underset{\sim}{X}_2(t)'\underset{\sim}{b}_2 \quad , \qquad a_2 \geq 0 \; .$$

Here D, S refer to quantities demanded and supplied (but not necessarily transacted), p is price and $\underset{\sim}{X}_1$, $\underset{\sim}{X}_2$ are exogenous vector functions of time, which may contain elements in common. The standard continuous competitive Walrasian adjustment mechanism is:

$$\text{(2)} \quad \dot{p} = \theta(D - S) \quad , \qquad \theta \geq 0 \; .$$

The above equations have standard discrete analogues, namely:

$$\text{(3) (a)} \quad D_t = \alpha_1 p_t + \underset{\sim}{X}'_{1t} \underset{\sim}{\beta}_1 \qquad \alpha_1 \leq 0$$

$$\text{(b)} \quad S_t = \alpha_2 p_t + \underset{\sim}{X}'_{2t} \underset{\sim}{\beta}_2 \qquad \alpha_2 \geq 0 \; ,$$

and

$$\text{(4)} \quad p_t = p_{t-1} + \lambda(D_t - S_t) \; , \qquad \lambda \geq 0 \; .$$

Note first that the timing of the discrete mechanism (4) is a little odd. Thus if p_t is taken to refer to price at the end of the period, equation (4) cannot refer to any behavioural hypothesis about price setters. The resolution of the apparent difficulty lies in the fact that (4) can be regarded as a solution of the continuous adjustment mechanism (2). Now it is quite possible to specify and estimate the system wholly in continuous time and we refer the reader to the collection by A.R. Bergstrom *et al* [1976]. Whether it is better to do so turns upon the limits of our ability to accurately specify economic processes together with available measurement techniques, and is not a question we shall discuss here. But for less ambitious projects, the discrete mechanism (4) nevertheless sits uncomfortably with our intuitive feeling that such adjustment processes should have some tangible correspondence with any presumptions we may have about the behaviour of market participants or about the nature of the market clearing process. We shall return later to this point.

The parameters θ or λ in the adjustment mechanisms (2) or (4) indicate the speed with which the system traverses to equilibrium. Referring first to (2), if $\theta = 0$ the variables do not respond to demand/supply imbalances and clearing is infinitely slow. On the other hand, as $\theta \to \infty$, the reaction becomes infinitely fast, and a demand/supply imbalance cannot persist for a finite length of time. Suppose, for instance that $X_1(t) = X_2(t) = 1$, and let the system initially be at price level p_o. Write the equilibrium price as $\bar{p} = \frac{b_2 - b_1}{a_1 - a_2}$. The resulting dynamic system has solution

$$p(t) = \bar{p} + (p_o - \bar{p})e^{-\theta(a_2 - a_1)t} .$$

We see that as $\theta \to \infty$, $p(t)$ approaches closer and closer to $\bar{p}$. In particular,

$$\theta = \frac{1}{a_1 - a_2} \log\left(\frac{p(1) - \bar{p}}{p_o - \bar{p}}\right) .$$

Arithmetic changes in the parameter θ are therefore directly related to changes in the proportion of an initial disequilibrium gap closed per unit of time. Suppose that we define a new parameter $\mu = e^{\theta(a_1 - a_2)}$. It will follow that

$$\mu = \frac{p(1) - \bar{p}}{p_o - \bar{p}} ,$$

so that μ directly measures the proportion mentioned above. Similar relationships hold for the discrete-time formulation, (3) and (4). There is indeed a functional relationship between the discrete time adjustment parameter λ and the parameters of the continuous version, namely

$$e^{\theta(a_1 - a_2)} = \frac{1}{1 - \lambda(\alpha_1 - \alpha_2)} .$$

Once again the parameter $\mu = \frac{1}{1 - \lambda(\alpha_1 - \alpha_2)}$ may be taken as a direct measure of the proportion of an initial gap closed per unit time and hence as an index of the speed of disequilibrium adjustment. In both cases, we note that $\mu = 0$ will correspond to instantaneous adjustment, which is the same as saying that the model is an equilibrium one, and $\mu = 1$ can be taken as indicating infinitely slow adjustment.

Consider now the econometric problem of testing whether the adjustment process is such as to allow disequilibrium states to persist. One might think, in the case of discrete data, of a test based on the magnitude of λ , of equation (4). That is, one could introduce disturbances into equations (3) and (4) and employ usual techniques of estimation and inference in respect of the parameters of these equations. The difficulty in doing so will immediately be apparent. The range of this parameter is from zero to infinity. On such a scale it is difficult to judge whether the market is slow or fast to clear. It would be more convenient from this point of view to estimate a parameter whose range is between zero and unity. More important is the difficulty which arises in testing the limiting case. We wish, say, to arrange "equilibrium" as a point, null hypothesis. (If we are to set up a point hypothesis there is no other option, since "disequilibrium" evidently is not a unique phenomenon so far as the parameters of the adjustment mechanism are concerned). But what procedure is appropriate for testing $\lambda = \infty$ as a null hypothesis? We might test $\frac{1}{\lambda} = 0$, but this is simply arbitrary. As we shall see, such troublesome questions can simply be bypassed with an appropriate respecification of the system.

3.2[1] PAMEQ: The Univariate Case

Let us now add disturbance terms to the discrete equations (3) and (4):

(5) (a) $D_t = \alpha_1 p_t + \underset{\sim}{X}'_{1t} \underset{\sim}{\beta}_1 + u_{1t}$

(b) $S_t = \alpha_2 p_t + \underset{\sim}{X}'_{2t} \underset{\sim}{\beta}_2 + u_{2t}$.

The adjustment equation may be either:

(6) (a) $p_t - p_{t-1} = \lambda(D_t - S_t)$

or

(b) $p_t - p_{t-1} = \lambda(D_t - S_t) + \varepsilon_t$.

In the above system of stochastic equations, the variables u_{1t}, u_{2t} and ε_t are all supposed white-noise disturbance terms. It will be observed according to (6)(a) and (b) that there are two possible specifications for the price adjustment equation; "error-free clearing" (EFC), which is an exact relationship, and "noisy clearing" (NC), which is not.

Let us now introduce an unobservable variable p_t^*. This represents the price at which the market would clear if it could. In other words, given the current values of the predetermined variables, p_t^* is defined by:

$$D_t = \alpha_1 p_t^* + \underset{\sim}{X}'_{1t} \underset{\sim}{\beta}_1 + u_{1t} = \alpha_2 p_t^* + \underset{\sim}{X}'_{2t} \underset{\sim}{\beta}_2 + u_{2t} = S_t ,$$

that is:

$$p_t^* = \frac{1}{\alpha_1 - \alpha_2} (\underset{\sim}{X}'_{2t} \underset{\sim}{\beta}_2 - \underset{\sim}{X}'_{1t} \underset{\sim}{\beta}_1) + \frac{1}{\alpha_1 - \alpha_2} (u_{2t} - u_{1t}) .$$

Evidently if the market is to be continuously in a state of equilibrium, $p_t = p_t^*$, all t . We propose replacing (6)(a) and (b) by:

(7) (a) $p_t = \mu p_{t-1} + (1-\mu) p_t^* \quad ; \quad 0 \le \mu \le 1$,

(b) $p_t = \mu p_{t-1} + (1-\mu) p_t^* + u_{3t} \; ; \; 0 \le \mu \le 1 , \; \lim_{\mu \to 0} \text{Var}(u_{3t}) = 0$.

To obtain the limiting case of instantaneous market equilibrium, we put $\mu = 0$; the other polar case of no response corresponds to $\mu = 1$. Thus we are employing the parameter μ as a measure of the drag in market clearing, a coefficient of friction as it were. It is evident that $p_t \gtrless p_t^*$ according as $D_t \lessgtr S_t$, so that the sign of $p_t - p_t^*$ can be taken to discriminate between periods of excess supply (+) or excess demand (-).

With regard to equation (7)(b), there are two possible specifications for the limiting variance of u_{3t}:

(i) With the condition $\lim_{\mu \to 0} \mathrm{Var}(u_{3t}) = 0$ as given above, the implication is that as market clearing becomes instantaneous, i.e. as $\mu \to 0$, the model in its entirety reduces to the standard equilibrium simultaneous model:

(8) $$Q_t = \underset{\sim}{X}'_{1t} \underset{\sim}{\beta}_1 + \alpha_1 p_t + u_{1t}$$

$$Q_t = \underset{\sim}{X}'_{2t} \underset{\sim}{\beta}_1 + \alpha_2 p_t + u_{2t} .$$

It will be noted that the disequilibrium models above are not complete as an estimable system, for there is no equation explaining the determination of observable quantities (Q) in disequilibrium. But however the missing equation is specified, putting $\mu = 0$ will reduce the disequilibrium model to the equilibrium system (8). To use statistical terminology, the standard simultaneous model of price and quantity determination can be regarded as nested, according to the parameter μ, within the class of models defined by equations (5) and (7). Our use of the word "nested" here refers to its usage in maximum-likelihood theory. The likelihood function of the equilibrium model may be obtained from the disequilibrium model by simply putting $\mu = 0$. No structural recasting of any equation is involved.

(ii) An alternative specification is that no such limiting process occurs for $\mathrm{Var}(u_{3t})$. Thus when $\mu = 0$ we can write the system as:

(9) $$Q_t = \underset{\sim}{X}'_{1t}\underset{\sim}{\beta}_1 + \alpha_1 p_t^* + u_{1t}$$

$$Q_t = \underset{\sim}{X}'_{2t}\underset{\sim}{\beta}_1 + \alpha_2 p_t^* + u_{2t}$$

$$p_t = p_t^* + u_{3t} \, .$$

The implication is that there is a certain price level p_t^* which, given the current values of the exogenous variables $\underset{\sim}{X}_1$ and $\underset{\sim}{X}_2$ and disturbances u_{1t}, u_{2t}, would clear the market, in the sense that demand and supply schedules would be equal. But the actual price level p_t differs from this clearing price by a random factor u_{3t}. This specification is not nested, in the sense described under (i), if part of our object is to derive estimates of the variances of the disturbance terms u_{1t} and u_{2t}. In this respect we note that there may be difficulties in identifying the disturbance process under this specification. To see this, write the equilibrium model as a two-equation system in the observable variables p and Q. Then there are just three reduced-form covariance equations available for the identification of the six elements of the covariance matrix of (u_{1t}, u_{2t}, u_{3t}). On the other hand, it may turn out that such difficulties disappear out of equilibrium. A systematic study of identification problems in disequilibrium processes remains to be accomplished. In the meantime, both for this reason and because we think it preferable from the point of view of interpretation, we are inclined to prefer the limiting specification (i).

We have not yet discussed the relationship of our respecification to existing formulations. But the adjustment equations (7) are attractive specifications in their own right. It is worth noting that these equations may be generalised. Equation 7(a), for instance, may be written in terms of past p_t^* by the distributed lag formulation:

$$p_t = (1-\mu)(p_t^* + \mu p_{t-1}^* + \mu^2 p_{t-2}^* + \ldots) \, .$$

One might accordingly think of more general distributed lag clearing mechanisms of the form

$$p_t = w_o p_t^* + w_1 p_{t-1}^* + \dots ,$$

which in turn may be augmented with an error process, not necessarily of white-noise type, as the generalisation of equation (7)(b). Although our specification lends itself readily to such generalisations of the Walrasian clearing mechanism, we shall confine our econometric discussion to the simpler schemes of equation (7).

We note finally that these equations may be recast in the following form:

(10) (a) $p_t = p_{t-1} + (1-\mu)(p_t^* - p_{t-1})$

(b) $p_t = p_{t-1} + (1-\mu)(p_t^* - p_{t-1}) + u_{3t}$.

Prices adjust each period partially to the moving equilibrium p_t^*. The partial adjustment parameter is $(1-\mu)$. This formulation motivates the PAMEQ pseudonym. It enables us to see also that although there are two natural "benchmark" figures, namely $\mu = 0$ and $\mu = 1$, to restrict μ to this interval (as is done above) is not logically necessary. Thus $\mu < 0$ would indicate overshooting of the equilibrium position, for in this case the parameter $(1-\mu)$ of equations (10) would exceed unity. It is also possible to imagine $\mu > 1$, although such an adjustment would surely be rather "pathological". In general, putting restrictions on the domain of μ corresponds to making definite *a-priori* statements about the possible modes of dynamic behaviour. The particular restriction $0 \le \mu \le 1$ gives in (7) above happens to correspond to dynamic modes possible under the standard Walrasian formulations discussed in section 3.1. There is however, no binding reason why we should not take advantage of the freedom of our respecification, and set no restrictions upon the parameter μ .

3.3 Relationship With Standard Adjustment Rules

In this section we shall show that, under suitable assumptions, the PAMEQ specification subsumes both standard discrete and continuous Walrasian adjustment mechanisms. Let us consider first the discrete case. Starting from equation (6)(b), we have:

$$\begin{aligned} p_t - p_{t-1} &= \lambda(D_t - S_t) + \varepsilon_t \\ &= \lambda[\alpha_1 p_t^* + \underset{\sim}{X}'_{1t} \underset{\sim}{\beta}_1 + u_{1t} + \alpha_1(p_t - p_t^*) - \{\alpha_2 p_t^* + \underset{\sim}{X}'_{2t} \underset{\sim}{\beta}_2 \\ &\qquad + u_{2t} + \alpha_2(p_t - p_t^*)\}] + \varepsilon_t \\ &= \lambda(\alpha_1 - \alpha_2)(p_t - p_t^*) + \varepsilon_t , \end{aligned}$$

employing the definition of p_t^*. Define now

$$\mu = \frac{1}{1 - \lambda(\alpha_1 - \alpha_2)} .$$

We obtain

$$(11) \qquad p_t = \mu p_{t-1} + (1 - \mu) p_t^* + u_{3t} ,$$

where $u_{3t} = \mu\varepsilon_t$. Observe that Var $u_{3t} = \mu^2$ Var $\varepsilon_t \longrightarrow 0$ as $\mu \to 0$ as required by (7)(b). We have already come across the mapping (11) in section 3.1. It tells us that $\lambda = 0$ (infinitely slow clearing) corresponds to $\mu = 1$ and that $\lambda = \infty$ (infinitely fast clearing) corresponds to $\mu = 0$. Note that if $\lambda \geq 0$, we must have $0 \leq \mu \leq 1$, under standard sign restrictions on the α_i. In short, the PAMEQ specification subsumes the discrete adjustment process.

Alternatively we might reject the idea that clearing is supposed to take place at discrete points in time. What sort of discrete specification we end up with depends upon the assumptions we make concerning continuous-time dynamics. Let us specify for the price adjustment equation in continuous time (denoted w) the following stochastic differential equation:

(12) $$dp = \theta(D(w) - S(w)) + d\xi(w) .$$

For the disturbance term we have introduced a random process $\xi(w)$ with orthogonal increments $d\xi(w)$. This is the natural generalisation to continuous time of the discrete white-noise process (e.g. D.R. Cox and H.D. Miller [1965]). We assume that

$$E\, d\xi(w) = 0 \qquad \text{all } w ,$$

$$E|d\xi(w)|^2 = \sigma^2 dw$$

and $$E\, d\xi(w)\overline{d\xi(w')} = 0 \qquad \text{if } w \neq w' .$$

As for the discrete case we may show that:

$$D(w) - S(w) = (a_1 - a_2)(p(w) - p^*(w)) .$$

So

(13) $$dp = \theta(a_1 - a_2)(p(w) - p^*(w))dw + d\xi(w) .$$

This equation can be rewritten as:

$$d(p - p^*) = \theta(a_1 - a_2)(p - p^*)dw - dp^* + d\xi(w) ,$$

which has the solution:

(14) $$p_t = p_t^* + e^{\theta(a_1 - a_2)}(p_{t-1} - p_{t-1}^*) - \int_{t-1}^{t} e^{\theta(a_1 - a_2)(t - w)} dp^*(w) + \int_{t-1}^{t} e^{\theta(a_1 - a_2)(t - w)} d\xi(w) .$$

Consider the first integral on the RHS of (14). Integrating by parts,

$$\int_{t-1}^{t} e^{-\theta(a_1 - a_2)w} dp^*(w) = \Big[e^{-\theta(a_1 - a_2)w} p^*(w)\Big]_{t-1}^{t} + \theta(a_1 - a_2)\int_{t-1}^{t} e^{-\theta(a_1 - a_2)w} p^*(w)\, dw$$

Writing $\mu = e^{\theta(a_1 - a_2)}$, equation (14) becomes:

$$(15) \qquad p_t = \mu p_{t-1} - \theta(a_1 - a_2)e^{\theta(a_1 - a_2)t}\int_{t-1}^{t} e^{-\theta(a_1 - a_2)w}\, p^*(w)\, dw + \int_{t-1}^{t} e^{\theta(a_1 - a_2)(t-w)}\, d\xi(w) \;.$$

The evaluation of (15) now depends on what sort of approximation procedure we employ for the first integral on the RHS of (15), namely

$$I = \int_{t-1}^{t} e^{-\theta(a_1 - a_2)w}\, p^*(w)\, dw \;.$$

(a) Let us assume that the processes $\underset{\sim}{X}_1$, $\underset{\sim}{X}_2$ and u_1, u_2 are slowly changing relative to the speed of price adjustment. An extreme version of this is to be found in some theoretical treatments in which market clearing is supposed to occur in "metatime" rather than actual time. For our purposes the assumption is obviously a poor one for extreme disequilibrium phenomena in which market clearing is very slow indeed. With this assumption, $p^*(w)$ is approximately constant over the interval $(t-1,t)$, so that over this interval we may write $p^*(w) = p_t^*$. In this case,

$$I = -\frac{e^{-\theta(a_1 - a_2)t}}{\theta(a_1 - a_2)} \cdot (1-\mu)p_t^* \;.$$

Substituting into (15) we obtain:

$$(16) \qquad p_t = \mu p_{t-1} + (1-\mu)p_t^* + u_{3t} \;,$$

where $u_{3t} \triangleq \int_{t-1}^{t} e^{\theta(a_1 - a_2)(t-w)}\, d\xi(w) = -\int_{0}^{1} e^{\theta(a_1 - a_2)w}\, d\xi(t-w)$.

Obviously $E\, u_{3t} = 0$. Since $\xi(t)$ is stationary, we must have

$$E\, u_{3t}^2 = \sigma^2 \int_{0}^{1} e^{2\theta(a_1 - a_2)w}\, dw \;.$$

Hence

(17) $$E\,u_{3t}^2 = \frac{\sigma^2}{2} \cdot \frac{\mu^2 - 1}{\log \mu} \ .$$

We observe by L'Hôpital's rule that

$$\lim_{\mu \to 0} E\ u_{3t}^2 = \frac{\sigma^2}{2} \lim_{\mu \to 0} \frac{1}{\left(\frac{1}{\mu}\right)}$$

$$= 0\ .$$

It follows that the derived form (16) is identical with the PAMEQ specification (7)(b).

(b) Instead of supposing $p^*(t)$ to be approximately constant over the interval $(t-1,t)$ we could consider other approximations to the integral I. According to the trapezoidal rule for numerical approximations we could write:

$$I \simeq \tfrac{1}{2}\left(e^{-\theta(a_1 - a_2)t}\ p_t^* + e^{-\theta(a_1 - a_2)(t - 1)}\ p_{t-1}^*\right) .$$

Inserting this approximation into equation (15) we obtain:

(18) $$p_t = \mu p_{t-1} - \gamma(p_t^* + \mu p_{t-1}^*) + u_{3t}\ ,$$

where $\gamma \overset{\Delta}{=} \frac{\theta}{2}(a_1 - a_2) = \tfrac{1}{2} \log \mu < 0$.

Equation (18) does not satisfy desirable consistency requirements. Observe that when $\mu \to 1$, $\gamma \to 0$ so $p_t \to p_{t-1}$. This is, of course, desirable. But when $\mu \to 0$, indicating instantaneous clearing, $\gamma \to -\infty$, so that (18) does not give a globally sensible adjustment mechanism.

In summary, the PAMEQ specification as given by equations (7) is a rather general price adjustment mechanism which includes as special cases the discrete Walrasian mechanism and an approximation to the continuous-time version of the latter. Perhaps more to the point, it constitutes an intuitively appealing adjustment procedure in its own right, with no prior appeal to existing standard discrete or continuous-time formulations. This is true either of the original formulas (7), or the alternative interpretations of equations (10). The idea that we should take the PAMEQ specification as a primitive notion, or starting point, becomes even more appealing when we consider the nature of observable price or quantity aggregates. In justifying PAMEQ in terms of standard continuous adjustment mechanisms we have implicitly assumed that point observations on p are available. But in practice, observations are usually derived from a process of sampling and aggregation which may extend over a substantial portion of the unit of time being considered (a month, or a quarter). The relationship of such a sampling/aggregation process to the theoretical point observations therefore needs a separate theory in its own right. The point gains force from the applicability of the excess-demand paradigm to national income statistics (see e.g. chapter 4 of the present study) which are explicitly aggregated over a unit period. In short we could if we wished posit an underlying continuous-time adjustment process and construct in addition a theory of time-aggregation, to end up with estimable relationships between observable magnitudes. The PAMEQ formulation is an economical and robust alternative. On these grounds we propose replacing the conventional adjustment parameters (λ or θ) as objects of primary interest by the adjustment parameter μ as defined in the PAMEQ specification.

3.4 Other Adjustment Modes

The PAMEQ specification can be extended to cover other modes of adjustment. We consider in this section two such applications.

3.4.1 Acceleration Modes. Let us consider an adjustment mechanism of a kind mentioned in chapter 1.2.2, where the rate of price change is dependent not only upon excess demand but also upon the rate of change of excess demand. The basic idea is the appealing one that a given state of excess demand will have different consequences for price change according to whether it is rising or falling. Thus we might write in continuous time, as a generalisation of equation (13),

$$dp = \theta_1(D(w) - S(w))dw + \theta_2(D(w) \dot{-} S(w))dw + d\xi(w), \qquad \theta_1, \theta_2 \geq 0 . \tag{19}$$

Following similar steps to those in connection with (13), we derive:

$$d(p - p^*) = \frac{\theta_1(a_1 - a_2)}{1 - \theta_2(a_1 - a_2)}(p - p^*)dw - \frac{1}{1 - \theta_2(a_1 - a_2)}dp^* + \frac{d\xi(w)}{1 - \theta_2(a_1 - a_2)} .$$

Write $\beta = \dfrac{\theta_1(a_1 - a_2)}{1 - \theta_2(a_1 - a_2)}$ and $\mu = e^{\beta}$.

Integrating the above stochastic differential equation, we have:

$$p_t = p_t^* + \mu(p_{t-1} - p_{t-1}^*) - \frac{1}{1 - \theta_2(a_1 - a_2)} \int_{t-1}^{t} e^{\beta(t - w)} dp^*(w) + \int_{t-1}^{t} \frac{e^{\beta(t - w)}}{1 - \theta_2(a_1 - a_2)} d\xi(w) .$$

Writing $\gamma = \dfrac{1}{1 - \theta_2(a_1 - a_2)}$ we obtain

$$p_t = p_t^* + \mu(p_{t-1} - p_{t-1}^*) - \gamma(p_t^* - \mu p_{t-1}^*) - \gamma\beta \int_{t-1}^{t} e^{\beta(t - w)} p^*(w)\, dw + v_t , \tag{20}$$

where $v_t = \gamma \int_{t-1}^{t} e^{\beta(t-w)} d\xi(w)$. Once again we have the problem of approximating the integral on the RHS of (20) involving p^* . Choosing the simplest approximation procedure (case (a) of section 3.3) we have

$$\int_{t-1}^{t} e^{\beta(t-w)} p^*(w)\, dw \simeq - \frac{1-\mu}{\beta} p_t^* .$$

Substituting into equation (20), the final form may be written as

(21) $$p_t = \mu p_{t-1} + (1-\gamma\mu) p_t^* - \mu(1-\gamma) p_{t-1}^* + v_t .$$

An attractive allelomorph of (21) is:

(22) $$p_t = p_{t-1} + (1-\mu)(p_t^* - p_{t-1}) + \mu(1-\gamma)(p_t^* - p_{t-1}^*) + v_t .$$

Equation (22) corresponds to the partial-adjustment interpretation (10) of section 3.2. The acceleration mode introduces an additional contribution from the change in the equilibrium price. If $\mu = 0$ we have $p_t = p_t^*$ as we should expect. On the other hand if $\mu = 1$, prices will nevertheless change, by a fraction of the change in equilibrium prices between the two periods. We note that

$$E v_t^2 = \gamma^2 \frac{\sigma^2}{2} \cdot \frac{\mu^2 - 1}{\log \mu} .$$

As before $\lim_{\mu \to 0} E v_t^2 = 0$. However since $\gamma < 1$, the effect of the acceleration specification is to reduce the residual variance in the clearing process. The higher the acceleration parameter θ_2 , the lower is γ . The coefficient $\mu(1-\gamma)$ of (22) can thus be taken as a measure of the acceleration contribution. The higher this contribution the lower is the residual clearing variance.

We remarked in section 3.2 that the basic Walrasian scheme (7)(a) could also be represented as an exponential distributed lag in present and past equilibrium prices. Equation (21) above yields another form for such a distributed lag. Introducing the lag operator L such that $Lp_t = p_{t-1}$ we observe from (21) that

$$p_t = \left(\frac{1 - \gamma\mu - \mu(1 - \gamma)L}{1 - \mu L}\right)p_t^* + \frac{v_t}{1 - \mu L} \quad .$$

In this case, therefore $w(L) = (1 - \gamma) + \frac{\gamma(1 - \mu)}{1 - \mu L}$ from which the individual weights of the distributed lag can be obtained as $w_o = 1 - \gamma\mu$, $w_i = \gamma(1 - \mu)\mu^i$, $i \geq 1$. Note that the sum of the weights is unity, as we should hope. It is evident that under the acceleration mechanism, current equilibrium prices receive extra weight. As we might expect, therefore, clearing is faster under this mechanism. More generally, we have now exhibited two different examples of clearing mechanisms generated as distributed lags of present and past imputed equilibrium prices. This might make a little more attractive the idea of an arbitrary weighting function $w(L)$, to be determined (if possible) from the data itself.

3.4.2 Administered Pricing Schemes. In chapter one various "administered" pricing schemes were discussed, according to which prices were set upon the basis of underlying cost factors ($\underset{\sim}{Y}_t$ say) tempered by influences from the demand side of the market. Consider first discrete time. As a representation of this adjustment behaviour we might write:

$$(22) \qquad p_t - p_{t-1} = \lambda(D_t - S_t) + \underset{\sim}{\delta}'\underset{\sim}{Y}_t + \varepsilon_t \ ,$$

where the $\underset{\sim}{Y}_t$ represent the "cost factors". Note that the variables incorporated in this vector may include variables also incorporated in $\underset{\sim}{X}_{1t}$ and $\underset{\sim}{X}_{2t}$, those occurring in the supply and demand equations. Potentially more troublesome is the contingency where $\underset{\sim}{Y}_t$ includes also the lagged price, p_{t-1}.

Defining once again p_t^* as the value of p such that $D_t^* = S_t^*$, we derive

$$p_t = p_{t-1} + \underset{\sim}{\delta}'\underset{\sim}{Y}_t + \lambda(\alpha_1 - \alpha_2)(p_t - p_t^*) \ ,$$

from which once again $\mu \triangleq \frac{1}{1 - \lambda(\alpha_1 - \alpha_2)}$. Rearranging, the PAMEQ version of equation (22) is:

$$p_t = \mu p_{t-1} + (1-\mu)p_t^* + \mu\underset{\sim}{\delta}'\underset{\sim}{Y}_t + v_t \; . \qquad (23)$$

We note of equation (23) that as market clearing becomes instantaneous - i.e. as $\mu \to 0$ - the influence of the variables $\underset{\sim}{Y}_t$ on on price determination vanishes. If this were not so, the equilibrium price level would be overdetermined. Thus the equilibrium price-level p_t^* is defined by $D_t^* = S_t^*$, equivalently by the system (8). If μ were not zero, equation (23) would, in equilibrium, constitute an additional defining relation independent of (8). There is therefore an elementary consistency requirement, usually ignored, that in equations like (22) the effect of the additional variables $\underset{\sim}{Y}_t$ must vanish toward equilibrium. The PAMEQ specification handles this requirement in a natural manner by requiring the coefficient of $\underset{\sim}{Y}_t$ to vanish with μ.

The same sort of property is true also of the continuous-time formulation. In the simplest version, wherein we imagine $\underset{\sim}{Y}_t$ to be roughly constant over the interval, the coefficient of this vector is $\frac{\mu - 1}{\log \mu}\underset{\sim}{\delta}'$. Again it can be verified that the contribution of $\underset{\sim}{Y}_t$ vanishes as $\mu \to 0$.

3.5 Multivariate Extensions

The extension to the case where $\tilde{p}$ is a vector of prices is relatively straightforward. Thus we might specify vector demand and supply functions as:

$$(24)\ (a)\quad \tilde{D}_t = A^d\tilde{p}_t + B^d\tilde{X}_{1t} + \tilde{u}_{1t}$$

$$(b)\quad \tilde{S}_t = A^s\tilde{p}_t + B^s\tilde{X}_{2t} + \tilde{u}_{2t}\ ,$$

where $\tilde{p}$ is of order g , as are the square matrices A^d , A^s .
The generalisation of the basic PAMEQ mechanism is:

$$(25)\ (a)\quad \tilde{p}_t = M\tilde{p}_{t-1} + (I - M)\tilde{p}^*_t$$

$$(b)\quad \tilde{p}_t = M\tilde{p}_{t-1} + (I - M)\tilde{p}^*_t + \tilde{u}_{3t}\ ; \qquad \lim_{M\to 0} \text{Cov}\ \tilde{u}_{3t} = 0$$

The matrix M of "friction coefficients" need not be diagonal. Off-diagonal elements refer to the effect of disequilibrium in one market upon price adjustment in another. We can regard (25) as a difference equation forced by the series $\tilde{p}^*_t$ (and, if present, a disturbance term). A natural scalar measure of the speed of convergence of the system to equilibrium is therefore the absolute value of the largest eigenvalue of M. The closer this is to zero, the faster is the rate of clearing. As a stability condition, one would require all characteristic roots of M to be less than one in absolute value.

As in section 3.3, the multivariate PAMEQ specification may be derived from conventional discrete - or continuous - time formulations. Consider, for instance, the following discrete-time adjustment mechanism (cf. (6)(b)):

$$\tilde{p}_t - \tilde{p}_{t-1} = \Lambda(\tilde{D}_t - \tilde{S}_t) + \tilde{\varepsilon}_t\ ,$$

where $\Lambda = ((\lambda_{ij}))$ is a g×g matrix and Cov $\tilde{\varepsilon}_t = Q$.
Following the arguments of section 3.3, one easily derives equation (25)(b)

with

(26) $$M = [I - \Lambda(A^d - A^s)]^{-1} ,$$

and $\underset{\sim}{u}_{3t} = M\underset{\sim}{\varepsilon}_t$.

We observe that Cov $\underset{\sim}{u}_{3t} = MQM' \to 0$ as $M \to 0$.

The generalisation to the multivariate case of the univariate continuous-time correspondence has some minor points of complication. Start with the multivariate version of equation (12) as:

$$d\underset{\sim}{p} = \Theta(\underset{\sim}{D}(w) - \underset{\sim}{S}(w))dw + d\underset{\sim}{\xi}(w) ,$$

where Θ is a g×g matrix and

$$E\, d\underset{\sim}{\xi}(w)\, d\underset{\sim}{\xi}(w') = \delta(w - w')Q ,$$

δ the Kronecker delta function. As in section 3.3, we obtain (25)(b), with[2]

(27) $$M = \exp[\Theta(A^d - A^s)] .$$

With regard to the disturbance term,

(28) $$\underset{\sim}{u}_{3t} = -\int_0^1 \exp[\Theta(A^d - A^s)]d\underset{\sim}{\xi}(t - w) .$$

The covariance matrix of $\underset{\sim}{u}_{3t}$ is therefore

(29) $$E\,\underset{\sim}{u}_{3t}\,\underset{\sim}{u}'_{3t} = \int_0^1 \exp[\Theta(A^d - A^s)w]Q\, \exp[\Theta(A^d - A^s)w]'dw .$$

The integral in (29) may be expressed analytically in terms of the eigenvalues of the matrix M, in a way which preserves the analogy with the univariate relation (17) of section 3.3. Write $C = \Theta(A^d - A^s)$, so that $M = \exp C$. Suppose C has distinct eigenvalues $\omega_1 \ldots \omega_g$, and write $C = U\Omega U^{-1}$, $\Omega = \mathrm{Diag}(\omega_1 \ldots \omega_g)$. Then

$$\exp C = U(\exp \Omega)U^{-1} .$$

Writing $D = U^{-1}QU'^{-1}$ the integral is

$$I = U\left(\int_0^1 \exp(\Omega w)\, D \exp(\Omega w)\, dw\right)U' .$$

Since $\exp(\Omega w)$ is a diagonal matrix, we may write this as:

$$I = U\left(\left(\int_0^1 d_{ij} e^{(\omega_i + \omega_j)w} \, dw\right)\right)U' ,$$

$$= U\left(\left(\frac{d_{ij}}{\omega_i + \omega_j}[e^{(\omega_i + \omega_j)} - 1]\right)\right)U' .$$

Recall now that $M = \exp C$. It follows that the eigenvalues μ_i of M are related to those of C by $\mu_i = e^{\omega_i}$, and the eigenvectors of M and C are the same. We may therefore write

(30) $$E\,\underset{\sim}{u}_{3t}\,\underset{\sim}{u}'_{3t} = U\left(\left(\frac{d_{ij}}{\log(\mu_i\mu_j)}[\mu_i\mu_j - 1]\right)\right)U' .$$

Equation (30) generalises equation (17) for the univariate case. The limiting condition $\mu \to 0$ generalises to $\mu_i \to 0$, all i. If this is so, the entire covariance matrix (30) tends to the zero matrix. What results is a standard simultaneous general equilibrium model defined by equations (24) above with $\underset{\sim}{D}_t = \underset{\sim}{S}_t = \underset{\sim}{Q}_t$ the vector of quantities actually transacted.

3.6 Estimation of the Excess-Demand Function

We turn now to the estimation of the set of equations comprising the demand and supply sets - which we shall take in multivariate form as equations (24)(a) and (b) - and the price adjustment equation, which we shall take as the PAMEQ specification (25)(a) or (b). As already remarked, these sets of equations are in general empirically incomplete. The addition of an extra set of clearing equations for quantities is needed to complete the system. Except in special cases (see chapter 4) we cannot therefore hope to identify the parameters of $A^{d,s}$, $B^{d,s}$ and M on the basis of the relationships so far considered. On the other hand, the specification of appropriate quantity equations may not be at all transparent, and it may be necessary to settle for something less ambitious. In other circumstances, the separate identification of the demand and supply schedules may not be needed. Such an instance could arise where only price dynamics are felt to be of interest. In yet other special cases, as already remarked, specification of quantity equations may not be necessary to identify the demand and supply parameters of interest. For a variety of reasons, therefore, it is useful to consider a class of estimation problems, of more limited scope than a complete price-quantity dynamics, which we have called the "excess-demand" problem.

Returning to equations (24) of section 3.5, we can write excess demand as:

$$(31) \qquad \underset{\sim}{D}_t - \underset{\sim}{S}_t = A\,\underset{\sim}{p}_t - B\,\underset{\sim}{z}_t - \underset{\sim}{v}_t ,$$

where $A = A^d - A^s$,

$$B^d \underset{\sim}{X}_{1t} - B^s \underset{\sim}{X}_{2t} = -B\,\underset{\sim}{z}_t ,$$

and $\underset{\sim}{v}_t = \underset{\sim}{u}_{2t} - \underset{\sim}{u}_{1t}$.

We have combined $\underset{\sim}{X}_{1t}$ and $\underset{\sim}{X}_{2t}$ into a common vector $\underset{\sim}{z}_t$. Redefinition of the parameter matrices B^d, B^s indicates that $\underset{\sim}{X}_{1t}$ and $\underset{\sim}{X}_{2t}$ may have elements in common, in which case their separate effects are not distinguished in our excess demand formulation. Recalling that $\underset{\sim}{p}_t^*$ is defined by the equality $D_t = S_t = 0$, we may now formalise the excess demand problem as that of estimation and inference in the system:

$$(25)\ (b) \quad \underset{\sim}{p}_t = M\underset{\sim}{p}_{t-1} + (I - M)\underset{\sim}{p}_t^* + \underset{\sim}{u}_{3t}$$

$$(32) \quad A\,\underset{\sim}{p}_t^* = B\,\underset{\sim}{z}_t + \underset{\sim}{v}_t \,.$$

We shall suppose that the disturbance vectors $\underset{\sim}{u}_{3t}$ and $\underset{\sim}{v}_t$ are serially uncorrelated, although they may be correlated with each other. The subsections following will consider the estimation theory for the parameters of the excess demand problem. These methods will find empirical application in chapter 4. We shall find it convenient to consider initially the problem as given with equation (25)(b), the competitive price-adjustment equations. However we indicate in §3.6.4 how to handle the "administered" price-adjustment mechanism discussed in section 3.4.

3.6.1 Indirect Least Squares. Combining equations (25)(b) and (32), we can write the observable dynamics as:

$$(33) \quad \underset{\sim}{p}_t = M\underset{\sim}{p}_{t-1} + (I - M)A^{-1}B\,\underset{\sim}{z}_t + \underset{\sim}{\varepsilon}_t \,,$$

$$\text{where} \quad \underset{\sim}{\varepsilon}_t = (I - M)A^{-1}\,\underset{\sim}{v}_t + \underset{\sim}{u}_{3t} \,.$$

Let us assume initially that the vector $\underset{\sim}{z}_t$ does not contain elements of the lagged price vector $\underset{\sim}{p}_{t-1}$. We assume also that $(I - M_o)^{-1}$ exists, where M_o denotes the true value of M. In other words, we suppose that at least some tendency to equilibrium is exhibited.

Under these conditions, the matrices M and $F = (I - M)A^{-1}B$ are consistently estimable by ordinary least squares and are *a-fortiori* identified. By Slutsky's theorem, the same remark is therefore true of the matrix

(34) $\Pi = (I - M)^{-1} F$.

Since no useful restrictions are usually available for the disturbance terms, the matrices A and B will thus be identified if and only if their elements can be uniquely deduced from the equations:

(35) $A^{-1}B = \Pi$.

It will be recognised that these are the equations relating the structural form to the reduced form for the set of equations (32). We therefore have:

Proposition 3.1

If $\underset{\sim}{z}_t$ and $\underset{\sim}{p}_{t-1}$ have no common elements, the parameter matrices A and B of the excess demand problem are identified if and only if the standard rank and order conditions[3] hold in respect of (32) as if $\underset{\sim}{p}^*_t$ were observable.

The indirect least squares method for the estimation of the elements of A and B follows from equations (33), (34) and (35) as for the classical treatment. However it may be, just as in the textbook development, that the parameters in A or B are overidentified. That is, equations (35) may have multiple solutions for the elements of A or B . For the remainder of the present subsection, we assume that there is no overidentification problem.

The task remains of finding the asymptotic covariance matrix of the resulting estimators. As with classical indirect least squares we start by defining the multivariate least squares matrix as $\hat{H} = [\hat{M} \vdots \hat{F}]$. We know that $E(\hat{H}) = H$. Now stack the columns of $\hat{H}$ one above the other, to form a supervector, $\hat{\underset{\approx}{h}}$ say. Using relationships (34) and (35), together with standard results for matrix differentiation (e.g. A.S. Goldberger [1964], §2.8.12), we can derive the Jacobian:

$$(36) \qquad \frac{\partial \underset{\approx}{h}}{\partial \begin{bmatrix} \underset{\approx}{\alpha} \\ \underset{\approx}{\beta} \end{bmatrix}} = J_{h,\alpha\beta} \ .$$

Here $\underset{\approx}{\alpha}$ and $\underset{\approx}{\beta}$ are the stacked forms of A and B. The covariance matrix of the vector $\hat{\underset{\approx}{h}}$ can be easily obtained from the multivariate OLS fit of (33). The required asymptotic covariance matrix is then:

$$(37) \qquad \mathrm{Cov}\begin{bmatrix} \hat{\underset{\approx}{\alpha}} \\ \hat{\underset{\approx}{\beta}} \end{bmatrix} = J_{h,\alpha\beta}\,\mathrm{Cov}(\hat{\underset{\approx}{h}})\,J'_{h,\alpha\beta}\ .$$

We have assumed up until now that the vector of predetermined variables $\underset{\sim}{z}_t$ does not include elements of $\underset{\sim}{p}_{t-1}$. If this is not the case, the classical rank and order conditions applied to equation (32) are no longer sufficient for the identification of the model. To see this, partition $B = (B_1, B_2)$, where B_1 contains the coefficients of $\underset{\sim}{p}_{t-1}$ and B_2 the remaining coefficients. Corresponding to the observed reduced-form (33) we have

$$\underset{\sim}{p}_t = \Pi_1 \underset{\sim}{p}_{t-1} + \Pi_2 \underset{\sim}{x}_t + \underset{\sim}{\varepsilon}_t\ ,$$

where $\underset{\sim}{x}_t$ refers to the true exogenous variables. Here

$$\Pi_1 = M + (1 - M)A^{-1}B_1$$
$$\Pi_2 = (I - M)A^{-1}B_2\ ,$$

from which the equations

$$A^{-1}(B_1, B_2) = (I - M)^{-1}(\Pi_1 - M, \Pi_2)$$

correspond to the reduced-form of system (32). Since the elements of M are unknown it is immediately apparent that the formal identifiability of (32) is no longer sufficient. If we define a new matrix $C = A(I - M)^{-1}$ we may decompose the identification problem into the solution for C, A, B_1, B_2 and M of the following "quasi-linear" sequence:

$$C(I - \Pi_1, \Pi_2) = (A - B_1, B_2)$$
$$(I - M)C = A\ .$$

It is evident from this series of equations that a considerable number of zero restrictions will be required on the matrices M and A in order to ensure identifiability. However no formal necessary conditions have yet been derived.

3.6.2 Two-Stage Least Squares. As indicated earlier the indirect least squares method may suffer from overidentification problems and, just as in the textbook development, it becomes necessary to consider two-stage least squares methods. As in §3.6.1 we shall initially assume that the vectors $\tilde{p}_{t-1}$ and $\tilde{z}_t$ contain no common elements. We start by writing

$$(38) \qquad \tilde{w}_t(\lambda) = \tilde{p}_{t-1} + \Lambda(\tilde{p}_t - \tilde{p}_{t-1}) ,$$

where $\Lambda = (I - M)^{-1}$ is a convenient relabelling.[4] We write $\tilde{w}_t(\lambda)$ to draw attention to the dependence of the variable $\tilde{w}_t$ on Λ. This variable will be recognised as $\tilde{p}_t^*$ less its disturbance term. The equations to be estimated may now be rewritten as:

$$(39) \qquad \tilde{p}_t = M\tilde{p}_{t-1} + F\tilde{z}_t + \tilde{\varepsilon}_t$$

$$(40) \qquad A\tilde{w}_t(\lambda) = B\tilde{z}_t + \tilde{u}_t .$$

The matrix F has already been defined in connection with equation (33), but we shall not employ here the relationship of F with the matrices A and B. The vector $\tilde{u}_t = A(I - M)^{-1}\tilde{u}_{3t} + \tilde{v}_t$ is a new disturbance term.

The 2SLS method proceeds as follows. We obtain $\hat{M}$ and hence $\hat{\Lambda} = (I - \hat{M})^{-1}$, from multivariate OLS applied to (39). Such estimates will be consistent, although not efficient. Using the calculated values $\hat{\Lambda}$ we form the variables $w_t(\hat{\lambda})$ from (38). Employing these computed variables as though they were actual observations, we apply standard 2SLS techniques to estimate the parameter matrices A and B in (40). With the substitution of $\tilde{w}_t(\hat{\lambda})$ for $\tilde{w}_t(\lambda)$, the latter system is now a standard linear simultaneous equation model.

We shall now demonstrate several propositions in connection with this method of estimation. We assume standard regularity conditions apply to the sequence of fixed constants $\tilde{z}_t$ and that the characteristic roots of M_o lie within the unit circle, indicating a stable system. Under these conditions the various limiting moment matrices employed in the subsequent arguments will exist.

Theorem 3.1

If the vectors of $\underset{\sim}{z}_t$ and $\underset{\sim}{p}_{t-1}$ share no common elements:

(i) The two-stage least squares procedure implicit in equations (39) and (40) yields consistent estimates.

(ii) These estimates are of order $\frac{1}{T}$ in sampling variance.

(iii) But the stage two estimates are not asymptotically the same as those obtained from (40) on the supposition that Λ is known. They are, however, asymptotically Normal.

Proof. It will be useful to write the equations to be estimated in data-matrix form. Define P as the T×G matrix of observations on $\underset{\sim}{p}_t$, and P_{-1} as the matrix of observations on $\underset{\sim}{p}_{t-1}$. Define $P_d = P - P_{-1}$. Denote by $W(\lambda)$ the data-matrix corresponding to $w_t(\lambda)$. The equivalent of (38) is thus:

$$W(\lambda) = P_{-1} + P_d\Lambda' . \tag{41}$$

Define Z as the data matrix of the exogenous variables $\underset{\sim}{z}_t$. We may therefore write the first of the equations (40) to be estimated as:

$$\underset{\sim}{w}_1(\lambda) = W_1(\lambda)\underset{\sim}{\alpha}_1 + Z_1\underset{\sim}{\beta}_1 + \underset{\sim}{u}_1 . \tag{42}$$

Here $W_1(\lambda)$ and Z_1 refer to submatrices of $W(\lambda)$ and Z corresponding to the endogenous and exogenous variables actually included in equation number one. The stage two regression is:

$$\underset{\sim}{w}_1(\hat{\lambda}) = \hat{W}_1(\hat{\lambda})\underset{\sim}{\alpha}_1 + Z_1\underset{\sim}{\beta}_1 + \underset{\sim}{\zeta}_1 . \tag{43}$$

Here $\hat{\lambda}$ indicates the consistent estimator obtained in stage one by employing equations (39). For our purposes, we shall treat $\hat{\lambda}$ as a consistent estimator of λ. We derive $\hat{W}_1(\hat{\lambda})$ in terms of $W_1(\hat{\lambda})$ as:

$$\hat{W}_1(\hat{\lambda}) = M_z\, W_1(\hat{\lambda}) ,$$

where $M_z = Z(Z'Z)^{-1}Z'$ is the OLS projection matrix from the first of the two stages of the 2SLS calculation. Finally $\underset{\sim}{\zeta}_1$ is a derived disturbance vector.

It will be convenient to set up the proof by comparing two estimators, in one of which Λ is known. The corresponding stage 2 Normal equations are:

(a) (Λ known)

$$(44)\ (a)\quad \begin{bmatrix} W_1(\lambda)'M_zW_1(\lambda) & W_1(\lambda)'Z_1 \\ Z_1'W_1(\lambda) & Z_1'Z_1 \end{bmatrix} \begin{bmatrix} \hat{\underset{\sim}{\alpha}}_1 \\ \hat{\underset{\sim}{\beta}}_1 \end{bmatrix} = \begin{bmatrix} W_1(\lambda)'M_z\underset{\sim}{w}_1(\lambda) \\ Z_1'\underset{\sim}{w}_1(\lambda) \end{bmatrix}$$

(b) ($\hat{\Lambda}$ consistently estimated)

$$(44)\ (b)\quad \begin{bmatrix} W_1(\hat{\lambda})'M_zW_1(\hat{\lambda}) & W_1(\hat{\lambda})Z_1 \\ Z_1'W_1(\hat{\lambda}) & Z_1'Z_1 \end{bmatrix} \begin{bmatrix} \hat{\hat{\underset{\sim}{\alpha}}}_1 \\ \hat{\hat{\underset{\sim}{\beta}}}_1 \end{bmatrix} = \begin{bmatrix} W_1(\hat{\lambda})'M_z\underset{\sim}{w}_1(\hat{\lambda}) \\ Z_1'\underset{\sim}{w}_1(\hat{\lambda}) \end{bmatrix}$$

In writing the second set we have used the fact that $M_z Z_1 = Z_1$, so that $\hat{W}(\lambda)'Z_1 = W_1(\lambda)'Z_1$, as written.

We know that $\hat{\underset{\sim}{\alpha}}_1$ and $\hat{\underset{\sim}{\beta}}_1$ are consistent, indeed have a limiting Normal distribution with a known covariance matrix. Subtracting set (a) from set (b) we obtain:

$$(45)\quad \frac{1}{T}\begin{bmatrix} W_1(\hat{\lambda})'M_zW_1(\hat{\lambda}) & W_1(\hat{\lambda})'Z_1 \\ Z_1'W_1(\hat{\lambda}) & Z_1'Z_1 \end{bmatrix} \begin{bmatrix} \hat{\hat{\underset{\sim}{\alpha}}}_1 - \hat{\underset{\sim}{\alpha}}_1 \\ \hat{\hat{\underset{\sim}{\beta}}}_1 - \hat{\underset{\sim}{\beta}}_1 \end{bmatrix} = \frac{1}{T}\begin{bmatrix} \Delta_{11} & \Delta_{12} \\ \Delta_{12}' & 0 \end{bmatrix} \begin{bmatrix} \hat{\underset{\sim}{\alpha}}_1 \\ \hat{\underset{\sim}{\beta}}_1 \end{bmatrix} - \frac{1}{T}\begin{bmatrix} \underset{\sim}{\delta}_1 \\ \underset{\sim}{\delta}_2 \end{bmatrix},$$

where:

$$\Delta_{11} = W_1(\lambda)'M_z W_1(\lambda) - W_1(\hat{\lambda})'M_z W_1(\hat{\lambda})$$

$$\Delta_{12} = [W_1(\lambda) - W_1(\hat{\lambda})]'Z_1$$

$$\underset{\sim}{\delta}_1 = W_1(\lambda)'M_z \underset{\sim}{w}_1(\lambda) - W_1(\hat{\lambda})'M_z \underset{\sim}{w}_1(\hat{\lambda})$$

$$\underset{\sim}{\delta}_2 = Z_1'[\underset{\sim}{w}_1(\lambda) - \underset{\sim}{w}_1(\hat{\lambda})]$$

Let us consider first the asymptotic behaviour of the matrix appearing on the LHS of (45). By using equations (41) it is easy, if a little tedious, to show that this matrix tends in probability to a nonsingular matrix of constants, $C(\lambda)$ say.[5] Let us turn now to the RHS of equations (45). All terms involved tend in probability to zero. For $\text{plim}\, \frac{1}{T} W_1(\hat{\lambda})'M_z W_1(\hat{\lambda}) = \text{plim}\, \frac{1}{T} W_1(\lambda)'M_z W_1(\lambda)$, by the consistency of $\hat{\lambda}$. Since $\text{plim}\, \hat{\underset{\sim}{\alpha}}_1 = \underset{\sim}{\alpha}_1$, a vector of finite constants, $\text{plim}\, \frac{1}{T} \Delta_{11} \hat{\underset{\sim}{\alpha}}_1 = \underset{\sim}{0}$. With similar arguments applied to the remaining terms, the assertion follows. Combining the limiting behaviour of the LHS of (45) with that of the RHS it follows that

$$\text{plim} \begin{bmatrix} \hat{\hat{\underset{\sim}{\alpha}}}_1 - \hat{\underset{\sim}{\alpha}}_1 \\ \hat{\hat{\underset{\sim}{\beta}}}_1 - \hat{\underset{\sim}{\beta}}_1 \end{bmatrix} = \underset{\sim}{0} ,$$

from which the desired consistency of $\begin{bmatrix} \hat{\hat{\underset{\sim}{\alpha}}}_1 \\ \hat{\hat{\underset{\sim}{\beta}}}_1 \end{bmatrix}$ follows, proving (i).

Let us now investigate the limiting behaviour of the vector $\sqrt{T} \begin{bmatrix} \hat{\hat{\underset{\sim}{\alpha}}}_1 - \hat{\underset{\sim}{\alpha}}_1 \\ \hat{\hat{\underset{\sim}{\beta}}}_1 - \hat{\underset{\sim}{\beta}}_1 \end{bmatrix}$. It will suffice to consider the asymptotic behaviour of the $\sqrt{T}$ times RHS of (45), namely:

$$\begin{bmatrix} E1 \\ E2 \end{bmatrix} = \frac{1}{\sqrt{T}} \begin{bmatrix} \Delta_{11} & \Delta_{12} \\ \Delta_{12}' & 0 \end{bmatrix} \begin{bmatrix} \hat{\underset{\sim}{\alpha}}_1 \\ \hat{\underset{\sim}{\beta}}_1 \end{bmatrix} - \frac{1}{\sqrt{T}} \begin{bmatrix} \underset{\sim}{\delta}_1 \\ \underset{\sim}{\delta}_2 \end{bmatrix} .$$

If we can show that terms such as $\frac{1}{\sqrt{T}} \Delta_{11}$ have a limiting distribution, it will make no difference[6] to the argument if we substitute $[\underset{\sim}{\alpha}_1 \quad \underset{\sim}{\beta}_1]'$

for its consistent estimate $[\hat{\underset{\sim}{\alpha}}_1 \ \ \hat{\underset{\sim}{\beta}}_1]'$. Accordingly, we may write

$$E1 = \frac{1}{\sqrt{T}} \{[W_1(\lambda)'M_z W_1(\lambda)\underset{\sim}{\alpha}_1 + W_1(\lambda)'Z_1\underset{\sim}{\beta}_1 - W_1(\lambda)'M_z\underset{\sim}{w}_1(\lambda)]$$

$$- [W_1(\hat{\lambda})'M_z W_1(\hat{\lambda})\underset{\sim}{\alpha}_1 + W_1(\hat{\lambda})'Z_1\underset{\sim}{\beta}_1 - W_1(\hat{\lambda})'M_z\underset{\sim}{w}_1(\hat{\lambda})]\}.$$

From equation (42), the first of the two terms in square brackets is equal to $-W_1(\lambda)'M_z\underset{\sim}{u}_1$. Now rewrite (42) in terms of $\hat{\lambda}$ rather than λ as

$$w_1(\hat{\lambda}) = W_1(\hat{\lambda})\underset{\sim}{\alpha}_1 + Z_1\underset{\sim}{\beta}_1 + [\underset{\sim}{u}_1 + \underset{\sim}{w}_1(\hat{\lambda}) - \underset{\sim}{w}_1(\lambda) + (W_1(\lambda) - W_1(\hat{\lambda}))\underset{\sim}{\alpha}_1] .$$

We can therefore write

$$E1 = \frac{1}{\sqrt{T}} [(W_1(\hat{\lambda}) - W_1(\lambda))'M_z\underset{\sim}{u}_1 + W_1(\hat{\lambda})'M_z(W_1(\lambda) - W_1(\hat{\lambda}))\underset{\sim}{\alpha}_1$$

$$+ W_1(\hat{\lambda})'M_z(\underset{\sim}{w}_1(\hat{\lambda}) - \underset{\sim}{w}_1(\lambda))] .$$

From equation (41) with appropriate partitions (see footnote 5),

$$W_1(\hat{\lambda}) - W_1(\lambda) = P_d(\hat{\Lambda}_1' - \Lambda_1') ,$$

and

$$\underset{\sim}{w}_1(\hat{\lambda}) - \underset{\sim}{w}_1(\lambda) = P_d(\hat{\underset{\sim}{\lambda}}_1 - \underset{\sim}{\lambda}_1) ,$$

where $\underset{\sim}{\lambda}_1$ is the column of Λ' corresponding to the first variable. With these substitutions, we may write

$$E1 = \sqrt{T}\left[(\hat{\Lambda}_1 - \Lambda_1)\left(\frac{1}{T}P_d' M_z \underset{\sim}{u}_1\right) - \frac{1}{T} W_1(\hat{\lambda})'M_z P_d (\hat{\Lambda}_1' - \Lambda_1)\underset{\sim}{\alpha}_1\right.$$

$$\left. + \frac{1}{T} W_1(\hat{\lambda})'M_z P_d (\hat{\underset{\sim}{\lambda}}_1 - \underset{\sim}{\lambda}_1)\right] .$$

From the exogeneity of Z_t, it follows that $\text{plim} \frac{1}{T}P_d' M_z \underset{\sim}{u}_1 = 0$. Moreover the expression $\frac{1}{T} W_1(\hat{\lambda})'M_z P_d$ tends in probability to a matrix of finite constants. Thus E1 has the same limiting distribution as

$$\text{plim}\left(\frac{1}{T} W_1(\lambda)'M_z P_d\right) \left[\sqrt{T}(\hat{\underset{\sim}{\lambda}}_1 - \underset{\sim}{\lambda}_1) - \sqrt{T}(\hat{\Lambda}_1' - \Lambda_1')\underset{\sim}{\alpha}_1\right] .$$

By using similar arguments for E2 we may now assert that the vector

$$\sqrt{T}\begin{bmatrix}\hat{\hat{\underset{\sim}{\alpha}}}_1 - \underset{\sim}{\alpha}_1 \\ \hat{\hat{\underset{\sim}{\beta}}}_1 - \underset{\sim}{\beta}_1\end{bmatrix}$$ has the same limiting distribution as:

$$(49) \quad \sqrt{T}\begin{bmatrix}\hat{\underset{\sim}{\alpha}}_1 - \underset{\sim}{\alpha}_1 \\ \hat{\underset{\sim}{\beta}}_1 - \underset{\sim}{\beta}_1\end{bmatrix} + C(\lambda)^{-1}\begin{bmatrix}\text{plim}\,\frac{1}{T}\,W_1(\lambda)'M_z P_d \\ \text{plim}\,\frac{1}{T}\,Z_1'M_z P_d\end{bmatrix}\{\sqrt{T}[\hat{\underset{\sim}{\lambda}}_1 - \underset{\sim}{\lambda}_1 - (\hat{\Lambda}_1' - \Lambda_1)\underset{\sim}{\alpha}_1]\}$$

We know that the standard 2SLS estimate $\sqrt{T}(\hat{\underset{\sim}{\alpha}}_1, \hat{\underset{\sim}{\beta}}_1)'$ has a limiting Normal distribution. The same remark is true of the consistent estimates $\hat{\Lambda}$, which have been derived in stage one by the use of ordinary least squares. It follows that the required estimate $\sqrt{T}(\hat{\hat{\underset{\sim}{\alpha}}}_1, \hat{\hat{\underset{\sim}{\beta}}}_1)'$ is also asymptotically Normal. On the other hand, as equation (46) shows, the asymptotic distribution of our estimator does not have the same covariance matrix as that obtained by assuming Λ known. We note finally that the sampling variance of $(\hat{\hat{\underset{\sim}{\alpha}}}_1, \hat{\hat{\underset{\sim}{\beta}}}_1)'$ is of order $\frac{1}{T}$. We have thus proved parts (ii) and (iii) of the theorem.

The specific interest of part (iii) of the theorem derives from comparison with a number of instances in econometrics where a nuisance parameter can be replaced by a consistent estimate. The asymptotic distribution of the estimates of substantive interest are then the same as if the nuisance parameters were known *a-priori*. Such instances arise particularly in considering the role of estimated error-process parameters in improving efficiency. Theorem 3.1(iii) remarks that if λ is regarded as such a nuisance parameter, this convenient state of affairs does not apply. Note also that we have not given an explicit statement for the asymptotic covariance matrix of our estimates. In equation (46), we cannot assume that $(\hat{\underset{\sim}{\alpha}}_1 - \underset{\sim}{\alpha}_1)$ and $(\hat{\Lambda} - \Lambda)$ are independent, since they depend upon common underlying disturbances. Hence no explicit formula for the required asymptotic covariance matrix exists. We should expect that the standard 2SLS asymptotic covariance matrix, treating λ as though it were known, will be an underestimate in respect of its diagonal elements.

Corollary 3.1. The disturbance covariance matrix $Q_u = E\,\underset{\sim}{u}_t\,\underset{\sim}{u}_t'$ of (40) may be consistently estimated in terms of the residuals of the 2SLS procedure.

Proof: Write the entire system (40) in data-matrix form as

$$W(\lambda)A' = Z\,B' + U\ .$$

The residual matrix is defined as:

$$\begin{aligned}\hat{U} &= W(\hat{\lambda})\hat{A}' - Z\,\hat{B}' \\ &= W(\lambda)A' - Z\,B' + (W(\hat{\lambda}) - W(\lambda))A' + W(\hat{\lambda})(\hat{A} - A)' - Z(\hat{B} - B)' \\ &= U + P_d(\hat{\Lambda}' - \Lambda')A' + (P_{-1} + P_d\hat{\Lambda}')(\hat{A} - A)' - Z(\hat{B} - B)'\ ,\end{aligned}$$

from equations (41). The remainder of the proof consists in forming the sample moment matrix $\frac{1}{T}\,\hat{U}'\hat{U}$ and demonstrating from the matrix version of Slutsky's theorem that all terms except $\frac{1}{T}\,U'U$ tend in probability to zero. The latter yields the required covariance matrix.

The question arises as to whether the covariance matrices Q_{u_3} and Q_v of the original disturbance terms $\underset{\sim}{u}_{3t}$ and $\underset{\sim}{v}_t$ can be obtained from Corollary 3.1. The defining relations involved are:

$$(I - M)A^{-1}\underset{\sim}{v}_t + \underset{\sim}{u}_{3t} = \underset{\sim}{\varepsilon}_t$$

$$A(I - M)^{-1}\underset{\sim}{u}_{3t} + \underset{\sim}{v}_t = \underset{\sim}{u}_t\ .$$

One might consider utilising the computed residuals $\hat{\underset{\sim}{\varepsilon}}_t$ from the multivariate ordinary least squares fit of equation (33), together with the computed residuals $\hat{\underset{\sim}{u}}_t$ from equation (40), in order to recover $\hat{\underset{\sim}{v}}_t$ and $\hat{\underset{\sim}{u}}_{3t}$ from the above relationships. Unfortunately such an estimation procedure for Q_{u_3} and Q_v will not work. To see why, we need only observe that $\underset{\sim}{u}_t = A(I - M)^{-1}\underset{\sim}{\varepsilon}_t$. The two sets of equations are therefore not independent, and no solution for the desired residuals is available. The required covariance matrices Q_{u_3} and Q_v are not separately identifiable. Such difficulties do not arise if the error-free clearing mechanism (25)(a) is employed. In this case $Q_{u_3} \equiv 0$

and $\hat{u}_t = \hat{v}_t$, yielding Q_v from the residuals of equation (40).

It will be observed that the central problem in the above estimation procedure is to obtain a consistent estimator $\hat{M}$ in stage one. As observed in the previous subsection, this is not possible under the present procedure if z_t and p_{t-1} contain common elements. A possible procedure is as follows. We may write equation (33) of section 3.6.1 as

$$(47) \qquad p_t = C(p_t - p_{t-1}) + A^{-1}Bz_t + \zeta_t ,$$

where

$$(48) \qquad C = -(I - M)^{-1}M$$

and $$\zeta_t = (I - M)^{-1}\varepsilon_t .$$

Equation (47), with endogenous variables on the RHS, is first estimated by two-stage least squares bearing in mind all *a-priori* restrictions on the elements of C and $A^{-1}B$. Assuming that this procedure yields consistent estimates of the elements of C, M may be recovered by inverting equations (48):

$$(49) \qquad \hat{M} = (I + \hat{C})^{-1}\hat{C} .$$

Once $\hat{M}$ is derived, the second series of two stage least squares calculations proceeds as outlined above. Evidently such a "double-barrelled" application of 2SLS would not be very efficient. A warning is also in order. Whether or not the suggested method works will depend upon the identifiability of the entire system for the case where z contains lagged prices. As pointed out in section 3.6.1, this matter is still unresolved. The method incorporated in equations (47)-(49) must therefore be regarded as strictly tentative.

3.6.3 Maximum-Likelihood. Equation (33) of §3.6.1 may be written in terms of the data matrices constructed in §3.6.2 as:

$$P = P_{-1}M' + ZB'A'^{-1}(I - M') + E . \tag{50}$$

The matrix E is the (unobservable) data-matrix on the disturbance terms $\underset{\sim}{\varepsilon}_t$. From (33) we know that $\underset{\sim}{\varepsilon}_t = (I - M)A^{-1}\underset{\sim}{v}_t + \underset{\sim}{u}_{3t}$ but we shall assume in this section that our object is to estimate $\Omega = E\,\underset{\sim}{\varepsilon}_t\,\underset{\sim}{\varepsilon}_t'$, together with the structural parameters M, B and A.

Assuming that the $\underset{\sim}{\varepsilon}_t$ are Normally distributed, the log-likelihood function is

$$\log L = -\frac{GT}{2}\log\pi - \frac{T}{2}\log(\det\Omega) - \tfrac{1}{2}\,\mathrm{trace}(\Omega^{-1}\hat{E}'\hat{E}) ,$$

where

$$\hat{E} = P - P_{-1}M' - ZB'A'^{-1}(I - M') . \tag{51}$$

As usual we may concentrate the likelihood function by inserting the M.L. estimates for Ω, namely $\frac{1}{T}E'E$. Note that in doing so we have ignored any *a-priori* information about the elements of Ω. The problem may then be cast as one of minimising $\log(\det(\hat{E}'\hat{E}))$ (e.g. A.S. Goldberger [1964], p.352 *et seq*). Now from (51),

$$\hat{E} = [P_{-1} + (P - P_{-1})(I - M')^{-1} - ZB'A'^{-1}][I - M'],$$

$$= [W(\lambda)A' - ZB']A'^{-1}\Lambda'^{-1} .$$

Here $W(\lambda)$ is defined in §3.6.2, and it will be recalled that $\Lambda = (1 - M)^{-1}$. The concentrated log-likelihood function may therefore be written, apart from a constant, as

$$\log\det(\hat{E}'\hat{E}) = -2\log(\det A) - 2\log(\det\Lambda) + \log[\det(AW'(\lambda) - BZ')(W(\lambda)A' - ZB')] . \tag{52}$$

Equation (52) is very similar to the likelihood function for a linear model. The difference is that the data matrices $W(\lambda)$ themselves depend upon the unknown parameter matrix Λ (see equation (44) above). The model is therefore nonlinear.

Nevertheless the similarity can be exploited. Observe that the first-order partial derivatives of log L with respect to A and B are exactly as for the linear model, on the assumption that W is an available data matrix. Differentiation with respect to the elements of Λ is also a straightforward matter. Indeed, since Λ is typically unrestricted, standard rules of matrix differentiation may be applied. In consequence it may not be a difficult matter to derive the sample covariance matrix of the gradient vector

$$\frac{1}{T}\frac{\partial}{\partial \underset{\sim}{\theta}} \log L \frac{\partial}{\partial \underset{\sim}{\theta}} \log L' ,$$

where $\underset{\sim}{\theta}$ stands for all the parameters in the likelihood function. Using the single-equation methods earlier described we may obtain consistent, although inefficient, estimates of these parameters. The covariance matrix above can be evaluated at these initial consistent estimates and the linearised maximum-likelihood estimator defined by Theorem 2.6 of chapter 2.4 may be employed. Since the basic problem is regular the asymptotic covariance matrix of the resulting estimates may be obtained in the manner described in sections 2.2 and 2.4. Alternatively, of course a full iterative solution of the likelihood function may be employed.

3.6.4 Extension to Administered Pricing. The multivariate version of the administered pricing rule discussed in section 3.4.2 may be written:

$$\underset{\sim}{p}_t = M\underset{\sim}{p}_{t-1} + (I - M)\underset{\sim}{p}^*_t + D\underset{\sim}{Y}_t + \underset{\sim}{u}_{3t} ,$$

where it will be recalled that $\underset{\sim}{Y}_t$ is a vector of exogenous variables. For consistency we must also have $\lim_{M \to 0} D = 0$, but such a requirement will not explicitly concern us here.

The techniques described in previous subsections extend without difficulty to this pricing model. Corresponding to the stage one equations (33) we have

(53) $$\underset{\sim}{p}_t = M\underset{\sim}{p}_{t-1} + (I - M)A^{-1}B\,\underset{\sim}{z}_t + D\,\underset{\sim}{Y}_t + \underset{\sim}{\varepsilon}_t\,.$$

In respect of the 2SLS technique the equations corresponding to (41) and (43) are:

(54) $$\underset{\sim}{w}_t(\lambda) = \underset{\sim}{p}_{t-1} + \Lambda(\underset{\sim}{p}_t - \underset{\sim}{p}_{t-1}) - \Lambda D\,Y_t$$

(55) $$A\underset{\sim}{w}_t(\lambda) = B\,\underset{\sim}{z}_t + \underset{\sim}{u}_t\,,$$

where once again $\Lambda = (I - M)^{-1}$.

Equations (53), as stage one, and equations (54) and (55), as stage two, can be combined into a two stage least squares procedure in a manner identical to the discussion of §3.6.2. Likewise the remarks of §3.6.3 concerning likelihood techniques are applicable. Note finally that we have implicitly assumed that the exogenous vectors $\underset{\sim}{z}_t$ and $\underset{\sim}{Y}_t$ contain no common elements. If this requirement is not met, the model is not fully identified.

3.7 Estimating the Equilibrium Values

The PAMEQ specification allows a decomposition of an observed series into an imputed equilibrium component and a disequilibrium component. In many instances this may be interpreted as a decomposition into short-run fluctuations and more "permanent" underlying long-run forces. Such a decomposition may be particularly attractive when it refers to percentage changes. In chapter 6.2.1 we exhibit an interpretation of the Phillips curve in which percentage wage changes are related on the one hand to unemployment, as a manifestation of the disequilibrium component, and on the other to changes in the equilibrium wage rate. The latter may reflect inflationary expectations or else structural changes in the underlying demand and supply schedules for labour. A similar decomposition into equilibrium and disequilibrium components has been exploited in the macro-econometric model by A.R. Bergstrom and C. Wymer [1976] discussed in chapter 1.4. In this case the model is cast in continuous time and the "steady-state" solution corresponding to equilibrium is an exponential growth path for all variables. Fluctuations (actually cycles) about this steady-state path are characterised by disequilibrium. These disequilibrium fluctuations are measured proportionately, so that the decomposition into equilibrium and disequilibrium states is a logarithmic one.

In the present, arithmetical, context we may write $\underset{\sim}{p}_t = (\underset{\sim}{p}_t - \underset{\sim}{p}_t^*) + \underset{\sim}{p}_t^*$ as a simple schematic indication of the decomposition referred to. It is therefore of interest to have available an estimate of the imputed equilibrium price level $\underset{\sim}{p}_t^*$, for it will be recalled that this is a random variable which depends upon unobservable disturbances as well as unknown parameters. In its full generality this is a difficult estimation problem, and it will be convenient to break it down into two facets. First we shall derive the "best" estimates for $\underset{\sim}{p}_t^*$ on the assumption that all parameter matrices are known. We shall then consider what happens when they are not.

The model with which we shall work is specified as follows:

$$(56) \qquad p^*_t = A^{-1}B\, z_t + A^{-1} v_t$$

$$(25)(b) \qquad p_t = M p_{t-1} + (I - M) p^*_t + u_{3t} \; .$$

We write $E\, v_t v_t' = Q_v$ and $E\, u_{3t} u_{3t}' = Q_{u_3}$. The problem to be investigated can be formalised: given $p_1 \ldots p_T;\ z_1 \ldots z_T$ as an observed sample, calculate the historical equilibrium imputed values $p^*_1 \ldots p^*_T$. We shall start from a standard result much used in the Control literature, where it forms the basis of Kalman/Bucy filter theory [1960], [1961]. The minimum quadratic loss[7] estimation of p^*_t , given $p_1 \ldots p_T;\ z_1 \ldots z_T$, is simply the conditional expectation $E(p^*_t / p_1 \ldots p_T;\ z_1 \ldots z_t)$. In the present instance, such an estimate will turn out, if we assume u_t and v_t to be Normally distributed, to be "maximum likelihood" estimates, which further increases the appeal of the quadratic loss criterion.

We turn, then, to the problem of obtaining the required expectation. Consider first the Jacobian matrix of the mapping implicit in equations (56) and (25)(b) from $(A^{-1} v_t \quad u_t)'_{t=1\ldots T}$ to $(p^*_t \quad p_t)'_{t=1\ldots T}$. This is triangular, with unity down the leading diagonal. Its determinant is therefore unity. Apart from constants (incorporating the covariance matrices Q_{u_3} and Q_v) the logarithm of the required joint density, on the assumption of independent Normal disturbances v_t and u_{3t} , is:

$$(57) \qquad -\tfrac{1}{2} \sum_t (p^*_t - A^{-1}B\, z_t)' \left[A^{-1} Q_v A'^{-1}\right]^{-1} (p^*_t - A^{-1}B\, z_t)$$

$$-\tfrac{1}{2} \sum_t (p_t - M p_{t-1} - (I - M)p^*_t)'\, Q_{u_3}^{-1} (p_t - M p_{t-1} - (I - M) p^*_t) \; .$$

By regrouping and completing the square in p^*_t the conditional density of $\underset{\sim}{p}_1^* \ldots \underset{\sim}{p}_T^*$ may be derived. This is Normal and the expectation $E(\underset{\sim}{p}_1^* \ldots \underset{\sim}{p}_T^* / \underset{\sim}{p}_1 \ldots \underset{\sim}{p}_T; \underset{\sim}{z}_1 \ldots \underset{\sim}{z}_T)$ may be isolated by inspection.

A quicker derivation, however, is to note that a Normal distribution is symmetric and unimodal at its mean, so that the desired expectation is identical with the maximum ordinate of the conditional density function. We may write

$$\text{prob}(\underset{\sim}{p}_1^* \ldots \underset{\sim}{p}_T^* / \underset{\sim}{p}_1 \ldots \underset{\sim}{p}_T; \underset{\sim}{z}_1 \ldots \underset{\sim}{z}_T) = \frac{\text{prob}(\underset{\sim}{p}_1^* \ldots \underset{\sim}{p}_T^*, \underset{\sim}{p}_1 \ldots \underset{\sim}{p}_T; \underset{\sim}{z}_1 \ldots \underset{\sim}{z}_T)}{\text{prob}(\underset{\sim}{p}_1 \ldots \underset{\sim}{p}_T)} .$$

Maximising the LHS with respect to the $\underset{\sim}{p}_t^*$ is therefore equivalent to maximising the numerator of the RHS. This is formally the same procedure as treating the unknown variables $\underset{\sim}{p}_t^*$ as parameters in the likelihood function (57). The symmetric properties of the relevant conditional density ensures that this "maximum-likelihood" estimator is identical with the required conditional expectation.

Accordingly, differentiating (57) with respect to $\underset{\sim}{p}_t^*$, t=1...T and setting the results equal to zero we obtain:

$$(A^{-1} Q_v A'^{-1})^{-1} \underset{\sim}{p}_t^* - (A' Q_v A'^{-1})^{-1} A^{-1} B \underset{\sim}{z}_t + (I - M)' Q_{u_3}^{-1} (I - M) \underset{\sim}{p}_t^*$$
$$- (I - M)' Q_{u_3}^{-1} (\underset{\sim}{p}_t - M \underset{\sim}{p}_{t-1}) = 0 , \qquad t=1 \ldots T .$$

So

$$\text{(58)} \quad \hat{\underset{\sim}{p}}_t^* = [A' Q_v^{-1} A + (I - M)' Q_{u_3}^{-1} (I - M)]^{-1} [A' Q_v^{-1} B \underset{\sim}{z}_t + (I - M)' Q_{u_3}^{-1} (\underset{\sim}{p}_t - M \underset{\sim}{p}_{t-1})]$$

is the desired point estimator. If desired the conditional variance of p_t^* can be obtained by finding the entire conditional density function as suggested above. A confidence ellipsoid for $\hat{\underset{\sim}{p}}_t^*$ may then be constructed.

A feature of the derived point estimate (58) of the equilibrium price is that it depends explicitly upon the covariance matrices of both disturbance series. There are two sources of information concerning the desired value $\underset{\sim}{p}_t^*$, embodied in equations (56) and (25)(b) above. If the disturbance $\underset{\sim}{v}_t$ were identically zero our "estimate" would be $\hat{p}^*_t = A^{-1} B \underset{\sim}{z}_t$. Likewise if the clearing disturbance $\underset{\sim}{u}_{3t}$ in (25)(b) were identically zero, the appropriate estimate is $\hat{p}^*_t = (I - M)^{-1}(\underset{\sim}{p}_t - M\underset{\sim}{p}_{t-1})$. Equation (58) may be interpreted in terms of a weighted average of these two extremes, with weights proportional to the precision attached to each source. To be sure, this is not entirely apparent from the general form (58). Observe however that as Q_{u_3} tends to the zero matrix, the expression (58) becomes dominated by:

$$[(I - M)'Q_{u_3}^{-1}(I - M)]^{-1} [(I - M)'Q_{u_3}^{-1}(\underset{\sim}{p}_t - M\underset{\sim}{p}_{t-1})] = (I - M)^{-1}(\underset{\sim}{p}_t - M\underset{\sim}{p}_{t-1}) .$$

This is just the estimator derived from equation (25)(b) by dropping the disturbance term. Similarly, as $Q_v \to 0$, (58) becomes dominated by $A^{-1} B \underset{\sim}{z}_t$ which is derived in the corresponding fashion from equation (56). We note finally that a similar, if more complicated, development can be designed for the case where the disturbances $\underset{\sim}{u}_{3t}$ and $\underset{\sim}{v}_t$ are not independent.

So far we have simply assumed that all the parameter matrices involved in e.g. (58) are known. If this is not the case, we might think of substituting consistent estimates in (58). This is quite feasible so far as the coefficient matrices (A,B,M) are concerned. Unfortunately, as pointed out in section 3.6.2, consistent estimates for the covariance matrices Q_{u_3} and Q_v are not available. Moreover even if they were, expressions like (58) lose their optimality (with respect to the quadratic loss criterion) when arbitrary consistent estimates of unknown parameters are employed in the manner suggested. These considerations motivate a search for alternative solutions to the problem of filtering out the unknown $\underset{\sim}{p}^*_t$. Ideally the two problems, of estimation and filtering, should be tackled simultaneously. This remains a topic for further research.

3.8 The Equilibrium-Disequilibrium Decomposition

Once estimates of the equilibrium values $\hat{p}^*_t$ have been obtained we may use the identity $\underset{\sim}{p}_t = (\underset{\sim}{p}_t - \underset{\sim}{p}^*_t) + \underset{\sim}{p}^*_t$ to decompose the series into estimated disequilibrium and equilibrium components. One naturally thinks of such a decomposition as coterminous with a frequency decomposition into shorter and longer-term fluctuations. Is this necessarily the case, or is it true only under special circumstances? To illuminate this question define $\underset{\sim}{\Delta}_t = \underset{\sim}{p}_t - \underset{\sim}{p}^*_t$ as the disequilibrium component of the price series. From (56) and (25)(b) above we may write the system jointly determining Δ_t and p^*_t as:

$$(59)(a) \quad \underset{\sim}{\Delta}_t = M\underset{\sim}{\Delta}_{t-1} - M(\underset{\sim}{p}^*_t - \underset{\sim}{p}^*_{t-1}) + \underset{\sim}{u}_{3t}$$

$$(b) \quad \underset{\sim}{p}^*_t = A^{-1} B \underset{\sim}{z}_t + \underset{\sim}{v}_t \ .$$

Let us again assume that $\underset{\sim}{u}_{3t}$ and $\underset{\sim}{v}_t$ are independent. Write $\zeta = e^{iw}$, so that $\bar{\zeta} = e^{-iw}$. Define G_* as the spectral density matrix of $\underset{\sim}{p}^*_t$. Assuming that the processes $\underset{\sim}{z}_t$ and $\underset{\sim}{v}_t$ are independent,

$$G_* = A^{-1} B G_z B' A'^{-1} + G_v \ ,$$

where G_z is the spectral density matrix of the process z_t and G_v that of the disturbance process $\underset{\sim}{v}_t$. (Alternatively, if $\underset{\sim}{z}_t$ is regarded as a sequence of fixed numbers G_{zz} can be regarded as its "pseudospectrum", in the sense of the limiting value of the Fourier sum used formally to define the spectrum).

We would usually conceive of the bulk of the power in $\underset{\sim}{p}^*_t$ as arising from the $\underset{\sim}{z}_t$ process, and the variation in the latter to be dominated by long run or low frequency components (the so-called "typical spectral shape"). To be sure the additional "noise" due to the disturbance process $\underset{\sim}{v}_t$ is high frequency variation, but we should not expect the power of this contribution to outweigh that of the $\underset{\sim}{z}_t$ process.

From (59)(b) the spectrum of $\underset{\sim}{\Delta}_t$ is given by

(60) $$G_{\Delta} = |1 - \zeta|^2 (I - M\zeta)^{-1} M G_{*} M' (I - M'\bar{\zeta})^{-1} + G_{u_3} .$$

Equation (60) relates the spectrum of the disequilibrium deviations Δ_t to that of the equilibrium process $\underset{\sim}{p}^*_t$. To obtain insight into this equation we may reconsider the effect of the dynamic relationship (59)(a). Let L be the lag operator such that $L\Delta_t = \Delta_{t-1}$. Equation (59)(a) may be written:

(61) $$\underset{\sim}{\Delta}_t = -(1 - L)(I - ML)^{-1} M \underset{\sim}{p}^*_t + (I - ML)^{-1} \underset{\sim}{u}_{3t} .$$

We see that $\underset{\sim}{\Delta}_t$ is related to $\underset{\sim}{p}^*_t$ by the transfer function

$$T(L) = -(1 - L)(I - ML)^{-1} M .$$

Write the "friction" matrix M in terms of its eigenvalues and eigenvectors $(\underset{\sim}{u}_i)$ as $M = U\Lambda U^{-1}$ where $\Lambda = \text{diag}(\mu_1 \ldots \mu_g)$ and $U = (\underset{\sim}{u}_1 \ldots \underset{\sim}{u}_g)$. We may define the mutually-orthogonal projection matrices $E_i = \underset{\sim}{u}_i \underset{\sim}{v}'_i$ where v'_i is the ith row of $V = U^{-1}$. The above transfer function may then be written as

(62) $$T(L) = -\sum_{i=1}^{n} \frac{\mu_i (1 - L)}{1 - \mu_i L} \cdot E_i .$$

This represents a decomposition of the transfer function into g mutually-orthogonal contributions, each corresponding to an eigenvalue of the adjustment matrix M. It will therefore be of assistance in our task of interpretation to examine the gain (as a function of frequency) of the representative filter element $\frac{\mu(1 - L)}{1 - \mu L}$. It will be recalled that the gain represents the extent to which the filter element T(L) magnifies or diminishes the spectral power at each frequency w of the series to which it applies, in this case to $\underset{\sim}{p}^*_t$. The required gain is given by:

$$T(w) = \frac{2\mu^2 (1 - \cos w)}{1 + \mu^2 - 2\mu \cos w} .$$

In figure 3.1 we have sketched the form of this function for three different values of μ , as indicated. The general effect of this transfer function is to diminish severely all lower frequencies, i.e. to attenuate longer-run components. Only for very high values of μ will the long-run movements retain any appreciable significance.

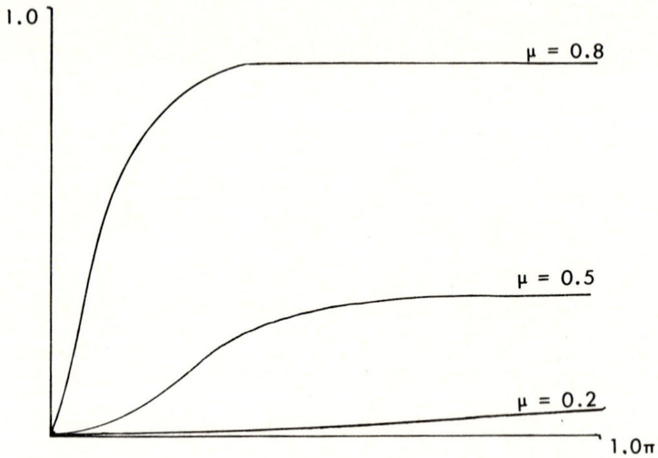

Figure 3.1

Returning now to equation (61), our results suggest that if M is moderate to low, the power of the low-frequency components of $\underset{\sim}{p}_t^*$ is appreciably diminished in the formation, as it were, of $\underset{\sim}{\Delta}_t$. In such circumstances, the deviations $\Delta_t = \underset{\sim}{p}_t - \underset{\sim}{p}_t^*$ will exhibit most power in the short-run fluctuations. In other words, the equilibrium-disequilibrium decomposition is likely to coincide with the decomposition into long- and short-run fluctuations. This conclusion may not hold if the "friction" matrix M is appreciable in size with one or more large positive eigenvalues (say 0.7 or above).

In the first place, not all of the low-frequency components of $\underset{\sim}{p}_t^*$ will be filtered out. Secondly, if M is appreciable in the sense described, there will be a non-negligible contribution to lower frequencies from the disturbance term $(I - ML)^{-1}\underset{\sim}{u}_{3t}$ of equation (61). On both counts, therefore, the existence of a considerable amount of friction or delay in market clearing may invalidate the intuitive correspondence between the equilibrium/disequilibrium decomposition on the one hand, and the long run/short run distinction, on the other.

3.9 Related Models

We have discussed in detail the excess demand paradigm expressed in equations (25)(b) and (32):

$$(25)(b) \qquad \underset{\sim}{p}_t = M\underset{\sim}{p}_{t-1} + (I - M)\underset{\sim}{p}^*_t + \underset{\sim}{u}_{3t}$$

$$(32) \qquad A\underset{\sim}{p}^*_t = B\underset{\sim}{z}_t + \underset{\sim}{v}_t \quad .$$

As earlier pointed out, equations (25)(b) could be generalised to encompass the expression of actual prices $\underset{\sim}{p}_t$ in terms of a more complex distributed lag pattern of present and past imputed equilibrium prices $\underset{\sim}{p}^*_t$. The above equations do not therefore constitute a definitive statement of the linear excess-demand model. Nevertheless it is useful to relate this basic model to some existing models in the econometric literature.

(a) The generalised adjustment model. Suppose that the desired asset composition $\underset{\sim}{y}^*$ of wealthholders is linearly related to a set of exogenous variables x :

$$(63) \qquad \underset{\sim}{y}^*_t = C\underset{\sim}{x}_t \ ,$$

where B is a $g \times k$ "long-run" coefficient matrix. There may, however, be costs involved in adjusting to this desired position. Under suitable cost functions it is possible to demonstrate a linear adjustment rule according to which actual asset positions adjust only partially in each period toward the optimal position:

$$(64) \qquad \Delta\underset{\sim}{y}_t = D(\underset{\sim}{y}^*_t - \underset{\sim}{y}_{t-1}) \ ,$$

which may be subject to a disturbance term.

Multivariate partial adjustment models of this kind have been used in a number of empirical studies. Examples are the choice of assets by households, interrelated factor demands by firms, and the production responses of firms. A convenient bibliography of the empirical applications and a collection of the econometric results is given by B.F. Hunt and M.R. Upcher [1977]. For our purposes, we note that the model is formally similar to the PAMEQ specification as given above, with the substitution A = I . In other words the desired composition $\underset{\sim}{y}^*$ is not simultaneously determined in the generalised asset adjustment model. There are therefore no identification problems and the task of estimation is much less difficult.

To see this, write the reduced form of equations (63) and (64) as:

$$(65) \qquad \underset{\sim}{y}_t = (I - D)\underset{\sim}{y}_{t-1} + F\underset{\sim}{x}_t + \underset{\sim}{v}_t \ ,$$

where $\underset{\sim}{v}_t$ is a disturbance term which may either be specified *ab initio* or else related to those attached to (63) and (64). From the application of unrestricted multivariate least squares to the equations (65), we may recover the desired matrix $\hat{C}$ from the closed-form relationship $C = D^{-1}F$. From the same reduced form estimation we may estimate the covariance matrix of the elements of D and F . This is done by stacking the columns of D to form a supervector $\underset{\approx}{d}$, doing the same with F , and creating the supervector $\begin{bmatrix} \underset{\approx}{d} \\ \underset{\approx}{f} \end{bmatrix}$. The covariance matrix $\Omega_{D,C}$ is then constructed according to the usual multivariate least squares procedure (e.g. A.S. Goldberger [1964], pp.207-210). Defining now the Jacobian

$$J_C = \begin{bmatrix} -D^{-1}F \otimes (D^{-1})' \\ \\ I \otimes (D^{-1})' \end{bmatrix} ,$$

the covariance matrix of C is given by

$$\Omega_C = J_C' \, \Omega_{D,F} \, J_C \ .$$

For further details we refer the reader to T.J. Valentine [1975] and Hunt and Upcher [1977].

Although the generalised asset adjustment model can be formally regarded as a specialisation of the basic PAMEQ form, the two models differ in their view of the underlying economics. Although the $\underset{\sim}{y}^*$ of the generalised asset adjustment models are often loosely referred to as "equilibrium" variables they indicate only the personal equilibrium that would prevail if the underlying stimuli (such as market prices) facing the representative individual were held constant for a long time. There is no necessary connection with the idea of market equilibrium as it appears in the PAMEQ formulation.

(b) Regressions with unobservable variables. There has in recent times been a revival of interest in regression specifications which involve the use of unobservable variables.[8] There are many such specifications in the socio-economic literature and some of them such as the errors in variables model and factor analysis have for some time constituted recognised areas of study in the statistical literature. More recently, A. Zellner [1970] showed that if we were willing to make assumptions about the generation of the unobservable variables, then not only is the errors in variables model now identified (which had been known earlier), but more efficient estimators could be derived by a systems approach. The model Zellner considered is:

(66) (a) $y_{1t} = y^*_{2t}\gamma + v_{1t}$

(b) $y_{2t} = y^*_{2t} + v_{2t}$

(c) $y^*_{2t} = \beta_0 + \beta_1 x_{1t} + \ldots + \beta_k x_{kt}$.

For instance, y_{1t} could be observed consumption, which is related to permanent income y^*_{2t}. Permanent income is a linear function of certain observable exogenous variables $x_1 \ldots x_k$. Observed income is permanent income plus a random measurement error. This system is identified and can be expressed in data-matrix form in terms of the observable variables y_1 and y_2 as:

$$\underset{\sim}{y}_1 = X\underset{\sim}{\beta}\gamma + \underset{\sim}{v}_1$$

$$\underset{\sim}{y}_2 = X\underset{\sim}{\beta} + \underset{\sim}{v}_2 ,$$

where X is the data matrix of the exogenous variables. Zellner shows that by considering the above two equations jointly, efficient estimation procedures may be derived in the "seemingly unrelated regression" framework.

The above model was further discussed by A.S. Goldberger [1972], who considered also the effect of adding a disturbance term to equation (66)(c). P.M. Robinson [1974] took up the development with a further generalisation, of the following form:

(70)(a) $$\underset{\sim}{y}_t = D\,\underset{\sim}{y}^*_t + E\,\underset{\sim}{x}_t + \underset{\sim}{u}_t$$

(b) $$\underset{\sim}{y}^*_t = C\,\underset{\sim}{z}_t + \underset{\sim}{v}_t \quad .$$

The model is now explicitly multivariate, with $\underset{\sim}{y}$ a vector of observed variables (of order g , say) and $\underset{\sim}{y}^*$ a vector of unobserved variables of order h , which may be either greater or less than g . The vectors $\underset{\sim}{u}_t$ and $\underset{\sim}{v}_t$ are disturbance terms, and the exogenous vectors $\underset{\sim}{x}_t$ and $\underset{\sim}{z}_t$ may contain common elements. In a time series context, some elements of $\underset{\sim}{x}_t$ could be lagged values of the observed y variables.

A discussion of restrictions which must be placed upon the coefficient matrices C, D, E, and the parameters of the disturbances, can be found in Robinson [1974]. We see that this framework is now broad enough to subsume the generalised asset adjustment equations. The presence of several unobservable variables in the equation defining the observable y variables looks to be a useful feature. However the model does not allow for the possibility that the unobservable y^*_t may themselves be simultaneously determined. It seems clear that a formidable number of *a-priori* parameter restrictions would be necessary to encompass such a possibility. Putting the matter another way, the

PAMEQ specification (e.g. equations (25)(b) and (32)) could be regarded as a contribution to the literature on unobserved variables, with stringent conditions placed on the parameter matrices to secure identification in a model where the unobservables are jointly determined.

Footnotes to Chapter 3

[1]Much of the material of this section is drawn from Bowden [1978b]. I am grateful to the editor and publishers of the *International Economic Review* for permission to reproduce material from this paper.

[2]If C is a matrix, $\exp C \triangleq I + C + \frac{C^2}{2} + \frac{C^3}{3!} + \ldots$, provided that the series on the RHS converges. Broadly speaking, the same sorts of differentiation and integration rules hold as for the case C scalar.

[3]For which see standard econometrics texts e.g. J. Johnston [1972], E. Malinvaud [1970] or H. Theil [1971].

[4]This is not the same matrix as that of §3.5. Note that we find it easier as a matter of notation to use λ to represent the entire matrix Λ.

[5]For instance write $W_1(\lambda) = P_{1,-1} + P_d\Lambda_1'$, where $P_{1,-1}$ and Λ_1 refer to appropriate partitions of P_{-1} and Λ. The term

$$\text{plim}\,\frac{1}{T} W_1(\hat{\lambda})' M_z W_1(\hat{\lambda}) = \text{plim}\,\frac{1}{T}\Big[P_{1,-1}' M_z P_{1,-1} + \hat{\Lambda}_1' P_d' M_z P_{1,-1} + P_{1,-1}' M_z P_d \hat{\Lambda}_1 + \hat{\Lambda}_1 P_d' M_z P_d \Lambda_1'\Big] .$$

Looking at the last term on the RHS, for instance,

$$\frac{1}{T} P_d' M_z P_d = \left(\frac{P_d'Z}{T}\right)\left(\frac{Z'Z}{T}\right)^{-1}\left(\frac{Z'P_d}{T}\right),$$

which in view of our earlier stability assumptions tends in probability to the product of three moment matrices. Since $\text{plim}\,\hat{\Lambda} = \Lambda$, the entire term tends to a matrix of finite constants. Similar arguments apply to the other terms on the RHS of the above expression and indeed, to the other elements of the matrix being considered.

[6] This is the matrix version of the well-known proposition that if $a_T \xrightarrow{p} a$, constant, and x_T tends in distribution to a random variable x, then $a_T x_T$ tends in distribution to the random variable ax.

[7]In other words, the implied loss function is quadratic in

$(\hat{\underset{\sim}{p}}{}_1^* - \underset{\sim}{p}_1^*,\ \hat{\underset{\sim}{p}}{}_2^* - \underset{\sim}{p}_2^*, \ldots\ \hat{\underset{\sim}{p}}{}_T^* - \underset{\sim}{p}_T^*)$. The most important particular case

is the M.S.E. criterion $\sum_i^G \sum_t^T c_{it}(\hat{p}_{it}^* - p_{it}^*)^2$, where the c_{it} are

preassigned weighting constants.

[8]For a useful collection of essays on this subject we refer the reader to D.J. Aigner and A.S. Goldberger [1977].

CHAPTER FOUR

DISEQUILIBRIUM AND THE DEMAND FOR MONEY

We are now ready to apply the specification and estimation techniques discussed in chapter 3 to a substantive economic problem. Accordingly the present chapter is a study of the implications of persistent disequilibrium states for the specification and estimation of the demand for money (in particular) and the important macro-economic nexus concerning the stock of money, income and the level of interest rates (in general). From the methodological point of view, it may seem odd that a treatment of the model referred to as the "excess demand" problem should be used to determine the demand for money function. The resolution of this apparent paradox, we shall see, is that in certain circumstances the parameters of the excess demand function are the same as those of the demand function. Explicit consideration of disequilibrium aspects of the estimation of the demand for money function has not been a feature of the econometrics literature, even though it abounds with references to partial adjustments, expectations and other dynamic devices of applied econometrics. For this reason we shall be at some pains to properly motivate different possibilities for the process of dynamic adjustment. This is done at a rather general level in section 4.1.

4.1 General Dynamics

It is now widely recognised that the adjustment of interest rates and incomes to the stock of money (or the monetary base) takes time, and may involve a good deal of uncertainty. This creates certain difficulties so far as the estimation of the demand for money is concerned. Any attempt to measure the demand for money must specify something about this process of dynamic adjustment, so that a compound hypothesis is involved, one about the form and variables of the demand function itself, the other about the disequilibrium dynamics. Indeed if one's view of the disequilibrium process is far-reaching enough, questions may be raised as to precisely what it is that we are, or ought to be, estimating. This section is concerned with some of these problems.

We have mentioned in chapter 1 the distinction between notional demand or supply and the effective schedules. In its most general usage, the former term refers to the outcome of the individual's decision process given that no quantity constraints on the variables under consideration serve to limit his options. The latter term refers to the situation where he may face one or more such constraints. Of course, no individual is ever entirely free of constraints on his economic behaviour. Thus the distinction between notional and effective demands usually assumes some given institutional setting.[1] This aside, there is evidently a special problem of stability (or better, "observability") with effective demand or supply schedules. For these schedules must at any given point in time depend not only upon individuals' perceptions of current or future prices, but upon the distribution of personal vectors of quantity constraints facing these agents.

Reservations about the stability of both individual and aggregate demand schedules during such a non-tatonnement process apply with special force to money holdings. For money has the peculiar attribute of being the sole repository of effective[2] purchasing power. Quantity constraints with respect to both the supply and demand of goods, bonds or labour services may thus be expected to affect the source or disposition of money holdings, so that the effective demand for money may be either above or below the notional quantity demanded.

Some of the above distinctions have been employed on the aggregate level as a matter of the theoretical reconciliation of common modes of macro-dynamic analysis. Thus H.I. Grossman [1971] suggested that the apparent paradox of Keynesian "liquidity preference" interest rate dynamics might be approached in such a way. According to this theory, the interest rate changes in response to a discrepancy between the demand and supply of money. As D. Patinkin [1965] pointed out, this is inconsistent with the loanable funds theory, in which the interest rate moves to balance the demand and supply of bonds. Grossman points out that if the interest rate changed in response to <u>effective</u> demand and supply in the bonds market, this might still be consistent with the liquidity preference theory if the latter referred to imbalance between the <u>notional</u> demand and supply of money. Of course, this leaves open the question as to why the time paths of the effective demand and supply of bonds should be precisely what is necessary to secure this result.

If we can generalise this example, it should now be clear that the new macrodynamics, if we can call it that, broadens the range of options and specifications for dynamic trajectories. One possible structure is that the relevant signals of imbalance, according to which prices or quantities change, are the purely notional demand and supply schedules. Another view might claim that only the immediately effective schedules have a role to play, and that the notional schedules have value only for exercises in comparative statics. Intermediate between the two might be the case where constraints in just one quantity variable (e.g. labour supply) determine the effective demands relevant for dynamic behaviour. It is apparent that the search for rules governing changes in prices, or interest rates, or incomes, becomes a great deal more complex and a considerable amount of empirical trial and error may be necessary to discover these rules, if indeed they do exist. It may be that such rules, once empirically established, may be rather opaque in terms of their justification from economic theory. A possible case in point, namely the popular partial adjustment mechanism for aggregate money holdings, is discussed below.

In summary, the "new macrodynamics" suggests that there is no unique theoretical demand for money function and no unique adjustment path to equilibrium. Instead it is an empirical matter as to which combination, of many possibilities, of demand and supply functions and disequilibrium dynamics best fits the available data. With regard to the demand for money function, we shall take the view that the natural construction is the Keynes/Hicks demand for money, called later the "H-effective" demand. As Clower has shown us, this corresponds to a demand for money in which just one constraint is assumed to be binding, namely the supply of labour. To identify the derived H-effective demand schedule, an explicit dynamic hypothesis determining the time path of income and the rate of income during disequilibrium periods, becomes necessary. But as we have argued above, there is no immediately obvious model for such a dynamics. The burden of finding it must rest on such empirical tools as are available. In some cases one may then be able to work back to the parameters of the desired demand for money function. In other cases, unfortunately, this will not be feasible. We will consider two possible dynamic paths in this paper. In the first we can certainly derive an estimate of the H-effective demand for money function; in the second, which coincides with the popular "partial adjustment" formulation, we shall argue that this may not be possible.

Of course, we have rather begged the question as to why a dynamic approach is needed in the first place. This seems to be part of the folklore, as it were, of this particular topic, but we shall illustrate with some actual results. This will also serve to illustrate the basic empirical model. Commensurate with the resources available and the complexity of the task, we chose a simple three-equation model involving the demand and supply of money with an expenditure equation to complete the system. The equations were (apart from one or two minor alterations to cope with data problems) lifted from among the series of alternative equations employed by R. Teigen [1964] and W.E. Gibson [1972] in their work on the demand and supply for money in the U.S.[3]

The money supply equation is linear in logs, of the form

$$(1)\quad \ln M_t = M^s(\ln r_t, \ln d_t, \ln R_t, \ln k_t, S2_t, S3_t, S4_t)\ ,$$

where[4]: M = M1. Notes and coin in the hands of the public plus demand deposits at trading banks.

r = interest rate (rate on 4-6 month commercial paper)

d = Federal Reserve discount rate

R = unborrowed Member-bank reserves

k = required reserve ratio, computed after Teigen [1964]

S2-4 = seasonal dummies.

The expenditure equation is also linear in logs, of the form

$$(2)\quad \ln Y_t = Y^d(\ln M_t, \ln r_t, \ln E_t, S2_t, S3_t, S4_t),$$

where in addition[5]:

Y = G.N.P.

E = Gross private domestic investment + exports + Government purchases of goods and services. Taken as exogenous.

At this stage of the development, detailed results for the above two functions are not presented, their role being merely to provide exogenous variables for the two-stage least squares estimation of the demand for money function. The following demand equation was estimated for U.S. quarterly data for the period[6] 1957 II - 1971 III, using 2SLS:

$$\text{(3)} \quad \ln M_t = \underset{(10.010)}{1.362} + \underset{(23.286)}{0.604} \ln Y_t - \underset{(-1.174)}{0.026} \ln r_t$$

$$- \underset{(-0.957)}{0.010}\, S2_t - \underset{(-0.727)}{0.008}\, S3_t + \underset{(1.127)}{0.012}\, S4_t$$

$$s^2 = 0.00073, \quad \text{V.N.} = 0.551.$$

(Here, as elsewhere, figures in parentheses beneath the estimated coefficients indicate t-values, or more correctly asymptotic coefficients of variation. V.N. and s^2 are the Von-Neumann ratio and standard error computed from the correct 2SLS residuals.)

Equation (3) will be useful for purposes of later comparison. For the moment we note only the very low figure for the Von-Neumann ratio, which suggests a specification problem.

4.2 Walrasian Dynamics and the H-Effective Demand Function

4.2.1 General Approach. It will be useful in motivating subsequent development not to plunge immediately into econometric discussion of the equation system outlined in section 4.1, but to consider instead a simple macro model involving money, bonds and goods very much along the lines of Part II of Patinkin [1965]. Write $M^d = M^d(Y,r;M,X)$, $Y^d = Y^d(Y,r;M,X)$, $B^d = B^d(Y,r;M,X)$ as the demand functions for money, goods and bonds, where X represents a set of exogenous variables. We suppose, to make matters simpler, that all money is of the outside, or fiat, variety.

The first question we have to resolve is the precise status of these aggregate demand functions. We have become so accustomed to writing down such functions, that this may seem an unnecessary proceeding. However, since the income term Y (rather than, say, the wage rate) appears in these schedules, we know from the work of Clower that there is an implied constraint on the supply of labour involved. Note however that no constraint on the demand for goods or the demand/supply of bonds is entertained. We might thus think of these schedules as notional with regard to the latter, but effective with regard to the labour constraint. We shall call such functions "H-effective". The H stands for J. Hicks who with his classic paper [1937] accustomed us all to think and work in terms of such schedules. We shall suppose that the determination of the H-effective demand function for money is the object of our investigation. That is, we are assuming, at least for the moment, that such schedules are stable empirically, and because of their comparative static properties are of basic policy interest.

Walras' law then tells us that:

$$\frac{B^d}{r} + M^d + Y^d = \frac{B^s}{r} + M + Y \; . \tag{4}$$

Note that since these schedules are at least partly notional it is Walras' law and not the truism which Clower calls "Say's identity" which applies. Let us now write the following Walrasian adjustment functions:

(5) $$\overset{\circ}{r} = -\lambda(B^d - B^s) , \qquad \lambda > 0$$

(6) $$\frac{\overset{\circ}{Y}}{Y} = \alpha(Y^d - Y) , \qquad \alpha > 0 .$$

From (4) it follows that

$$\frac{\overset{\circ}{r}}{r} = \lambda(Y^d - Y) + \lambda(M^d - M) .$$

These equations suggest a slightly more general adjustment mechanism for the rate of interest and income:

(7) $$\frac{\overset{\circ}{Y}}{Y} = \theta_{11}(Y^d - Y) + \theta_{12}(M^d - M)$$
$$\frac{\overset{\circ}{r}}{r} = \theta_{21}(Y^d - Y) + \theta_{22}(M^d - M) .$$

As a further detail of specification, we may replace the arithmetic excess demand on the RHS with the logarithmic version (the difference of the logarithms of demand and supply). Since $\frac{\overset{\circ}{Y}}{Y}$ and $\frac{\overset{\circ}{r}}{r}$ refer to the differentiation of logarithms, the result is evidently a standard Walrasian excess demand adjustment mechanism cast in terms of the logarithms of the variables.

Let us now define, given M and X, equilibrium values Y^* and r^* such that:

(8) $$Y^* = Y^d(Y^*, r^*; M, X) ,$$

(9) $$M = M^d(Y^*, r^*; M, X) .$$

If we could suppose for the moment that observations on Y^*, r^* were available, then we should be able to deduce from (8) and (9) the parameters of the H-effective demand schedule for money.

Since the system is not always in equilibrium observations on Y^*_t and r^*_t are not directly available. However at this point the development of chapter 3 becomes useful. Instead of the adjustment equations in the form (7), or its logarithmic version, we may employ the PAMEQ specification. As we saw in chapter three, the latter subsumes the former. The parameters of the equations determining the imputed equilibrium values, namely equations (8) and (9), may therefore be estimated by the methods of chapter 3. In particular, the parameters of equation (9) are those of the desired H-effective demand for money function.

4.2.2 Endogenous Money Supply and Disequilibrium. Before we proceed to details, we must discuss in general terms the role of the supply of money function. It will be recalled that we have specified (equation (1) above) M as dependent upon the endogenous rate of interest r, in addition to a further set of exogenous variables. In formulating this supply function, we have assumed that banks manage their reserves in such a way that the stock of money adjusts instantaneously to the rate of interest, unborrowed reserves, the discount rate and other determinants. Some work reported in chapter 6.4 of the present study supports this contention, at least over the period in question. Thus given all these variables - and in particular given r - the stock of money M is determined by the banking system. Hence following an increase in the stock of money (say because of an influx of unborrowed reserves), incomes Y and rates of interest r must change so that the new stock of money is absorbed into private portfolios. Naturally this process is simultaneous, for the rate of interest will react back to alter the stock of money according to equation (1).

This simultaneity is of importance in the present context, for the presumed nature of the causal links involved will help to determine our model. The "traditional" view is that the money stock is determined independently of the actions of the private non-bank public, who then react to an imbalance between their demand for money and the quantity actually in existence. The point has been well put by Tobin [1963] in his criticism of this view:

> "In this time-honoured exposition two characteristics of commercial banks - both of which are alleged to differentiate them sharply from other financial intermediaries - are intertwined. One is that their liabilities - well at least their demand deposit liabilities - serve as widely acceptable means of payment. Thus they count, along with coin and currency in public circulation, as "money". The other is that the preferences of the public normally play no role in determining the total volume of deposits or the total quantity of money. For it is the beginning of wisdom in monetary economics to observe that money is like the "hot potato" of a children's game: one individual may pass it to another but the group as a whole cannot get rid of it. If the economy and the supply of money are out of adjustment, it is the economy that must do the adjusting. This is as true, evidently, of money created by bankers' fountain pens as of money created by public printing presses. On the other hand, financial intermediaries other than banks do not create money and the scale of their assets is limited by their liabilities, i.e. by the savings the public entrusts to them. They cannot count on receiving "deposits" to match every extension of their lending."

According to this view, then, an addition to the stock of money, in the process of being passed from hand to hand, lowers interest rates (increases asset prices) and increases incomes. This is the "traditional view". "New view" theorists, such as J.G. Gurley and E.S. Shaw [1960], argue for the endogeneity of money in terms - *inter alia* - of the effect of interest rates on reserves desired by banks. In these terms, the asset preferences of the public also have a role in determining the quantity of money. Thus suppose that the public suddenly wished to hold more savings deposits. Initially this would merely result in a transfer of demand deposits from individual accounts to those of nonbank intermediaries. However with increased liabilities, the latter will now offer lower interest rates on their own assets (e.g. personal loans or mortgages). By normal arbitrage processes, interest rates will fall across the board. Trading banks will now have less incentive to economise on reserves. By a familiar process bank deposits and the quantity of money fall, validating (so to speak) the changed asset preferences of the non-bank public. Such effects are incorporated, admittedly in a rather crude way, in the money supply equation (1) above.

However, when we come to consider disequilibrium states the matter is not so simple. Suppose in the above analysis that interest rates do not immediately adjust to reflect changed conditions in the demand and supply of funds of all kinds. Our first question is: who or what determines the stock of money at any interest rate currently holding? That is, we fix the interest rate and consider what schedule it is that determines the stock of money actually in existence at this interest rate. Now for a given interest rate and a given stock of bank reserves the preferences of the public may help determine this schedule only through the quantity of bank loans outstanding, and then only if there happens to be deficient demand for bank loans. This point is considered in detail in chapter 6.4. The results of that section suggest that deficient demand for bank loans has played no role in the determination of the stock of money over the period considered. For the given rate of interest, and for a given stock of bank reserves, the quantity of money is therefore determined solely by the behaviour of banks, and it is to this behaviour that equation (1) appertains.

Still continuing to assume that the interest rate is fixed, the stock of money so determined may not coincide with the preferences of the public, who will react to this discrepancy in the ways suggested above. Out of equilibrium, therefore, there is still a considerable amount of truth in the "hot-potato" analogy. This analogy will be valid so long as (i) the stock of money and the demand for money are determined by two different classes of economic agent and (ii) the system is in a state of disequilibrium, so that the two are unequal. We note finally that none of the above analysis has suggested in any way that the banks "foist unwanted new money balances onto unwilling holders". It is true that out of equilibrium the money balances as such may be unwanted. These money balances may originate through government payments, or through the receipt of a bank loan. There can be no suggestion of involition on the part of recipients of such cheques. Nevertheless their receipt amounts to the creation of new money balances which at existing interest rates does not accord with the preferences of the public.

The representation of a monetary dynamics which incorporates the contributions of the "new" and "traditional" views in and out of equilibrium can be conveniently handled by use of the PAMEQ specification. We preserve equations (8) and (9) as referring now to the "hot-potato" effects out of equilibrium, where Y_t^* and r_t^* refer to the imputed equilibrium values specific to the current money stock M_t. But we also preserve the endogenous money supply equation (1) above, in which we regard M_t as endogenously determined in terms of current interest rates rather than imputed interest rates. This reflects the discussion above concerning the determination of the actual stock of money by the decisions of banks. Our equations for the determination of the imputed moving equilibrium are:

$$(10) \qquad \ln M_t = \beta_{11} \ln Y_t^* + \beta_{12} \ln r_t^* + \gamma_{10} + \gamma_{15} S2_t + \gamma_{16} S3_t + \gamma_{17} S4_t + u_{1t}$$

$$(11) \qquad \ln Y_t^* = \beta_{22} \ln r_t^* + \beta_{23} \ln M_t + \gamma_{20} + \gamma_{21} \ln E_t + \gamma_{25} S2_t + \gamma_{26} S3_t + \gamma_{27} S4_t + u_{2t}$$

$$(12) \qquad \ln M_t = \beta_{32} \ln r_t + \gamma_{32} \ln d_t + \gamma_{33} \ln R_t + \gamma_{34} \ln k_t + \gamma_{35} S2_t + \gamma_{36} S3_t + \gamma_{37} S4_t + u_{3t}.$$

Equation (12) is the standard supply function, cast in terms of the actual rate of interest r_t. Equation (10) expresses equilibrium between the demand and stock of money (cf. equation (9)). Here Y_t^* and r_t^* are the imputed equilibrium values; naturally they will depend upon the current values of the exogenous variables and upon M_t. Equation (11) refers to equilibrium in the goods market. The u_{it} are disturbances, supposed serially uncorrelated.

Thus given M as determined by the decisions of banks according to (12), the values of Y and r which would clear the money and goods "markets" in the private sector are given by (10) and (11). The values so defined will constitute an input into the dynamic hypothesis outlined below. In particular they will not coincide with those values which would equilibrate the entire system (10)-(12) simultaneously.

Having defined the imputed clearing values Y_t^* and r_t^*, we specify that actual Y_t and r_t adjust partially towards these values according to a PAMEQ specification of the following form:

$$(13) \qquad \begin{bmatrix} \ln Y_t \\ \\ \ln r_t \end{bmatrix} = M \begin{bmatrix} \ln Y_{t-1} \\ \\ \ln r_{t-1} \end{bmatrix} + (I - M) \begin{bmatrix} \ln Y_t^* \\ \\ \ln r_t^* \end{bmatrix} + \underset{\sim}{v}_t$$

where $M = \begin{bmatrix} \mu_{11} & \mu_{12} \\ \mu_{21} & \mu_{22} \end{bmatrix}$. As usual $\underset{\sim}{v}_t$ is a disturbance vector with the limiting properties discussed in sections 3.2 and 3.3. The question arises as to the relationship between the matrix of adjustment factors M with the adjustment parameters θ_{ij} defined in terms of the conventional formulation (7) above. In the general excess demand problem the transformation involved is estimable, in the sense that we can obtain θ from a knowledge of M. Here, unfortunately, the analysis of chapter 3.3 in respect of this transformation is not applicable. For equation (11) of the goods market is a quasi-reduced form of the demand and supply relationship expressed by equation (8) above. The required excess demand parameters are not identified. As usual, however, an impression of the dynamic behaviour of the system is to be had by studying the characteristic roots of the matrix M. In particular, we recall the stability requirement that the eigenvalues of this matrix should be less than one in absolute value.

In summary, the system (10)-(13) consists in five equations in the five endogenous variables Y_t, Y_t^*, r_t, r_t^* and M_t. It is worth reiterating that (13) is a hypothesis about dynamic adjustments in the private sector, reflecting the presumed role of money in disequilibrium. Money is fully endogenous in the complete system.

4.3 Estimation

We adopted a limited-information approach to the estimation of the H-effective demand for money function. Apart from computational convenience, this was indicated from the 2SLS fitting of the supply function, which was not entirely satisfactory (see equation (12) below). To avoid the effects of specification error in the demand equation, we therefore confined the role of the supply equation to supplying the appropriate instruments for the 2SLS estimation of the rest of the system. We estimated the H-effective demand function in two quite distinct ways, corresponding to the methods discussed at length in chapters 2.6.1 and 2.6.2.

Method (1): (Indirect least-squares analogue; cf. §2.6.1)

We start by considering the money and expenditure quasi-equilibrium conditions (10) and (11). Define

$$A = \begin{bmatrix} -\beta_{11} & -\beta_{12} \\ 1 & -\beta_{22} \end{bmatrix},$$

$$G = \begin{bmatrix} -1 & 0 & \gamma_{10} & \gamma_{15} & \gamma_{16} & \gamma_{17} \\ \beta_{23} & \gamma_{21} & \gamma_{20} & \gamma_{25} & \gamma_{26} & \gamma_{27} \end{bmatrix}.$$

The equations (10) and (11) can thus be written:

$$(14) \qquad A\underset{\sim}{z}_t^* = G\underset{\sim}{x}_t + \underset{\sim}{u}_t ,$$

where for the sake of brevity we define

$\underset{\sim}{z}_t' = [\ln Y_t, \ln r_t]$ and redefine $\underset{\sim}{x}_t' = [\ln M_t, \ln E_t, 1, S2_t, S3_t, S4_t]$.

Combining this with the clearing mechanism, we obtain

$$(15) \qquad \underset{\sim}{z}_t = M\underset{\sim}{z}_{t-1} + F\underset{\sim}{x}_t + \underset{\sim}{\varepsilon}_t ,$$

where $F = (I - M)A^{-1}G$ and $\underset{\sim}{\varepsilon}_t$ is the resulting (white-noise) disturbance matrix (cf. equation (33) of chapter 3.6.1).

The equations (15) are estimable in straightforward fashion. The vector $\underset{\sim}{x}_t$ contains one variable $\ln M_t$ which is endogenous to the system (10)-(13). Thus a 2SLS procedure is appropriate. The results, together with the supply equation, are shown for the period 1957 II - 1971 III:

(12)(Supply):
$$\ln M_t = \underset{(0.066)}{0.183} + \underset{(0.249)}{0.063} \ln r_t + \underset{(0.066)}{0.020} \ln d_t + \underset{(5.714)}{1.050} \ln R_t$$
$$- \underset{(-1.477)}{1.109} \ln k_t + \underset{(0.355)}{0.013}\, S2_t + \underset{(0.409)}{0.014}\, S3_t + \underset{(0.009)}{0.0003}\, S4_t$$
$$s^2 = 0.0078, \quad \text{V.N.} = 1.0387.$$

(16)(a)
$$\ln Y_t = \underset{(4.391)}{0.495} \ln Y_{t-1} - \underset{(-0.952)}{0.009} \ln r_{t-1} + \underset{(2.187)}{0.173} \ln M_t + \underset{(0.848)}{0.098}$$
$$+ \underset{(5.527)}{0.404} \ln E_t - \underset{(-0.136)}{0.001}\, S2_t - \underset{(-0.626)}{0.003}\, S3_t - \underset{(-1.497)}{0.006}\, S4_t$$
$$s^2 = 0.00013, \quad \text{V.N.} = 1.1591.$$

(16)(b)
$$\ln r_t = \underset{(-1.737)}{-1.922} \ln Y_{t-1} + \underset{(9.257)}{0.851} \ln r_{t-1} - \underset{(-0.154)}{0.119} \ln M_t + \underset{(1.347)}{1.523}$$
$$+ \underset{(2.876)}{2.064} \ln E_t + \underset{(0.056)}{0.002}\, S2_t + \underset{(1.618)}{0.070}\, S3_t + \underset{(1.714)}{0.072}\, S4_t$$
$$s^2 = 0.0123, \quad \text{V.N.} = 1.1049.$$

Our next task is to derive from these parameters consistent estimates for the parameters of the demand for money function (10). The matrices $\Lambda = (I - M)^{-1}$ and F are obtained from (16)(a) and (b). Partition

$$G = [G_1 \vdots G_2] = \begin{bmatrix} -1 & 0 & \cdot & \gamma_{10} & \gamma_{15} & \gamma_{16} & \gamma_{17} \\ & & \cdot & & & & \\ \beta_{23} & \gamma_{21} & \cdot & \gamma_{20} & \gamma_{25} & \gamma_{26} & \gamma_{27} \end{bmatrix} .$$

Thus G_1 refers to the coefficients of $\ln M_t$ and $\ln E_t$.
Conformably partition $F = [F_1 \vdots F_2]$. Hence we can write
(cf. equation (15)):

$$A\Lambda F_1 = G_1 ,$$

so that in particular

$$[-\beta_{11} \quad -\beta_{12}]\Lambda F_1 = [-1 \quad 0] .$$

Write $\underset{\sim}{e}_i$ as the ith column of I, the identity matrix.
Thus since F_1 has full rank,

(17) $$[\hat{\beta}_{11} \quad \hat{\beta}_{12}] = \underset{\sim}{e}_1' F_1^{-1} \Lambda^{-1} .$$

The remaining coefficients of the demand for money schedule can be established from:

(18) $$[\hat{\gamma}_{10} \quad \hat{\gamma}_{15} \quad \hat{\gamma}_{16} \quad \hat{\gamma}_{17}] = -[\hat{\beta}_{11} \quad \hat{\beta}_{12}]\Lambda F_2 .$$

Finally we have to establish estimates for the variances of our coefficients. This was a little more involved, and we carried out the calculations only for the important coefficients β_{11} and β_{12}. To do this, we started from the 2SLS estimation of the coefficients of (16)(a) and (b), namely

(19) $$H = [M \vdots F] .$$

Stack the rows h_i' of H into a supervector

$$\underset{\approx}{h} = \begin{bmatrix} \underset{\sim}{h}_1 \\ \underset{\sim}{h}_2 \end{bmatrix} .$$

Then the asymptotic covariance matrix of H is given by

(20) $$\text{Cov}\ \underset{\approx}{h} = S \otimes (X'X)^{-1} .$$

Here $S = ((s_{ij}))$ denotes the estimated covariance matrix of the residuals from 16(a) and (b), e.g. $s_{11} = s_1^2$. The data matrix X contains the observations on the variables [$\ln \hat{M}$, ln E, 1, S2, S3, S4] employed in the second stage of the 2SLS calculation. Recall now that

(21) $$\underset{\sim}{\beta}_1' = [\hat{\beta}_{11}, \hat{\beta}_{12}] = \underset{\sim}{e}_1' F_1^{-1}(I-M) .$$

Denote by $\underset{\sim}{\theta}$ the coefficients of the matrices F and M, arranged in a vector according to any convenient order. The matrix Cov($\underset{\sim}{\theta}$) can be obtained from Cov($\underset{\approx}{h}$) as defined above, simply by picking out the appropriate elements. Using (21) and rules for differentiating the matrix inverse (e.g. A.S. Goldberger [1964] §2.8.12), one can now form the Jacobian J' , where

$$\frac{\partial \underset{\sim}{\beta}_1}{\partial \underset{\sim}{\theta}} = J \quad \text{of order } 6\times 2 .$$

Then

(22) $$\text{Cov}(\underset{\sim}{\beta}_1) = J' \ \text{Cov}\ \underset{\sim}{\theta}\ J$$

yields the required asymptotic covariance matrix for $\hat{\beta}_{11}$, $\hat{\beta}_{12}$.

It will be evident that the above method traces out in detail the indirect least squares calculation of chapter 2.6.1. There is, however, a slight complication in the appearance among variables formally exogenous to the clearing mechanism (13) a variable which is in fact endogenous to the entire system being estimated, namely ln M_t . The method therefore starts from an initial 2SLS calculation, instead of OLS.

Our results for the H-effective demand for money function are:

$$(10) \quad \ln M_t = \underset{(4.301)}{0.658} \ln Y_t^* - \underset{(-0.037)}{0.103} \ln r_t^* + 1.022$$

$$+ 0.005\, S2_t + 0.083\, S3_t + 0.105\, S4_t .$$

<u>Method (2)</u>: (Two-stage least squares analogue; cf. §2.6.2)

Following chapter 3.6.2 we define

$$(23) \quad \underset{\sim}{w}_t(\lambda) = \underset{\sim}{z}_{t-1} + \Lambda(\underset{\sim}{z}_t - \underset{\sim}{z}_{t-1}) ,$$

where it will be recalled that $\Lambda = (I - M)^{-1}$. We can now write

$$(24) \quad A\underset{\sim}{w}_t = G\underset{\sim}{x}_t + \underset{\sim}{\zeta}_t ,$$

where $\underset{\sim}{\zeta}_t$ is a compound white-noise disturbance term. Having obtained $\hat{\Lambda}$ from the OLS fitting of equations (16), the resulting values $w_t(\hat{\lambda})$ are employed for the 2SLS estimation of equations (24). It will be recalled from chapter 3.6.2 that the estimates of A and G are consistent but that the usual 2SLS asymptotic covariance matrix is likely to be an underestimate. The t-values as presented will therefore be overestimated.

Results from this technique for the demand for money function are:

$$(10)' \quad \ln M_t = \underset{(36.427)}{0.572} \ln Y_t - \underset{(-0.568)}{0.004} \ln r_t + \underset{(17.518)}{1.503} - \underset{(-0.485)}{0.006}\, S2_t$$

$$+ \underset{(0.504)}{0.067}\, S2_t + \underset{(1.880)}{0.025}\, S3_t .$$

Some comment is now in order on all the above results. Turning first to the dynamic adjustment equations (16)(a) and (b), the characteristic roots of the matrix M are 0.4519 and 0.8943. The large root (0.8943) suggests that convergence to the moving equilibrium is rather slow (a "long" if not "variable" lag?).

In both versions, income is highly significant in the demand for money function. The income-elasticity is about 0.6 in each case. Likewise in both (10) and (10)', the interest rate has a negative sign but is quite insignificant. On the other hand, the Von-Neumann statistic in both (16)(a) and (b) is rather low, suggesting a specification problem. Thus these results although very interesting, are not as conclusive as we should like. We shall return to a discussion of the significance of these results after considering an alternative disequilibrium dynamics.

4.4 Autoregressive-M Dynamics

Teigen [1964] and other authors (e.g. D. Laidler and M. Parkin [1970] for the U.K.) have employed the lagged stock of money among the independent regressors in the demand for money equation. In the present context, the suggested equation would be of the form:

$$\text{(25)} \qquad \ln M_t = \gamma \ln M_{t-1} + \beta_{11} \ln Y_t + \beta_{12} \ln r_t + \underset{\sim}{\gamma}_1' \underset{\sim}{x}_t + u_t ,$$

where $\underset{\sim}{x}_t$ refers to additional exogenous variables.

The interpretation of such an equation most often[7] given is that it refers to a partial adjustment mechanism. According to this, individuals adjust their holdings of money only part way toward the desired level, as indexed by Y_t and r_t. Define $\bar{M}$ as the "desired" holdings of money. Neglecting the disturbance term,

$$\ln M_t = \ln M_{t-1} + (1-\lambda)(\ln \bar{M}_t - \ln M_{t-1}) ,$$

and

$$\text{(26)} \qquad \ln \bar{M}_t = \frac{\beta_{11}}{1-\lambda} \ln Y_t + \frac{\beta_{12}}{1-\lambda} \ln r_t + \frac{1}{1-\lambda} \underset{\sim}{\gamma}' x_t .$$

Equation (26) is taken as the demand for money schedule of basic interest. However while this may be true enough as a description of <u>individual</u> behaviour, it is very important to bear in mind that an equation like (25) refers to <u>aggregate</u> behaviour. If the good involved were motor cars, the stock of motor cars is determined by the behaviour of consumers, the same decision-making agents to whom the structural equation in question is supposed to apply. Thus there are no logical problems in adding up individual demands to obtain an estimable aggregate demand schedule. But we have argued already that the stock of money (M) is, given r and unborrowed reserves, determined by the decisions of banks. <u>Out of equilibrium</u>, it is a given datum so far as the private non-banking sector is concerned.

In the aggregate, therefore, an equation like (25) can only be taken as a hypothesis about market clearing. For given M_t and M_{t-1}, the path of Y_t and r_t must be such that this equation is satisfied; it is the behaviour of individuals in trying to get rid of unwanted money balances, or build up more, that determines this path. As a dynamic hypothesis, it is of course not fully determinate, for it must be combined with two more equations to fully identify the time path for M, Y and r. However this will not prevent the estimation of (25) as it stands.

The question arises as to whether (25) is merely a transformation of the Walrasian mechanism expressed in equations (10)-(13). The answer turns out to be no. If M, Y, r are constrained to lie along (25), this may be a brand of dynamics in which H-effective demand or supply schedules do not appear to provide the appropriate signals of demand or supply pressure. As we have argued in section 4.1, it is not a matter of logical necessity or of economic theory that this should be the case. Thus if equation (25) represents an empirically determined clearing path it is not at all obvious that we can derive from it the H-effective demand for money, or any other schedule of this kind judged to be meaningful or useful for purposes of comparative statics. In short, the comparison of the "autoregressive-M" dynamics with the "Walrasian" dynamics considered in section 4.3 is full of interest and we move on to discuss our empirical results.

It will be helpful to reproduce first Teigen's 2SLS results,[8] spanning the period 1946 IV - 1952 IV (Teigen [1964], p.490 equation (3.1a')).

$$(27) \quad \ln M_t = \underset{(3.179)}{0.551} + \underset{(9.731)}{0.715} \ln M_{t-1} + \underset{(4.172)}{0.148} \ln Y_t - \underset{(-2.778)}{0.020} \ln r_t - \underset{(-9.846)}{0.064}\, S1_t - \underset{(6.676)}{0.025}\, S2_t - \underset{(-5.525)}{0.022}\, S3_t$$

$$^{9}R^2 = 0.992, \qquad {}^{9}\text{D.W.} = 1.652.$$

Results from our study, for the period 1957 II - 1971 III are:

$$\text{(28)} \quad \ln M_t = \underset{(-2.797)}{-0.215} + \underset{(24.502)}{0.997} \ln M_{t-1} + \underset{(1.816)}{0.043} \ln Y_t - \underset{(-4.263)}{0.026} \ln r_t$$

$$- \underset{(-0.605)}{0.002} S2_t + \underset{(3.156)}{0.009} S3_t + \underset{(10.224)}{0.031} S4_t$$

$$s^2 = 0.00005, \quad V.N. = 1.3284, \quad D.W. = 1.799.$$ [9]

In both equations, the interest-rate is negative and significant. The main differences between the two equations are (a) the much reduced significance level for income in the later period and (b) the higher coefficient, now approximately unity, for the lagged money stock. The coefficient of the lagged money stock is somewhat at variance with other studies. When we confined the regressions to the first 40 of the 58 observations employed in fitting (28) (i.e. to 1967 I), we obtained the following results:

$$\text{(29)} \quad \ln M_t = \underset{(1.084)}{0.434} + \underset{(4.360)}{0.742} \ln M_{t-1} + \underset{(1.943)}{0.145} \ln Y_t - \underset{(-2.552)}{0.020} \ln r_t$$

$$- \underset{(-1.980)}{0.007} S2_t + \underset{(0.623)}{0.003} S3_t + \underset{(5.186)}{0.025} S4_t .$$

Equation (29) is remarkably similar to the much earlier period covered by Teigen's equation (27). This suggests that there was a structural change in the latter half of the sixties, a not altogether surprising conclusion which may result from the omission of price considerations. For our present purposes we note that all three equations exhibit a significant interest-rate coefficient. In this important feature they differ from the Walrasian dynamics considered in section 4.3.

4.5 Conclusions

Each of the two approaches considered has a certain amount of coherence so far as their empirical testing is concerned. Thus if we assume Walrasian-type dynamics, the stationary or stable H-effective demand for money function is significantly related only to income, and in particular is not related to the rate of interest. Moreover the lag involved is long. The combination of this brand of dynamics with this specification for a demand for money function calls to mind monetarist doctrines. On the other hand, a different kind of dynamics produces a different view of the demand for money function. We argued above that conventional "autoregressive-M" formulations do in fact constitute part of a hypothesis about disequilibrium dynamics. If we accept the long-run equation (26) as the appropriate demand for money, then the rate of interest will be highly significant. Earlier, however we argued that the parent equation (25) may be a hypothesis about market clearing, on a macro-economic level. To call the "long-run" construction (26) a demand for money function is therefore not well grounded theoretically, even if it is very suggestive empirically.

There has in recent years been a tendency to regard the estimation (let alone the existence) of a demand for money function as a more or less settled matter. We have tried to show that there are serious problems of specification and identification to be approached before such questions can be safely relegated to the econometrician's out-basket. Undoubtedly a great deal of further experimentation with different variables and lag distributions will be necessary, and in this respect we acknowledge the limited scope of the present chapter. It is greatly to be desired, however, that we do not become so immersed in the folklore of applied econometrics that we cannot pause and enquire into the meaning and interpretation of our partial adjustment mechanisms or distributed lags. In the present contribution we hope to have at least asked some of the right questions.

Footnotes to Chapter 4

[1]Even this may be a matter of debate. An outstanding example is Friedman's demand for money function [1956]. In omitting actual income in favour of permanent income, Friedman argues against transactions motives (related to actual income) on the grounds that, for example, payment procedures are themselves determined by other current arguments in the demand function. Thus whereas most others would view payments mechanisms as an institutional datum given in the short-run - certainly longer dated, as it were, than interest rate or price movements - Friedman would not.

[2]We use the word "effective" in the special sense of the "Keynesian reinterpretation", in terms of the medium of exchange necessary to effect transactions.

[3]Such equations have been widely used in the literature, although their basis in price theory has attracted some criticism. In the present explanatory study there seems some virtue in starting along such a well trodden path.

[4]The source of this data was the Federal Reserve Bulletin. In general, quarterly averages of monthly figures were used, following W.E. Gibson [1972].

[5]Source: U.S. Commerce Department's *Survey of Current Business*.

[6]There is no special significance in the particular period considered in this study; it was determined simply by the particular data readily available to the author. We did feel, however, that there was some virtue in choosing more recent data than that considered by both Teigen and Gibson.

[7]An alternative explanation is that the income variable included in the H-effective demand for money function is Friedman's time-series proxy for permanent income, as a Koyck-type weighted average of past observed incomes. Equation (25) is then the transformed, or autoregressive version. Apart from possible serial correlation in the residual term, comments on permanent income as an argument of the demand for money function have been made already (see footnote 1).

[8]Teigen's results were subsequently the subject of some debate (W.E. Gibson [1976] and Teigen [1976]). After comparing the results from Gibson's and Teigen's work with our own, we decided to reproduce only Teigen's, but we did decide to employ quarterly averages of monthly figures. Teigen's results as given refer to end-of-quarter figures. Note also that Teigen includes a net worth variable among his exogenous (sic) variables, not included in our work.

[9]We reproduce these figures although there is some doubt about their interpretation in a 2SLS context. R^2 plainly refers to the stage 2 regression and is thus an overestimate of the goodness of fit. Presumably D.W. also refers to the stage 2 regression, so that it may again be an overestimate of the V.N. ratio applied to the correct residuals. We reproduce the D.W. statistic from our own results for the stage 2 regression, in addition to the correct V.N. ratio (see equation (28)).

CHAPTER FIVE

QUANTITIES AS THE SHORT SIDE[1]

We have explored in chapters three and four models in which information about market clearing is confined to price adjustment, or more generally to just one dimension of interest. The econometric limitation of such a procedure is that in general the supply and demand relations cannot be separately identified (although as we found in chapter four, there are some circumstances where they may be). It is time now to consider the incorporation of information about quantities. As noted in chapter one, there are many possible trajectories for the adjustment or clearing of market quantities. In this chapter we shall consider what in many ways is the simplest of these possibilities. According to this, if prices do not immediately move to clear an imbalance of supply and demand, the quantities actually transacted are determined as the minimum of the quantity demanded and the quantity supplied. It is this formulation which has so far received the bulk of attention from econometricians. The probabilistic structure of the "short" or "Fair-Jaffee" model is not straightforward, and indeed the derivation of its likelihood function strains one's grasp of intuitive probability notions. It is consequently not surprising that authors have in the past fallen into error. Fortunately exploitation of the PAMEQ specification allows an uncomplicated derivation and presentation of the leading possibilities for estimation, and points up clearly certain failures of the method of maximum-likelihood. The present chapter is largely an exposition of the estimation theory, with certain ancillary properties, of these models. Some applications will be considered in following chapters.

5.1 Non-simultaneous Models

We consider two models in this section. They have this in common, that there is no equilibrating tendency specified as part of the model, between the forces of supply and demand. For this reason the models are not of the greatest intrinsic interest and we shall not consider their estimation in minute detail. The derivation of their likelihood functions is, however, of interest and significance for more truly simultaneous forms and we shall therefore be at some pains to elucidate their probability structure. The two models differ according to whether or not it is possible to tell from inspection of the sample whether a particular period is one of excess demand or excess supply. We shall refer to the latter property in terms of "sample separation" of the two regimes. We consider first the model with no sample separation.

5.1.1 No Sample Separation.

This model is of the following form:

$$(1)\ (a)\quad D_t = \underset{\sim}{X}'_{1t}\underset{\sim}{\beta}_1 + u_{1t}$$

$$(b)\quad S_t = \underset{\sim}{X}'_{2t}\underset{\sim}{\beta}_2 + u_{2t}$$

$$(c)\quad Q_t = \min(D_t, S_t)\ .$$

Here X_{1t} and X_{2t} are observable vectors of fixed numbers, which may contain common elements. The quantities D_t and S_t - demand and supply - are not directly observable. Their minimum or short side defines the observable transacted quantity Q. (A basic discussion of the short-side models is to be found in section 1.2.1.)

Let us derive[2] the likelihood function for the observable sample $Q_1 \ldots Q_T$. We may write schematically:

(2) $\text{prob}(Q_t) = \text{prob}(Q_t/Q_t$ belongs to supply function$) \times \text{prob}(Q_t$ belongs to supply function$) + \text{prob}(Q_t/Q_t$ belongs to demand function$) \times \text{prob}(Q_t$ belongs to demand function$)$.

Write $\text{prob}(Q_t \in \text{supply}) = \pi_t$, so that $\text{prob}(Q_t \in \text{demand}) = 1 - \pi_t$. Now

(3) $$\text{prob}(Q_t/Q_t \in \text{supply}) = \frac{\text{prob}(Q_t \text{ and } Q_t \in \text{supply})}{\pi_t} .$$

In considering the numerator of the R.H.S. of (3), a diagrammatic interpretation may be helpful.

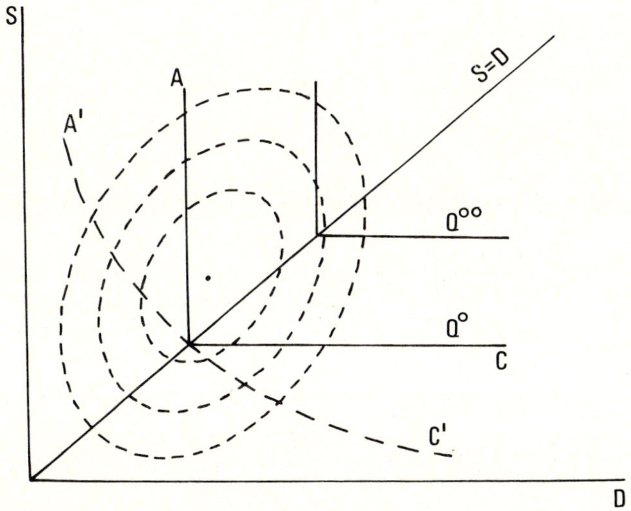

Figure 5.1

In figure 5.1 the heavy shaded lines represent isoquants for differing values of Q, the quantity actually transacted ($Q^{oo} > Q^{o}$). The dotted ellipses are contours of the joint density of D and S. Consider the isoquant for the particular quantity Q^o. Along the stretch CB, $Q^o = S$. We may write:

$$\text{prob}(Q^o \text{ and } Q^o \in \text{supply}) = \int_{BC} \text{prob}(D,Q^o)dD ,$$

where prob(D,S) refers to the joint density of D and S. Similarly for prob(Q^o and $Q^o \in$ demand). Write f and F for the joint density and (cumulative) distribution function of D,S.

From (2) and (3), we therefore have:

$$\text{(4)} \qquad \text{prob } Q^o = \text{prob}(Q^o \text{ and } Q^o \in \text{supply}) + \text{prob}(Q^o \text{ and } Q^o \in \text{demand})$$

$$= \int_{Q^o}^{\infty} f(D,Q^o)\,dD + \int_{Q^o}^{\infty} f(Q^o,S)\,dS\,.$$

A useful particular case is where u_{1t} and u_{2t} are independent. Then $f = f_1 f_2$, as the product of the marginal distributions of D and S, and the density g of Q is:

$$\text{(5)} \qquad g(Q) = f_2(Q)[1 - F_1(Q)] + f_1(Q)[1 - F_2(Q)]\,.$$

It is evident from (5) that

$$g(Q) = -\frac{d}{dQ}\,(1 - F_1(Q))(1 - F_2(Q))\,.$$

The distribution function G of g is therefore

$$G(Q^o) = \text{prob}(Q \le Q^o) = 1 - (1 - F_1(Q^o))(1 - F_2(Q^o))\,.$$

This result (for f_1 and f_2 independent) may also be derived by noting that the required distribution is that of the smaller order statistic of two independent drawings from the two distributions f_1 and f_2. We have

$$\text{prob}(Q \le Q^o) = 1 - \text{prob}(Q \ge Q^o)\,.$$

Now $Q \ge Q^o$ if and only if values in excess of Q^o were drawn from both f_1 and f_2. Since the drawings are independent

$$\text{prob}(Q \ge Q^o) = (1 - F_1(Q^o))(1 - F_2(Q^o))\,,$$

from which the desired result follows.

Thus let us assume that u_{1t} and u_{2t} are Normal, with variances σ_1^2 and σ_2^2 respectively. Denote by $N(\cdot;0,1)$ the cumulative distribution function of the standard Normal distribution (i.e. mean zero, variance unity). Then

$$1 - F_1(Q_t) = 1 - N\left(\frac{Q_t - X'_{1t}\beta_1}{\sigma_1};0,1\right)$$

$$= N\left(-\frac{(Q_t - X'_{1t}\beta_1)}{\sigma_1};0,1\right)$$

Hence

$$G(Q_t) = 1 - N\left(-\frac{(Q_t - X'_{1t}\beta_1)}{\sigma_1};0,1\right) N\left(-\frac{(Q_t - X'_{2t}\beta_2)}{\sigma_2};0,1\right) .$$

Whichever assumption we employ in deriving the density g, the log-likelihood function is

$$\log L = \sum_t^T \log(g(Q_t)) .$$

It will be apparent from the form of the density function g (e.g. (5)) that log L is a very complicated function of the desired parameters. The first and second derivatives have been tabulated by G.S. Maddala and F.D. Nelson [1974] for the case where u_{1t} and u_{2t} are independent, and for the more general case by M.J. Hartley and P. Mallela [1977]. From the additive form of (4) or (5) one might expect trouble with the regularity of this likelihood function, but a moment's thought in respect of (5) will show that the "cross-products" involved will rule out any of the mixed-distribution difficulties discussed in chapter 2.3. Indeed, Hartley and Mallela [1977] showed that the general likelihood function based on (4) is regular, with the standard properties discussed in chapter 2.2. Computational experience is still limited, but Maddala and Nelson [1974] found that quadratic hill climbing (see chapter 2.4) gave acceptable results. Both for actual data (the Fair-Jaffee data) and artificially generated data, the unmodified Newton method performed poorly.

It may be seen that the complicated nature of the probability element g(Q) arises out of the fact that the minimum of two Normal variates is not itself Normal, or again any other simple distribution. It would be convenient if we could find an underlying distribution which was preserved under the operation of taking the minimum. The classic instance of such a reproductive property is the Weibull distribution, much used in reliability theory (see e.g. K.V. Bury [1975], ch. 12 onwards). The minimum of two identical Weibull variates is itself Weibull. Unfortunately this very convenient property does not extend to general non-identical Weibull variates. The Weibull distribution is therefore not applicable. The existence of any distributions f_1 and f_2, alternative to the Normal which, while being adequate from the representational viewpoint, allow a simpler expression of the likelihood function remains an unsolved matter.

A final remark concerning figure 5.1 may be made. Loci such as ABC are formally the same as the "isoquants" of production or consumer demand theory. Such discontinuous isoquants are characteristic of simple linear-programming technologies. Continuous technologies such as the Cobb-Douglas production function exhibit smooth isoquants convex to the origin. This suggests by analogy that we might replace our discontinuous clearing path ABC with such a convex curve as illustrated in Figure 5.1 by A'BC'. Algebraically, we might thus specify a clearing path of the form $Q = D^{\alpha}S^{\beta}$ with $\alpha + \beta = 1$. Unfortunately, this carries the implication that the clearing path lies between the demand and supply curves, i.e. quantities transacted are greater than the minimum of demand and supply. As a matter of logic, this is hard to justify. It may arise, however, that D and S are to refer to notional schedules, while the clearing path might be determined in terms of unidentifiable effective schedules (see sections 1.3, 4.1 and 6.3 for the difference). In such circumstances, the clearing path might lie strictly between the notional demand and supply schedules, although whether its position in this respect would remain a stable function of prices remains another matter.

5.1.2 Sample Separation Available. The second model we consider shares equations 1(a),(b),(c) with the model just discussed. What distinguishes it from this model is that extra information, which is nevertheless extraneous to the model, is available to discriminate periods of excess supply from excess demand. We assume that an ancillary variable z is available in first-difference form Δz, such that:

$$\begin{array}{ll} \Delta z_t > 0 & D_t > S_t \\ \Delta z_t = 0 & D_t = S_t \\ \Delta z_t < 0 & D_t < S_t . \end{array}$$

It will be apparent that Δz plays the role of price changes in competitive theory, and is indeed so labelled in the original studies dealing with this model (Fair and Jaffee [1972], Fair and H.H. Kelejian [1974]). It should be remarked, however, that the variable Δz is not itself assumed to be related to the current state of excess demand. In other words Δz_t is considered an exogenous variable. Later we shall introduce truly simultaneous versions of this model.

Since we now have available information as to which of the two possible regimes - excess demand or excess supply - the regime is currently in, we have in effect not one but two "observations" in each period, namely:

(i) the value Q_t of transacted quantities,

(ii) a variable indicating whether or not we are currently in excess demand or excess supply. We can proxy this switch by the variable:

$$R_t = 1 \quad \text{if } \Delta z_t < 0$$
$$= 0 \quad \text{otherwise.}$$

We therefore seek the likelihood function:

(6) $$L(Q_1 \ldots Q_T, R_1 \ldots R_T) = \prod_{t \in \psi_a} g(Q_t/R_t = 1).\text{prob}(R_t = 1) \times \prod_{t \in \psi_b} g(Q_t/R_t = 0).\text{prob}(R_t = 0) .$$

Here ψ_a indicates the set of points for which $\Delta z_t < 0$, i.e. $R_t = 1$, and ψ_b the complementary set. Now

$$g(Q_t/R_t = 1) = \frac{\text{prob}(Q_t \text{ and } R_t = 1)}{\text{prob}(R_t = 1)} .$$

By a similar process to that leading up to equation (4) of §5.1.1,

$$\text{prob}(Q_t \text{ and } R_t = 1) = \int_{Q_t}^{\infty} f(Q_t, S)dS .$$

We may therefore write:

(7) $$L = \prod_{t \in \psi_a} \left(\int_{Q_t}^{\infty} f(Q_t, S)dS \right) \times \prod_{t \in \psi_b} \left(\int_{Q_t}^{\infty} f(D, Q_t)dD \right)$$

Again, in the particular case where the disturbances u_{1t} and u_{2t} are independent, we can simplify (7) to

(8) $$L = \prod_{t \in \psi_a} f_1(Q_t)(1 - F_2(Q_t)) \times \prod_{t \in \psi_b} f_2(Q_t)(1 - F_1(Q_t)) .$$

This can be rewritten

(9) $$L = \left[\prod_{t \in \psi_a} f_1(Q_t) \prod_{t \in \psi_b} (1 - F_1(Q_t)) \right] \left[\prod_{t \in \psi_b} f_2(Q_t) \prod_{t \in \psi_a} (1 - F_2(Q_t)) \right] ,$$

$$= L_{(i)} . L_{(ii)} , \text{ say.}$$

Since $L_{(i)}$ and $L_{(ii)}$ have no common factors, maximising L amounts to maximising them separately. Expressions $L_{(i)}$ and $L_{(ii)}$ have a useful similarity to the likelihood function of the Tobit model (J. Tobin [1958]), which has been shown by T. Amemiya [1973] to be regular. We should therefore expect a similar property to hold of the likelihood function (9).

5.2 Simultaneous Models

Much of the interest in this study centres around models in which price movements, while not always clearing the market in every period, are nevertheless responsive to forces of supply and demand. Price and quantity therefore form a simultaneous system. The system we shall consider in subsequent sections is of the following form:

$$(10)\quad (a)\quad D_t = \underset{\sim}{X}'_{1t}\underset{\sim}{\beta}_1 + \alpha_1 p_t + u_{1t}$$

$$(b)\quad S_t = \underset{\sim}{X}'_{2t}\underset{\sim}{\beta}_2 + \alpha_2 p_t + u_{2t}$$

$$(c)\quad Q_t = \min(D_t, S_t)$$

$$(d)\quad p_t = \mu p_{t-1} + (1-\mu)p_t^* + u_{3t} .$$

Equation (d) is the competitive PAMEQ specification considered in detail in chapter 3. It will be recalled from §3.4.2 that this may be augmented with further exogenous variables (the "administered" price adjustment equation). Although it will be convenient to treat fully only the competitive mechanism, we shall consider any complications of the administered scheme in section 5.6.2.

It will be recalled from chapter 3 that the imputed market clearing price p_t^* is defined by the relation:

$$D(p_t^*) = S(p_t^*) ,$$

$$\text{i.e. } (11)\quad p_t^* = \frac{1}{\alpha_1 - \alpha_2}(\underset{\sim}{X}'_{2t}\underset{\sim}{\beta}_2 - \underset{\sim}{X}'_{1t}\underset{\sim}{\beta}_1) + \frac{1}{\alpha_1 - \alpha_2}(u_{2t} - u_{1t}) .$$

The disturbance term u_{3t} of (10)(d) may not appear. We shall refer to this as error-free clearing (the E.F.C. model). Where it does occur (the noisy clearing model, N.C.M.), we shall assume following the discussion of chapter 3 that Eu_{3t}^2 collapses to zero as the "friction" parameter $\mu \to 0$. If this is the case, equations (10) reduce for $\mu = 0$ to the standard simultaneous model:

$$(12) \qquad Q_t = \underset{\sim}{X}'_{1t}\underset{\sim}{\beta}_1 + \alpha_1 p_t + u_{1t}$$

$$Q_t = \underset{\sim}{X}'_{2t}\underset{\sim}{\beta}_2 + \alpha_2 p_t + u_{2t} \;.$$

It will be convenient at this stage to recast the model (11) in various different forms. From (10)(a) and (b), we have:

$$(13) \qquad \underset{\sim}{X}'_{1t}\underset{\sim}{\beta}_1 + \alpha_1 p_t + u_{1t} - (\underset{\sim}{X}'_{2t}\underset{\sim}{\beta}_2 + \alpha_2 p_t + u_{2t}) = (\alpha_2 - \alpha_1)(p^*_t - p_t) \;.$$

Now equations (10)(a), (b) and (c) can be combined into:

$$(14) \qquad Q_t = R_t(\underset{\sim}{X}'_{1t}\underset{\sim}{\beta}_1 + \alpha_1 p_t + u_{1t}) + (1 - R_t)(\underset{\sim}{X}'_{2t}\underset{\sim}{\beta}_2 + \alpha_2 p_t + u_{2t}) \;.$$

Here $R_t = R(p_t - p^*_t)$, where the ramp function R is defined by:

$$R(X) = \begin{cases} 1 & \text{if } X \geq 0 \\ 0 & \text{otherwise} \;. \end{cases}$$

Thus if $p_t - p^*_t > 0$ (excess supply), $R_t = 1$, so that $Q_t = \underset{\sim}{X}'_{1t}\underset{\sim}{\beta}_1 + \alpha_1 \beta_t + u_{1t}$.

And if $p_t - p^*_t < 0$, the Q-observations lie on the supply curve.

From (14)

$$Q_t = \underset{\sim}{X}'_{2t}\underset{\sim}{\beta}_2 + \alpha_2 p_t + u_{2t} + R_t(\underset{\sim}{X}'_{1t}\underset{\sim}{\beta}_1 + \alpha_1 p_t + u_{1t} - (\underset{\sim}{X}'_{2t}\underset{\sim}{\beta}_2 + \alpha_2 p_t + u_{2t})) \;.$$

Using (13) this yields:

$$(15)(b) \quad Q_t = \underset{\sim}{X}'_{2t}\underset{\sim}{\beta}_2 + \alpha_2 p_t - (\alpha_2 - \alpha_1)(p_t - p^*_t)R(p_t - p^*_t) + u_{2t} \;.$$

Similarly, we can obtain:

$$(15)(a) \quad Q_t = \underset{\sim}{X}'_{1t}\underset{\sim}{\beta}_1 + \alpha_1 p_t + (\alpha_2 - \alpha_1)(p_t - p^*_t)(1 - R(p_t - p^*_t)) + u_{1t} \;.$$

Equations 15(a) and (b) are formulations of the demand and supply curve which bear a closer analogy with conventional equilibrium models. They will form the basis of analysis in section 5.6.

Note that if $p_t = p^*_t$ they reduce to the standard equilibrium model.

For maximum likelihood estimation it is useful to consider the behaviour of the model in regimes of excess supply and excess demand.

(a) Excess Supply. (Corresponds to $p_t > p_t^*$ and $R_t = 1$)

$$
\begin{aligned}
Q_t &= X'_{1t}\beta_1 + \alpha_1 p_t + u_{1t} \\
Q_t &= X'_{2t}\beta_2 + \alpha_2 p_t - (\alpha_2 - \alpha_1)(p_t - p_t^*) + u_{2t} \qquad (16)(a) \\
p_t &= \mu p_{t-1} + (1-\mu)p_t^* + u_{3t} \, .
\end{aligned}
$$

(b) Excess Demand. (Corresponds to $p_t < p_t^*$ and $R_t = 0$)

$$
\begin{aligned}
Q_t &= X'_{1t}\beta_1 + \alpha_1 p_t + (\alpha_2 - \alpha_1)(p_t - p_t^*) + u_{1t} \\
Q_t &= X'_{2t}\beta_2 + \alpha_2 p_t + u_{2t} \qquad (16)(b) \\
p_t &= \mu p_{t-1} + (1-\mu)p_t^* + u_{3t} \, .
\end{aligned}
$$

Finally one can specialise to the E.F.C. model by putting $u_{3t} \equiv 0$ where it occurs in the above equations.

5.3 The General Likelihood Function

In this section we shall establish the general form of the likelihood function for both the error-free and noisy clearing models. To do so we shall draw on arguments very similar to those utilised in section 5.1 in respect of the non-simultaneous models.

5.3.1 Noisy Clearing Mechanism. Equations (16)(a) and (b) define a probability density in the three variables p_t, p_t^* and Q_t. The observable variables, on the other hand, are just p_t and Q_t. The problem is therefore to find the marginal density of the latter two variables. Following the general schemes of section 5.1 we write:

$$\begin{aligned}\text{prob}(p,Q) &= (\text{prob}(p,Q)/p < p^*).\text{prob}(p < p^*) \\ &\quad + (\text{prob}(p,Q)/p \geq p^*).\text{prob}(p \geq p^*) \\ &= \frac{\text{prob}(p,Q \text{ and } p < p^*)}{\text{prob}(p < p^*)}.\text{prob}(p < p^*) \\ &\quad + \frac{\text{prob}(p,Q \text{ and } p \geq p^*)}{\text{prob}(p \geq p^*)}.\text{prob}(p \geq p^*).\end{aligned}$$

So

$$\text{prob}(p,Q) = \text{prob}(p,Q \text{ and } p < p^*) + \text{prob}(p,Q \text{ and } p > p^*),$$

(17) $$= \int_p^{\infty} f(p,Q,p^*)dp^* + \int_{-\infty}^{p} f(p,Q,p^*)dp^*,$$

where f refers to the joint density defined in terms of equations (16)(a) and (b). In fact, formally speaking these equations define two different densities. Given a certain density defined for the disturbance terms (u_{1t},u_{2t},u_{3t}) equations (16)(a) define an implied density $f^a(p,Q,p^*)$ for p,Q,p^*, in terms of ordinary mechanical transformation processes from one set of variables to another. Likewise equations (16)(b) define formally a different density, $f^b(p,Q,p^*)$. The two terms of equation (17) are then expressible in terms of these formal densities as:

(18) $$\text{prob}(p,Q) = \int_p^{\infty} f^b(p,Q,p^*)dp^* + \int_{-\infty}^{p} f^a(p,Q,p^*)dp^*.$$

Once $\text{prob}(p_t, Q_t)$ has been found as in (18), the likelihood function is:

(19) $$L(p_1 \ldots p_T,\ Q_1 \ldots Q_T) = \prod_{t=1}^{T} \text{prob}(p_t, Q_t)\ .$$

We note that because of the PAMEQ clearing specification, $\text{prob}(p_t, Q_t)$ will depend upon p_{t-1}. In other words the individual terms $\text{prob}(p_t, Q_t)$ refer to the densities conditional upon p_{t-1}. As pointed out in chapter 2.2.2, this circumstance in itself does not necessarily affect the regularity of the resulting likelihood functions.

5.3.2 The EFC Mechanism. It will be recalled that in this case the clearing mechanism is not subject to a disturbance and reads:

$$p_t = \mu p_{t-1} + (1-\mu) p_t^* ,$$

from which

(20) $$(p_t - p_t^*) = -\frac{\mu}{1-\mu}(p_t - p_{t-1})\ .$$

The sign of $(p_t - p_t^*)$ is therefore the same as that of $p_{t-1} - p_t$. This is observable, so that the fact of whether or not we are in a position of excess demand or excess supply is itself an observation, as well as the actual values p_t, Q_t. The likelihood function is therefore:

(21) $$L(p_1 \ldots p_T,\ Q_1 \ldots Q_T,\ \text{sign}\ \Delta p_1 \ldots \text{sign}\ \Delta p_T)$$
$$= \prod_{t\in\psi_b}\left(\int_{p_t}^{\infty} f^b(p_t, Q_t, p^*)\,dp^*\right) \cdot \prod_{t\in\psi_a}\left(\int_{-\infty}^{p_t} f^a(p_t, Q_t, p^*)\,dp^*\right) ,$$

where ψ_a indicates the set of periods for which $p_t < p_{t-1}$ and ψ_b the complementary set. In the present case, p_t^* is functionally related by (20) to p_t. Hence f^a and f^b are degenerate distributions and we may write, for example, $f^a(p_t, Q_t, p^*) = g^a(p_t, Q_t)$. The likelihood function is then expressible as:

(22) $$L = \prod_{t\in\psi_a} g^a(p_t, Q_t) \prod_{t\in\psi_b} g^b(p_t, Q_t)\ .$$

5.4 Normal Disturbances

We may now proceed to evaluate the likelihood functions in the particular case of Normally distributed disturbances.

5.4.1 Noisy Clearing. We proceed by obtaining the densities f^a and f^b of equation (18) above. It will bear reiterating that f^a, for instance, is only formally a density function; integrating out p^*, for instance, will not give the marginal density of p and Q. However we can proceed in mechanical fashion as if f^a were in fact the density function defined by a standard linear simultaneous model. The equations of regime (a), as defined by (16)(a), may accordingly be written in the following form.

$$(23)(a) \qquad B_a \begin{bmatrix} p_t \\ Q_t \\ p_t^* \end{bmatrix} = \Gamma_a \begin{bmatrix} p_{t-1} \\ \underset{\sim}{X}_{1t} \\ \underset{\sim}{X}_{2t} \end{bmatrix} + \underset{\sim}{u}_t$$

where:

$$B_a = \begin{bmatrix} -\alpha_1 & 1 & 0 \\ -\alpha_1 & 1 & \alpha_1 - \alpha_2 \\ 1 & 0 & -(1-\mu) \end{bmatrix}$$

and

$$\Gamma_a = \begin{bmatrix} 0 & \underset{\sim}{\beta}_1' & 0 \\ 0 & \underset{\sim}{0}' & \underset{\sim}{\beta}_2' \\ \mu & \underset{\sim}{0}' & \underset{\sim}{0}' \end{bmatrix}, \quad \underset{\sim}{u}_t = \begin{bmatrix} u_{1t} \\ u_{2t} \\ u_{3t} \end{bmatrix}.$$

Write the covariance matrix $E\underset{\sim}{u}_t\underset{\sim}{u}_t' = \Sigma = ((\sigma_{ij}))$. The corresponding formal reduced form may be written

$$(24)(a) \qquad \begin{bmatrix} p_t \\ Q_t \\ p_t^* \end{bmatrix} = \Pi_a \begin{bmatrix} p_{t-1} \\ \underset{\sim}{X}_{1t} \\ \underset{\sim}{X}_{2t} \end{bmatrix} + \underset{\sim}{v}_t^a ,$$

where $\Pi_a = B_a^{-1}\Gamma_a$ and $\underset{\sim}{v}_t^a = B_a^{-1}\underset{\sim}{u}_t$. Thus $\Omega_a = E\underset{\sim}{v}_t^a \underset{\sim}{v}_t^{a'} = B_a^{-1}\Sigma B_a^{'-1}$ is the covariance matrix of the reduced form residuals for regime (a). Next, write

$$(25)(a) \qquad \underset{\sim}{\mu}_t^a = \Pi_a \begin{bmatrix} p_{t-1} \\ \underset{\sim}{X}_{1t} \\ \underset{\sim}{X}_{2t} \end{bmatrix} = E^a \begin{bmatrix} p_t \\ Q_t \\ p_t^* \end{bmatrix} .$$

The notation E^a indicates the <u>formal</u> conditional (upon p_{t-1}) expectation of the endogenous variables for regime (a). Once again this is not to be confused with the true expectation of these variables, or with the expectation conditional upon regime (a) holding. These are purely mechanical operations, motivated by comparison with linear models. To accommodate sub- or super-scripts we shall on occasion write Ω^a rather than Ω_a. We may now write

$$(26)(a) \qquad f^a(p,Q,p^*) = (2\pi)^{-\frac{3}{2}}|\Omega_a|^{-\frac{1}{2}} \exp(-\tfrac{1}{2}\underset{\sim}{x}_a' \Omega_a^{-1} \underset{\sim}{x}_a) ,$$

where $\underset{\sim}{x}_a' = [p - \mu_1^a,\ Q - \mu_2^a,\ p^* - \mu_3^a]$. One can similarly derive the formal density $f^b(p,Q,p^*)$ in terms of equations (23)(b), (24)(b) and (25)(b) with "a" everywhere replaced by "b".

We shall now perform the integration of the second term in (18), i.e. that corresponding to regime (a). Partition

$$\underset{\sim}{x}_a = \begin{bmatrix} p - \mu_1^a \\ Q - \mu_2^a \\ \hline p^* - \mu_3^a \end{bmatrix} = \begin{bmatrix} \underset{\sim}{y}_a \\ \hline p^* - \mu_3^a \end{bmatrix}$$

Partition conformably:

$$\Omega_a = \left[\begin{array}{c|c} \Omega_{11}^a & \underset{\sim}{\phi}_a \\ \hline \underset{\sim}{\phi}_a' & w_{33}^a \end{array}\right] .$$

According to the partitioned inverse,

$$\Omega_a^{-1} = \begin{bmatrix} K_{11}^a & \underset{\sim}{k}_a \\ \\ \underset{\sim}{k}'_a & d_a^{-1} \end{bmatrix} = \begin{bmatrix} \Omega_{11}^{a^{-1}}\left(I + \dfrac{\underset{\sim}{\phi}_a \underset{\sim}{\phi}'_a \Omega_{11}^{a^{-1}}}{d_a}\right), & \dfrac{-\Omega_{11}^{a^{-1}} \underset{\sim}{\phi}_a}{d_a} \\ \\ \dfrac{-\phi'_a \Omega_{11}^{a^{-1}}}{d_a} & , \quad d_a^{-1} \end{bmatrix} ;$$

where

(27) $$d_a = w_{33}^a - \underset{\sim}{\phi}'_a \Omega_{11}^{a^{-1}} \underset{\sim}{\phi}_a .$$

Thus

$$\exp -\tfrac{1}{2}\, \underset{\sim}{x}' \Omega_a^{-1} \underset{\sim}{x} = \exp -\tfrac{1}{2}\left[y'_a K_{11}^a y_a + 2 \underset{\sim}{y}'_a \underset{\sim}{k}_a (p^* - \mu_3^a) + \frac{(p^* - \mu_3^a)^2}{d_a} \right] .$$

Completing the square in $(p^* - \mu_3^a)$ on the R.H.S. we obtain:

$$\exp -\tfrac{1}{2}\, \underset{\sim}{x}' \Omega_a^{-1} \underset{\sim}{x} = \exp -\tfrac{1}{2}\left[\underset{\sim}{y}'_a K_{11}^a \underset{\sim}{y}_a - d_a (\underset{\sim}{y}'_a \underset{\sim}{k}_a)^2 \right] .$$

$$\exp \frac{-1}{2d_a} (p^* - \mu_3^a + d_a \underset{\sim}{y}'_a \underset{\sim}{k}_a)^2 ,$$

(28) $$= \exp -\tfrac{1}{2}\, (\underset{\sim}{y}'_a \Omega_{11}^{a^{-1}} \underset{\sim}{y}_a) . \exp \frac{-1}{2d_a} (p^* - \mu_3^a - \underset{\sim}{y}'_a \Omega_{11}^{a^{-1}} \underset{\sim}{\phi}_a)^2 .$$

Write $\underset{\sim}{\beta}_a = \Omega_{11}^{a^{-1}} \underset{\sim}{\phi}_a$. This vector will be recognised as the vector of <u>formal</u> theoretical least-squares regression coefficients in the regression of p* on p and Q. The term d_a as defined by (27) is <u>formally</u> the residual variance in this theoretical regression. Combining (27) and (28), the second term on the R.H.S. of (18) can be written

(29) $$(2\Pi)^{-\frac{3}{2}} |\Omega_a|^{-\frac{1}{2}} \int_{-\infty}^{P} \exp(-\tfrac{1}{2}\, \underset{\sim}{y}'_a \Omega_{11}^{a^{-1}} \underset{\sim}{y}_a) . \exp \frac{-1}{2d_a} (p^* - \mu_3^a - \underset{\sim}{y}'_a \underset{\sim}{\beta}_a)^2 \, dp^* .$$

Write $N(.;\mu,\sigma^2)$ as the (cumulative) normal distribution function for mean μ, variance σ^2. Now[3]

(30) $$|\Omega_a| = |\Omega_{11}^a| . d_a .$$

Performing the integration in (29), we can by using (30) write the second term on the R.H.S. of (18) as

$$(2\Pi)^{-1}|\Omega_{11}^a|^{-\frac{1}{2}} \exp\left(-\tfrac{1}{2}\, \underset{\sim}{y}_a' \Omega_{11}^{a^{-1}} \underset{\sim}{y}_a\right) N\,(p; \mu_3^a + \underset{\sim}{y}_a' \underset{\sim}{\beta}_a, d_a) .$$

Doing the same[4] for regime (b) in respect of the first term of (18) and changing to N(.;0,1) in each case we have:

(31) $$\text{prob}(p,Q) = (2\Pi)^{-1}|\Omega_{11}^a|^{-\frac{1}{2}} \exp\left(-\tfrac{1}{2}\, \underset{\sim}{y}_a' \Omega_{11}^{a^{-1}} \underset{\sim}{y}_a\right) N\left[\frac{p - \mu_3^a - \underset{\sim}{y}_a' \underset{\sim}{\beta}_a}{d_a^{\frac{1}{2}}}; 0,1\right]$$

$$+ (2\Pi)^{-1}|\Omega_{11}^b|^{-\frac{1}{2}} \exp\left(-\tfrac{1}{2}\, \underset{\sim}{y}_b' \Omega_{11}^{b^{-1}} \underset{\sim}{y}_b\right) N\left[-\left(\frac{p - \mu_3^b - \underset{\sim}{y}_b' \underset{\sim}{\beta}_b}{d_b^{\frac{1}{2}}}\right); 0,1\right] .$$

$$= n(\underset{\sim}{y}_a; \underset{\sim}{0}, \Omega_{11}^a)\, N\left[\frac{p - \mu_3^a - \underset{\sim}{y}_a' \underset{\sim}{\beta}_a}{d_a^{\frac{1}{2}}}; 0,1\right]$$

$$+ n(\underset{\sim}{y}_b; \underset{\sim}{0}, \Omega_{11}^b)\, N\left[-\left(\frac{p - \mu_3^b - \underset{\sim}{y}_b' \underset{\sim}{\beta}_b}{d_b^{\frac{1}{2}}}\right); 0,1\right] ,$$

where it will be recalled that $\underset{\sim}{y}_a' = [p - \mu_1^a, Q - \mu_2^a]$. Here n denotes the joint Normal density with mean and covariance matrix as indicated.

The probability density for p,Q consists in a weighted sum of the formal probability densities of the reduced forms in each period. The weights involved are cast in terms of what can (formally) be viewed as the conditional distribution functions of the imputed equilibrium variable in each period. We might then set up the likelihood function as

(32) $$L = \prod_{t=1}^{T} \text{prob}(p_t, Q_t) .$$

Let us now examine the regularity of the proposed maximum-likelihood estimator. The representative likelihood element (31) has a strong resemblance to that for the mixed distribution estimator discussed in chapter 2.3, with the two N terms playing the role of weights. The question therefore arises as to whether, by appropriate choice of Ω_{11}^{a}, it is possible to render the likelihood function (32) unbounded. In fact this undesirable state of affairs turns out all too simple to arrange. Given a sample $(p_1,Q_1),\ldots(p_T,Q_T)$ we need only choose values for Π_a such that $\underset{\sim}{y}_a = 0$. Now let the elements of Ω_a tend to zero in such a way that $|\Omega_{11}^{a}| \to 0$ but the conditional variance d_a remains a finite constant. Then $\text{prob}(p_1,Q_1) = 0(|\Omega_{11}^{a}|^{-\frac{1}{2}}) \to \infty$ but $\text{prob}(p_2,Q_2)\ldots\text{prob}(p_T,Q_T)$ remain bounded as $\Omega_a \to 0$, in a manner identical to the mixed distribution case discussed in §2.3. In short, the M.L. of the general model is not consistent. It may be possible to overcome this problem if something is known *a priori* about the relationship between Ω_a and Ω_b. Since we cannot expect this as a general rule, it is evident that the method of maximum-likelihood breaks down. On the other hand the development of the present subsection will be useful in considering later problems of estimating the equilibrium values.

Note finally that we have so far simply assumed the identifiability of the model. As pointed out in the context of mixed distributions (chapter 2.3) the unboundedness of the likelihood function does not necessarily mean that the model is not identified. From equation (31) it is evident that the probability structure of the model may be cast entirely in terms of the reduced-form parameters Π_a,Ω_a and Π_b,Ω_b. From this it will certainly follow that a necessary condition for the identification of the structural parameters $B_{a,b}$, $T_{a,b}$ and $\Sigma_{a,b}$ is that they are uniquely deducible from the corresponding reduced-form parameters. For this to be so, the classical rank and order conditions must hold in respect of each regime for equations (16)(a) and (b). On the other hand, it is not entirely clear under what conditions the reduced-form parameters are themselves identified, so that the rank and order conditions referred to may not be sufficient. In short, a systematic study of the identification of the short-side model remains to be accomplished.

5.4.2 Error-free Clearing. Using equation (20) of section 5.3.2 we may write the formal structural form for regime (a) as:

$$(33)(a) \qquad Q_t = \underset{\sim}{X}'_{1t}\underset{\sim}{\beta}_1 + \alpha_1 p_t + u_{1t}$$

$$Q_t = \underset{\sim}{X}'_{2t}\underset{\sim}{\beta}_1 + \left(\frac{\alpha_2 - \alpha_1\mu}{1-\mu}\right) p_t - \frac{(\alpha_2 - \alpha_1)\mu}{1-\mu} p_{t-1} + u_{2t} \, .$$

We may now define the densities g^a and g^b referred to in section 5.3.2 (equation (22)) in terms of the reduced forms $\Pi_{a,b}$, $\Omega_{a,b}$ corresponding to the structural forms (33)(a) and (b). Define now

$$\underset{\sim}{y}_{at} = \begin{bmatrix} p - \mu_1^a \\ Q - \mu_2^a \end{bmatrix}, \qquad \underset{\sim}{\mu}^a = \Pi_a \begin{bmatrix} p_{t-1} \\ \underset{\sim}{X}_{1t} \\ \underset{\sim}{X}_{2t} \end{bmatrix}.$$

With sample separation now available, the likelihood function is:

$$(34) \qquad \log L = \text{const.} - \frac{T_a}{2}\log|\Omega_a| - \tfrac{1}{2}\sum_{t\in\psi_a} \underset{\sim}{y}'_{at}\Omega_a^{-1}\underset{\sim}{y}_{at}$$

$$- \frac{T_b}{2}\log|\Omega_b| - \tfrac{1}{2}\sum_{t\in\psi_b} \underset{\sim}{y}'_{bt}\Omega_b^{-1}\underset{\sim}{y}_{bt} \, .$$

Here $T_a = \dim(\psi_a)$, $T_b = \dim(\psi_b)$, i.e. the numbers of observations in regimes (a) and (b) respectively. The form of equation (34) suggests that this is a regular estimation situation of the kind discussed in chapter 2.

A special case of the EFC which has found application is:

$$D_t = X'_{1t}\beta_1 + u_{1t}$$

$$D_t = X'_{2t}\beta_2 + u_{2t}$$

$$Q_t = \min(D_t, S_t)$$

$$p_t - p_{t-1} = \gamma(D_t - S_t) \ .$$

The predetermined vectors X_{1t} and X_{2t} may include p_{t-1} but not p_t . Note the recursive nature of the relationship between D, S and p . Provided that u_{1t} and u_{2t} are independent (see below), the relationship between p and Q is also recursive, in the sense that Q_t is defined independently of p_t .

Since contemporaneous price is not included in either the demand or supply schedules, the definition of p^*_t as an imputed equilibrium price is no longer possible. The PAMEQ specification is therefore not available. Instead we proceed from first principles to write the model in terms of the two regimes as follows:

Regime (a) (excess supply)

$$Q_t = X'_{1t}\beta_1 + u_{1t}$$

$$p_t = p_{t-1} + \gamma(Q_t - X'_{2t}\beta_2) - \gamma u_{2t}$$

Regime (b) (excess demand)

$$Q_t = X'_{2t}\beta_2 + u_{2t}$$

$$p_t = p_{t-1} + \gamma(X'_{1t}\beta_1 - Q_t) + \gamma u_{1t} \ .$$

We can use this decomposition to derive the likelihood function. For the sake of simplicity we assume that the disturbances

u_{1t} and u_{2t} are independent. If this is so, the model is recursive in each regime. The likelihood function may therefore be written down directly as:

$$\log L = \text{const.} - T\log\sigma_1 - T\log\sigma_2 - T\log\gamma - \frac{1}{2\sigma_1^2}\sum_{t\in\psi_a}(Q_t - \underset{\sim}{X}'_{1t}\underset{\sim}{\beta}_1)^2$$

$$- \frac{1}{2\gamma^2\sigma_2^2}\sum_{t\in\psi_a}[p_t - p_{t-1} - \gamma(Q_t - \underset{\sim}{X}'_{2t}\underset{\sim}{\beta}_2)]^2 - \frac{1}{2\sigma_2^2}\sum_{t\in\psi_b}(Q_t - \underset{\sim}{X}'_{2t}\underset{\sim}{\beta}_2)^2$$

$$- \frac{1}{2\gamma^2\sigma_1^2}\sum_{t\in\psi_b}[p_t - p_{t-1} - \gamma(\underset{\sim}{X}'_{1t}\underset{\sim}{\beta}_1 - Q_t)]^2 .$$

The Normal equations may now be obtained by differentiating log L with respect to the unknown parameters and equating the results to zero. The Normal equation for γ may be written

$$T\gamma^2 - \frac{1}{\sigma_2^2}\sum_{t\in\psi_a}[p_t - p_{t-1} - \gamma(Q_t - X'_{2t}\beta_2)](p_t - p_{t-1})$$

$$- \frac{1}{\sigma_1^2}\sum_{t\in\Psi_b}[p_t - p_{t-1} + \gamma(Q_t - X'_{1t}\beta_1)](p_t - p_{t-1}) = 0 .$$

The Normal equations for the remaining parameters $\underset{\sim}{\beta}_1$, $\underset{\sim}{\beta}_2$, σ_1^2 and σ_2^2 have a particularly interesting form. Observe that we may, as in section 5.2, combine the two regimes into a simultaneous equation system for quantities:

$$Q_t = X'_{1t}\beta_1 - \frac{1}{\gamma}(p_t - p_{t-1})R(p_t - p_{t-1}) + u_{1t}$$

$$Q_t = X'_{2t}\beta_2 + \frac{1}{\gamma}(p_t - p_{t-1})(1 - R(p_t - p_{t-1})) + u_{2t} .$$

It turns out (see T. Amemiya [1974]) that the M.L. Normal equations for $\underset{\sim}{\beta}_1$, $\underset{\sim}{\beta}_2$, σ_1^2 and σ_2^2 are just those obtained from the O.L.S. fit of the above two equations on the assumption that γ^2 is known. Amemiya therefore suggested an iterative scheme based on the value of γ.

For a given value of γ, one obtains estimates of $\underset{\sim}{\beta}_1$, $\underset{\sim}{\beta}_2$, σ_1^2 and σ_2^2 by using ordinary least squares in the manner suggested. The resulting values are substituted into the M.L. Normal equation for γ and the process iterated with the new value for γ. J.J. Laffont and R. Garcia [1977] showed that the (quadratic) Normal equation for γ has a unique positive root and that Amemiya's algorithm is uphill in the sense discussed in chapter 2.4.

The special "recursive" case where the demand and supply functions do not contain p_t has therefore very convenient computational features, whatever the shortcomings of this model as a matter of specification. From the form of the likelihood function (34), it seems a reasonable conjecture that the more general model shares these concavity properties. However no formal proof either of the regularity or global concavity of the general likelihood function (34) has yet been published.

5.5 The Suits Model: A Digression

A model which turns out to have the same probability structure as the noisy clearing model was originated by D. Suits [1955], who used it to analyse the dynamics of the U.S. watermelon market. The model incorporates the decision as to how much of a crop to harvest. If the going price is too low, the quantity actually harvested may be less than the available crop. On the other hand, if the price is high enough, the quantity sold may be restricted by the predetermined size of the harvest. The quantity actually sold is the minimum of the crop and the harvest.

Specifically, there are four equations:

(35)

(a) $q_t = b_1 z_{1t} + b_2 + u_{1t}$ (crop)

(b) $x_t = b_3 p_t + b_4 q_t + b_5 z_{2t} + b_6 + u_{2t}$ (harvest)

(c) $p_t = b_7 z_{3t} + b_8 Q_t + b_9 + u_{3t}$ (demand)

(d) $Q_t = \min(q_t, x_t)$ (quantity sold).

Here the z_{it} are exogenous variables, condensed in number from the original Suits model. According to (a) and (b) it may not be worthwhile harvesting the entire crop if the going price is too low. The two regimes correspond to whether $Q_t = q_t$ or $Q_t = x_t$, i.e. according to whether $q_t \lesseqgtr x_t$. In either case Q_t denotes the observed quantity and we suppose the minimum of information so that neither q_t nor x_t as such are actually observed.

Let $\tilde{p}_t$ be such that $q_t = x_t$, i.e.

$$q_t = b_3 \tilde{p}_t + b_4 q_t + b_5 z_{2t} + b_6 + u_{2t} .$$

Thus

$$(36) \qquad \tilde{p}_t = \frac{(1-b_4)b_5 - b_6}{b_3} + \frac{b_1(1-b_4)}{b_3} z_{1t} - \frac{b_5}{b_3} z_{1t} + \frac{1-b_4}{b_3} u_{1t} - \frac{1}{b_3} u_{2t} .$$

Observe that

$$x_t = q_t + b_3(p_t - \tilde{p}_t) \; .$$

Since it is reasonable to specify *a priori* that $b_3 > 0$, it follows that $p_t \gtrless \tilde{p}_t$ according as $x_t \gtrless q_t$. In other words, just as in the disequilibrium model, the sign of $p_t - \tilde{p}_t$ can be taken to discriminate between the two regimes involved:

Regime (a): $p_t > \tilde{p}_t$

(a) $Q_t = b_1 z_{1t} + b_2 + u_{1t}$

(37)(a) (b) $p_t = b_7 z_{3t} + b_8 Q_t + b_9 + u_{3t}$

(c) $$\tilde{p}_t = \frac{(1-b_4)b_2 - b_6}{b_3} + \frac{b_1(1-b_4)}{b_3} z_{1t} - \frac{b_5}{b_3} z_{2t} + \frac{1-b_4}{b_3} u_{1t} - \frac{1}{b_3} u_{2t} \; .$$

Regime (b): $p_t < \tilde{p}_t$

(a) $Q_t = b_1 z_{1t} + b_2 + b_3(p_t - \tilde{p}_t) + u_{1t}$

(37)(b) (b) $p_t = b_7 z_{3t} + b_8 Q_t + b_9 + u_{3t}$

(c) $$\tilde{p}_t = \frac{(1-b_4)b_2 - b_6}{b_3} + \frac{b_1(1-b_4)}{b_3} z_{1t} - \frac{b_5}{b_3} z_{2t} + \frac{1-b_4}{b_3} u_{1t} - \frac{1}{b_3} u_{2t} \; .$$

As with the disequilibrium model, we can formally define reduced forms in each regime for the endogenous variables p_t, Q_t and $\tilde{p}_t$, with parameter matrices Π_a, Ω_a and Π_b, Ω_b. In terms of these reduced form matrices, the likelihood function for $(p_t, Q_t)_{t=1...T}$ is identical with equations (31) and (32) for the disequilibrium noisy-clearing model.

It is interesting to observe that the device of an imputed price or clearing variable, central to the PAMEQ specification, is applicable to other contexts. However it should not be inferred from this that the Suits model is itself a disequilibrium model. To see that this is not the case, we start by recalling the definition of the ramp function $R(x) = \begin{cases} 1 & \text{if } x \geq 0 \\ 0 & \text{otherwise} \end{cases}$. Then equations (37)(a) and (b) can be combined into:

$$\text{(38)} \quad \begin{aligned} &\text{(a)} \quad Q_t = b_1 z_{1t} + b_2 + b_3(1 - R(p_t - \tilde{p}_t))(p_t - \tilde{p}_t) + u_{1t} \\ &\text{(b)} \quad p_t = b_7 z_{3t} + b_8 Q_t + b_9 + u_{3t} \\ &\text{(c)} \quad \tilde{p}_t = \frac{(1-b_4)b_2 - b_6}{b_3} + \frac{b_1(1-b_4)}{b_3} z_{1t} - \frac{b_5}{b_3} z_{2t} + \frac{1-b_4}{b_3} u_{1t} - \frac{1}{b_3} u_{3t} . \end{aligned}$$

Substitute for $\tilde{p}_t$ from (c) into (a). What results is a supply function $Q_t = Q(z_{1t}, z_{2t}, p_t, u_{1t}, u_{2t})$. This is highly nonlinear but is nevertheless a stochastic supply function which forms, together with the demand function (b), a standard equilibrium simultaneous system. This, therefore, is an example of an equilibrium structure which does not possess a regular likelihood function, a fact pointed out by S.M. Goldfeld and R.E. Quandt [1975]. As with the disequilibrium system, further information is required for regularity. For instance, we may have available values of the actual harvest x_t or the crop q_t for all periods, rather than merely those in which they happen to coincide with the transacted quantity Q_t. The value of such information is fully discussed by Goldfeld and Quandt [1975].

5.6 Least-Squares Methods

In this section we shall consider the application to the short-side problem of methods based on two-stage least squares or instrumental variables.

5.6.1 EFC model. In the absence of a disturbance to the price adjustment equation we may combine equation (20), the definition of p_t^* in equation (11), and equations (16)(a) and (b) to obtain a single system:

$$(39) \qquad p_t = \mu p_{t-1} + \frac{1-\mu}{\alpha_1 - \alpha_2}(\underset{\sim}{X}'_{2t}\underset{\sim}{\beta}_2 - \underset{\sim}{X}'_{1t}\underset{\sim}{\beta}_1) + \frac{1-\mu}{\alpha_1 - \alpha_2}(u_{2t} - u_{1t})$$

$$(40)(a) \quad Q_t = \underset{\sim}{X}'_{1t}\underset{\sim}{\beta}_1 + \alpha_1 p_t - \frac{\mu(\alpha_2 - \alpha_1)}{1-\mu}(p_t - p_{t-1})(1 - R(p_{t-1} - p_t)) + u_{1t}$$

$$(40)(b) \quad Q_t = \underset{\sim}{X}'_{2t}\underset{\sim}{\beta}_2 + \alpha_2 p_t + \frac{\mu(\alpha_2 - \alpha_1)}{1-\mu}(p_t - p_{t-1})R(p_{t-1} - p_t) + u_{2t} .$$

Note first that the estimation of equation (39) involves no consistency problems. Application of OLS will yield estimates of μ and of the compound parameters $\left(\frac{1-\mu}{\alpha_1 - \alpha_2}\beta_2\right)$ and $\left(\frac{1-\mu}{\alpha_1 - \alpha_2}\beta_1\right)$. We turn now to the problem of estimating equations (40)(a) and (b). One might think immediately of the following procedure: First regress p_t upon the predetermined variables p_{t-1}, X_{2t} and X_{1t} as in (39). The predicted value $\hat{p}_t$ is then employed in equations (40), in the second-stage. For the nonlinear term $(p_t - p_{t-1})R(p_{t-1} - p_t)$ we substitute $(\hat{p}_t - p_{t-1})R(p_{t-1} - \hat{p}_t)$. For reasons discussed at length in chapter 2.5, this method will not in general yield consistent estimates. Nevertheless it deserves attention on grounds of simplicity. We shall refer to it as "naive 2SLS".

A consistent procedure is to regress the compound variable $g_t = (p_t - p_{t-1})R(p_{t-1} - p_t)$ upon the exogenous variables of the system and to use the fitted values $\hat{g}_t$ in the second stage. Possibly a more precise version of this technique is to regress g_t upon a polynomial in the predetermined variables (see chapter 2.5). The difficulty with these methods lies in the pronounced non-linearity of the function g_t. Unless the polynomial involved is of a high order - which carries its own problems - the result may not yield a very close substitute for g_t in stage two.

Fortunately, the problem allows an application of the conditional expectation technique discussed at length in chapter 2.6. According to this technique, we must be able to write $E g_t = h_t(\theta)$. A consistent estimate of θ, $\hat{\theta}_T$ say, must be available. Then $h_t(\hat{\theta}_T)$ is either used as an instrument in the second stage or else it is simply substituted for g_t in an ordinary least squares calculation (the "strict 2SLS" calculation).

Let us therefore derive an expression for $h_t(\theta)$, the expected value of $g_t = (p_t - p_{t-1})R(p_{t-1} - p_t)$, conditional upon the predetermined variables p_{t-1}, X_{1t} and X_{2t}. Write $m_t = E(p_t - p_{t-1})$, where E refers to the conditional expectation in question. It follows from equation (39) that:

$$m_t = (\mu-1)p_{t-1} + \frac{1-\mu}{\alpha_1 - \alpha_2}(\underset{\sim}{X}'_{2t}\underset{\sim}{\beta}_2 - \underset{\sim}{X}'_{1t}\underset{\sim}{\beta}_1)$$

(41) and

$$\sigma^2 = \mathrm{Var}(p_t - p_{t-1}) = \mathrm{Var}\left(\frac{1-\mu}{\alpha_1 - \alpha_2}\right)(u_{2t} - u_{1t}) .$$

Let n denote the density and N the distribution function (cumulative density) of the Normal distribution. The distribution of $p_t - p_{t-1}$ conditional upon p_{t-1}, X_{1t}, X_{2t} is therefore $N(.;m_t,\sigma^2)$. From the definition of the ramp function R,

$$h_t(\theta) = \int_{-\infty}^{0} xn(x;m_t,\sigma^2)dx .$$

Now[5] $\int_{-\infty}^{0} (x-m)n(x;m,\sigma^2)dx = \frac{-\sigma}{\sqrt{2\pi}} e^{-\frac{1}{2}m_t^2/\sigma^2}$.

It follows that

$$h_t(\theta) = m_t N(o;m_t,\sigma^2) - \frac{\sigma}{\sqrt{2\pi}} e^{-\frac{1}{2}m_t^2/\sigma^2} .$$

Moreover, it is easy to show that

$$N(o;m_t,\sigma^2) = 1 - N(m_t;o,\sigma^2) .$$

Thus

$$h_t(\theta) = m_t(1 - N(m_t;o,\sigma^2) - \frac{\sigma}{\sqrt{2\pi}} e^{-\frac{1}{2}m_t^2/\sigma^2} . \tag{42}$$

The parameters θ are the compound parameters referred to in equation (41), namely $\mu-1$, $\frac{1-\mu}{\alpha_1-\alpha_2}\beta_2$, $\frac{1-\mu}{\alpha_1-\alpha_2}\beta_1$, and $\mathrm{Var}\left(\frac{1-\mu}{\alpha_1-\alpha_2}(u_{2t}-u_{1t})\right)$. Application of OLS to equation (39) will yield estimates of these compound parameters which are consistent, indeed converge almost everywhere to the true values. From the practical point of view, we calculate $\hat{m}_t$ as $\hat{p}_t - p_{t-1}$, where $\hat{p}_t$ is the fitted value from the OLS regression of p_t on p_{t-1}, X_{2t}, X_{1t}, as in equation (39). The term $\hat{\sigma}^2$ is the estimated standard error from this regression. We can therefore write:

$$h_t(\hat{\theta}_T) = \hat{m}_t(1 - N(\hat{m}_t;o,\hat{\sigma}^2)) - \frac{\hat{\sigma}}{\sqrt{2\pi}} e^{-\frac{1}{2}\hat{m}_t^2/\hat{\sigma}^2} . \tag{43}$$

With reference to the second-stage calculation for the estimation of the supply equation (40)(b), two options are open: (i) instrumental variables, with $h_t(\hat{\theta}_T)$ as an instrument for g_t, and $\hat{p}_t$ for p_t or (ii) OLS with $\hat{p}_t$ substituted for p_t and $h_t(\hat{\theta}_T)$ for g_t (strict 2SLS). Both procedures are easy to compute, the second especially so. The only extra burden in this respect is that the Normal distribution function must be calculated for every value of $\hat{m}_t$. This is easily done with standard programs.[6] Finally, in the case of equation (40)(a), the required instrument, or second-stage variable, is the estimate of $E(p_t - p_{t-1})(1 - R(p_{t-1} - p_t))$, namely $\hat{m}_t N(\hat{m}_t;o,\hat{\sigma}^2) + \frac{\hat{\sigma}}{\sqrt{2\pi}} e^{-\frac{1}{2}\hat{m}_t^2/\hat{\sigma}^2}$.

5.6.2 Administered Pricing. Some remarks on specific points are now in order:

1. Although we have implicitly assumed so far that the vectors $\underset{\sim}{X}_{1t}$ and $\underset{\sim}{X}_{2t}$ appearing in the demand and supply equations have no common elements, this assumption is easily relaxed. It will be apparent from the development leading up to equation (43) that all we require in stage one is an estimate of $\hat{p}_t$ based on equation (39). In this equation, we simply regress p_t upon p_{t-1} and the distinct parts of $\underset{\sim}{X}_{1t}$ and $\underset{\sim}{X}_{2t}$. The appearance of the lagged p_{t-1} in either $\underset{\sim}{X}_{1t}$ or $\underset{\sim}{X}_{2t}$ is a little more awkward to handle. The determination of $\hat{p}_t$ in stage one is unchanged, but μ cannot now be determined from this regression. Given α_1 and α_2 from stage two as applied to (40)(a) and (b), $\hat{\mu}$ can be derived from the coefficient of the nonlinear terms in these equations. To avoid overidentification problems, these coefficients must be constrained to sum to zero across (12)(a) and (b).

2. The 2SLS method described for the competitive price adjustment model can in certain circumstances be adapted to handle the administered pricing equation. Following the discussion of chapter 3.4.2, we shall specify this - in contrast to the competitive equation (10)(d) - as

(10)(d") $p_t = \mu p_{t-1} + (1-\mu)p_t^* + \mu\underset{\sim}{\delta}'\underset{\sim}{Z}_t$.

Here $\underset{\sim}{Z}_t$ is a vector of exogenous variables. We shall assume that this does not contain the lagged price term p_{t-1} (see below). Observe first that from (10)(d"),

$$(44) \qquad p_t - p_t^* = \frac{-\mu}{1-\mu}(p_t - p_{t-1} - \underset{\sim}{\delta}'\underset{\sim}{Z}_t) .$$

Returning to equations (15)(a) and (b), we have

$$(45) \qquad (p_t - p_t^*)R(p_t - p_t^*) = \frac{-\mu}{1-\mu}(p_t - p_{t-1} - \delta'Z_t)R(p_{t-1} - p_t + \underset{\sim}{\delta}'\underset{\sim}{Z}_t) .$$

The stage one regression corresponding to (39) is

$$(46) \qquad p_t = \mu p_{t-1} + \frac{1-\mu}{\alpha_1 - \alpha_2}(\underset{\sim}{X}'_{2t}\underset{\sim}{\beta}_2 - \underset{\sim}{X}'_{1t}\underset{\sim}{\beta}_1) + \mu\delta' Z_t + \frac{1-\mu}{\alpha_1 - \alpha_2}(u_{2t} - u_{1t}) .$$

As usual denote by $\hat{p}_t$ the fitted value from this regression, and by $\hat{\sigma}^2$ the estimate of its residual variance. Redefine:

$$(47) \qquad m_t = E(p_t - p_{t-1} - \underset{\sim}{\delta}'\underset{\sim}{Z}_t), \text{ given } p_{t-1} .$$

Considering now the expectation of the nonlinear term (45), it can be seen that apart from a constant, this is precisely the same as that defined by equation (42) for the competitive case, with the redefinition (47) of m_t. The empirical implementation is similar. Write $\hat{m}_t = \hat{p}_t - p_{t-1} - \hat{\underset{\sim}{\delta}}'\underset{\sim}{Z}_t$ where $\hat{\delta}$ is estimated from the regression based on (46). The estimated variance $\hat{\sigma}^2$ of $(p_t - p_{t-1} - \underset{\sim}{\delta}'\underset{\sim}{Z}_t)$ is again obtained as the estimated disturbance variance in (46). In the case of the supply function, we may therefore write the second stage regression as

$$(48)(b) \qquad Q_t = \underset{\sim}{X}'_{2t}\underset{\sim}{\beta}_2 + \alpha_2\hat{p}_t + \frac{\mu(\alpha_2 - \alpha_1)}{1-\mu}\left[\hat{m}_t(1 - N(\hat{m}_t;0,\hat{\sigma}^2)) - \frac{\hat{\sigma}}{\sqrt{2\pi}} e^{-\frac{1}{2}\hat{m}_t^2/\hat{\sigma}^2}\right] + v_t ,$$

where v_t is a disturbance. This has exactly the same form as the second stage of the 2SLS technique for the competitive model. The only difference is the redefinition of m_t to incorporate the exogenous variables $\underset{\sim}{Z}_t$. Similarly for the demand function. In the case of the administered pricing model, however, the instrumental variables estimation is not available, for we do not have prior knowledge of the value of δ in equation (45). In terms of remark 1 above, observe also that if $\underset{\sim}{X}_{1t}$ or $\underset{\sim}{X}_{2t}$ contain p_{t-1} we may not be able to estimate μ and hence δ from the stage one regression. Formation of $\hat{m}_t$ would then not be possible, so that the technique breaks down in such a contingency. In these respects, therefore, the competitive pricing model is more amenable to estimation than is the administered model.

5.6.3 Simulation. To compare some of the alternative methods of estimation suggested for the EFC model, we carried out a modest simulation exercise. The methods to be compared are:

(a) The strict 2SLS technique.

(b) Instrumental variables, with $h_t(\hat{\theta}_T)$ used as an instrument for g_t, and $\hat{p}_t$ for p_t.

(c) The technique described above as "naive 2SLS". Specifically, we obtain $\hat{p}_t$ from the stage one regression as for (a) or (b). In stage two we substitute $\hat{p}_t$ for p_t and $(\hat{p}_t - p_{t-1})R(p_{t-1} - \hat{p}_t)$ for $(p_t - p_{t-1})R(p_{t-1} - p_t)$.

(d) In the stage two regression, replace p_t by $\hat{p}_t$ but maintain the natural $(p_t - p_{t-1})R(p_{t-1} - p_t)$ unchanged. We shall refer to this as the "OLS" or "natural separation" technique, although the OLS aspect strictly refers only to the handling of the nonlinear terms.

It will be observed that the "naive" technique (c) corresponds to the 2SLS (a) with σ^2 set arbitrarily at zero. The rationale for including technique (d) in our discussion is as follows. Some techniques for such switching phenomena divide the sample into regimes of excess demand or excess supply, and estimate separate regression equations for each. In the present context this would amount to incorporating in equation (40)(a) or (b) the natural variable $(p_t - p_{t-1})R(p_{t-1} - p_t)$. Such a procedure will not yield consistent estimates, even if $\hat{p}_t$ is employed for the term in p_t, for the simple reason that the switch is itself endogenously determined. It will be useful to investigate the performance of such a natural switch as a fourth alternative in our simulation exercise.

We generated observations for the following model:[7]

$$D_t = \underset{(\beta_{10})}{20.52} + \underset{(\beta_{11})}{1.90X_{1t}} - \underset{(\alpha_1)}{1.42p_t} + \underset{(Var = 0.317)}{u_{1t}}$$

$$S_t = \underset{(\beta_{20})}{14.60} - \underset{(\beta_{21})}{0.42X_{2t}} + \underset{(\alpha_2)}{0.62p_t} + \underset{(Var = 0.937)}{u_{2t}}$$

$$p_t = \underset{(\mu)}{0.7p_{t-1}} + \underset{(1-\mu)}{0.3p_t^*} .$$

Market clearing was thus assumed to be rather slow. Observations on the exogenous variables X_1 and X_2 were generated as independent normal variates with means 4.956 and 8.840, variances 0.3973 and 1.207 respectively. The required initial value for p_o was set at 9.23. The disturbance terms u_{1t}, u_{2t} and u_{3t} were generated as mutually independent. Note that with each replication we generated the exogenous variables afresh, so that the specification involved was that of stochastic exogenous variables.

We generated 50 observations and estimated equation (39) using OLS as step one of the estimation. This yielded the estimates for μ. Since the derivation of μ is thus straightforward and no problems were experienced, we do not present the results for this parameter. This initial regression also yielded $\hat{p}_t$ to replace p_t in the second-stage regression, and $\hat{m}_t$ and $\hat{\sigma}^2$ for the consistent techniques. In the second-stage regression we employed the four alternatives outlined above. The whole experiment was replicated 50 times. Thus each sample consisted of 50 observations and there were 50 samples. We computed the mean and mean-square-error for the important parameters β_{i1} and α_i, i=1,2. The results are given in Table 5.1.

Table 5.1: Simulation Results

Demand (equation (40)(a))

Technique:		2SLS	Instrumental Variables	Naive	Natural Separation
Parameter					
β_{11} (1.90)	Mean	1.968	1.934	1.793	1.878
	M.S.E.	0.148	0.095	0.093	0.040
α_1 (-1.42)	Mean	-1.498	-1.477	-1.333	-1.421
	M.S.E.	0.270	0.212	0.213	0.170

Supply (equation (40)(b))

Technique:		2SLS	Instrumental Variables	Naive	Natural Separation
Parameter					
β_{21} (-0.42)	Mean	-0.418	-0.422	-0.408	-0.340
	M.S.E.	0.015	0.015	0.014	0.016
α_2 (0.62)	Mean	0.712	0.713	0.727	0.824
	M.S.E.	0.242	0.224	0.237	0.297

A clue to the similarity of the first three techniques lies in the low value for σ^2 (see equation (41)) namely 0.028. We have already observed that if $\sigma^2 = 0$, the naive technique and the 2SLS technique are the same. As a second experiment, we doubled the standard deviations of the terms u_{1t} and u_{2t}, increasing the implied value of σ^2 by a factor of four to 0.108. With this change, we repeated the simulation runs as described above, for the demand function. The results are given in Table 5.2.

Table 5.2: Inflated Disturbance Variances (Expt. 2)

Demand (equation (12)(a)

Technique:		2SLS	Instrumental Variables	Naive	Natural Separation
Parameter					
β_{11} (1.90)	Mean	2.082	1.707	1.688	1.882
	M.S.E.	0.812	1.522	0.326	0.097
α_1 (-1.42)	Mean	-1.656	-1.071	-1.224	-1.477
	M.S.E.	1.131	3.590	0.557	0.389

The relative performance of the various estimators varies between the demand and supply estimation. Thus the natural separation performs very well for the demand equation and very poorly for the supply equation. Instrumental variables has good bias properties for a low σ^2, but does not perform so well when the underlying variance of the system is increased. With regard to M.S.E. as a summary measure Table 5.3 ranks the various estimators over the two experiments.

Table 5.3: M.S.E. Rankings

Demand				Supply	
Expt. 1		Expt. 2		Expt. 1	
β_{11}	α_1	β_{11}	α_1	β_{21}	α_2
Natural	Natural	Natural	Natural	Naive	I.V.
Naive	I.V.	Naive	Naive	2SLS	Naive
I.V.	Naive	2SLS	2SLS	I.V.	2SLS
2SLS	2SLS	I.V.	I.V.	Natural	Natural

From the point of view of mean square error, the best all-round estimator is perhaps the Naive technique. The fact that such a technique is not consistent does not therefore rule it out of consideration, particularly for the size of sample that one is likely to meet with in practice.

5.6.4 Noisy-clearing Model. Let us turn to consideration of the short-side model with a disturbance incorporated in the price adjustment equation. We shall confine our discussion to the competitive scheme (10)(d). Combining equations (15)(a) and (b) with the definition (11) of p_t^* yields the following simultaneous system:

(49) $$p_t = \mu p_{t-1} + \frac{1-\mu}{\alpha_1 - \alpha_2}(X'_{2t}\beta_2 - X'_{1t}\beta_1) + \frac{1-\mu}{\alpha_1 - \alpha_2}(u_{2t} - u_{1t}) + u_{3t}$$

(50)(a) $$Q_t = X'_{1t}\beta_1 + \alpha_1 p_t + (\alpha_2 - \alpha_1)(p_t - p_t^*)(1 - R(p_t - p_t^*)) + u_{1t}$$

(50)(b) $$Q_t = X'_{2t}\beta_2 + \alpha_2 p_t - (\alpha_2 - \alpha_1)(p_t - p_t^*)R(p_t - p_t^*) + u_{2t}.$$

Note that we can write

(51) $$p_t - p_t^* = \mu p_{t-1} - \frac{\mu}{\alpha_1 - \alpha_2}(X'_{2t}\beta_2 - X'_{1t}\beta_1) - \frac{\mu}{\alpha_1 - \alpha_2}(u_{2t} - u_{1t}) + u_{3t}.$$

Define now a new variable $\delta_t = \frac{\mu - 1}{\mu}(p_t - p_t^*)$. From (51) it follows that

(52) $$\delta_t = (\mu-1)p_t + \frac{1-\mu}{\alpha_1 - \alpha_2}(X'_{2t}\beta_2 - X'_{1t}\beta_1) + \frac{1-\mu}{\alpha_1 - \alpha_2}(u_{2t} - u_{1t}) - \frac{1-\mu}{\mu}u_{3t}.$$

Thus δ_t has conditional mean m_t, as defined by equation (41). Denote by w^2 the conditional variance of δ_t, i.e. $\mathrm{Var}\left(\frac{1-\mu}{\alpha_1 - \alpha_2}(u_{2t} - u_{1t}) - \frac{1-\mu}{\mu}u_{3t}\right)$. The non-linear term $(p_t - p_t^*)R(p_t - p_t^*)$ appearing in (50)(a) and (b) can be written (apart from a multiplicative constant) as $\delta_t R(-\delta_t)$. By a development identical with that for the EFC model, this has expectation:

(53) $$E\,\delta_t\,R(-\delta_t) = m_t(1 - N(m_t;o,w^2)) - \frac{w}{\sqrt{2\pi}}e^{-\frac{1}{2}m_t^2/w^2}.$$

Once again, we substitute for m_t its estimate $m_t = \hat{p}_t - p_{t-1}$ where $\hat{p}_t$ is the fitted value in the regression of p_t on p_{t-1}, X_{2t} and X_{1t}. However it is no longer possible to estimate w^2 on the basis of this preliminary regression. Suppose, for instance that it is known that u_{3t} is independent of u_{1t} and u_{2t}. Writing (from (49)) $\sigma^2 = \mathrm{Var}\left(\frac{1-\mu}{\alpha_1 - \alpha_2}(u_{2t} - u_{1t}) + u_{3t}\right)$, we have $w^2 = \sigma^2 - \sigma_3^2\left(1 - \left(\frac{1-\mu}{\mu}\right)^2\right)$, where $\sigma_3^2 = \mathrm{Var}\, u_{3t}$. Now σ^2 and μ can be estimated from the OLS regression based on (49), but unless σ_3^2 is known an initial estimate for w^2 is not available. The method described in §5.6.1 for the EFC model is therefore not directly applicable to the more general model.

Equations (50)(a) and (b) can, however, be rewritten with the endogenous terms on the R.H.S. replaced by their expectations (conditional upon p_{t-1}, X_{1t} and X_{2t}), as follows:

(54)(a) $$Q_t = X'_{1t}\beta_1 + \alpha_1(m_t + p_{t-1}) + (\alpha_2 - \alpha_1)\left(m_t N(m_t;o,w^2) + \frac{w}{\sqrt{2\pi}} e^{-\frac{1}{2}m_t^2/w^2}\right) + \zeta_{1t}$$

(54)(b) $$Q_t = X'_{2t}\beta_2 + \alpha_2(m_t + p_{t-1}) - (\alpha_2 - \alpha_1)\left(m_t(1 - N(m_t;o,w^2)) - \frac{w}{\sqrt{2\pi}} e^{-\frac{1}{2}m_t^2/w^2}\right) + \zeta_{2t}$$

where: $$\zeta_{1t} = \alpha_1\varepsilon_{1t} - (\alpha_2 - \alpha_1)\varepsilon_{2t} + (\alpha_2 - \alpha_1)\varepsilon_{3t} + u_{1t}$$

$$\zeta_{2t} = \alpha_2\varepsilon_{1t} - (\alpha_2 - \alpha_1)\varepsilon_{2t} + u_{2t}$$

$$\varepsilon_{1t} = p_t - E(p_t)$$

$$\varepsilon_{2t} = (p_t - p_t^*)R(p_t - p_t^*) - E(p_t - p_t^*)R(p_t - p_t^*)$$

$$\varepsilon_{3t} = p_t - p_t^* - E(p_t - p_t^*) .$$

In other words the ε_{it} represent the deviations of the indicated variables from their expectations, conditional upon the predetermined variables. The derived ζ_{it} will have zero expectations, but are not homoscedastic.

Since m_t is a function of the predetermined variables above, equations 54(a) and (b) comprise a nonlinear regression model. Let us investigate the consistency of the resulting estimates. The conditional means m_t depend upon unknown parameters which are nevertheless consistently estimated by OLS applied to the stage one regression based upon equation (49). Denote by $\hat{\theta}_T$ the resulting estimates of the compound parameters referred to, namely $\mu - 1$, $\frac{1-\mu}{\alpha_1 - \alpha_2} \cdot \beta_1$ and $\frac{1-\mu}{\alpha_1 - \alpha_2} \cdot \beta_2$. Let us write one of the equations (50)(a) or (b) in schematic form as:

$$Q_t = q(p_{t-1}, x_t, \theta, \gamma) + \zeta_t ,$$

where γ denotes the structural parameters β_i or α_i and w^2. Write $q_t(\gamma) = q(p_{t-1}, x_t, \theta_o, \gamma)$, where θ_o denotes the true value of θ. The sum of squares to be minimised is $\Sigma[Q_t - q(p_{t-1}, x_t, \hat{\theta}_T, \gamma)]^2$. Note that joint minimisation of (50)(a) and (b) will be required, since the same value of w^2 must serve for both to make sense of the ramp functions involved. For consistency arguments, however, it will suffice to consider the residual sum of squares of just one equation. It may be shown[8] that $\frac{1}{T}$ times the above sum of squares tends almost everywhere to the limit a.e. of the expression

$$\frac{1}{T} \sum_t \zeta_t^2 + \frac{1}{T} \Sigma[q_t(\gamma) - q_t(\gamma_o)]^2 .$$

We need, therefore, to show that the second term is uniquely maximised at $\gamma = \gamma_o$ (R.I. Jennrich [1969]). From inspection of equation (54)(a), we conjecture this to be true, although the point is hard to make with a desirable degree of rigour.

With the aim of throwing some light on the performance of nonlinear least squares, we continued the simulation experiment described in detail in §5.6.3. We added to the price-adjustment equation a disturbance term (u_{3t}) whose variance was set at 0.09. The resulting true value of w^2 was 0.044 (about twice the size of σ^2

used in the EFC experiment). We compared two estimation methods, the "naive" two-stage method as described in §5.6.2 and the non-linear least squares approach. With respect to the latter, our technique was as follows. As usual, our preliminary OLS regression yielded $\hat{m}_t$. A form of weighted least squares was used to combine 54(a) and (b) into a single scheme. Without such a combination one would have no guarantee that the value of w^2 estimated from 54(a) would be the same as that obtained from 54(b). To obtain these weights we set $w^2 = 0$ and estimated equations 54(a) and (b), obtaining the error variances ϕ_1^2 and ϕ_2^2. The inverses of these estimated variances were then used in subsequent calculations as weights to be attached to the computed residuals from each equation. The criterion sum of squares used to estimate 54(a) and (b) is thus: choose α_i, β_i and w^2 to minimise

$$S = \frac{1}{\phi_1^2} \sum_t e_{1t}^2 + \frac{1}{\phi_2^2} \sum_t e_{2t}^2, \tag{55}$$

where the e_{it} are the sample equivalent of the ζ_{it}. The form of weighting adopted may be viewed as a very crude but computationally undemanding form of generalised least squares.

With respect to the crucial parameter w^2 - the cause of the trouble, so to speak - two different search procedures were employed. The first was based on Fibonacci search, while the second employed a simple partitioning of the one-dimensional maximum interval within which w^2 was presumed to lie. For each value of w^2, ordinary least squares (with m_t already available from stage one) was employed to calculate the α_i and β_i on the basis of equations (54)(a) and (b). This procedure should theoretically locate the desired minimum of the criterion sum of squares function (55).

Table 5.4 illustrates the results when Fibonacci search was employed for w^2.

Table 5.4

Noisy-clearing Model: Simulation Results

(Sample size T = 50)

Parameter		Naive Two-Stage	Nonlinear Least Squares
Demand			
β_{11} (1.90)	Mean	0.027	0.060
	M.S.E.	3.579	3.496
α_1 (-1.42)	Mean	0.002	-0.044
	M.S.E.	2.202	2.132
Supply			
β_{21} (-0.42)	Mean	-0.020	-0.018
	M.S.E.	0.165	0.167
α_2 (0.62)	Mean	0.048	0.044
	M.S.E.	0.451	0.453

The results are very poor. A similar performance was obtained when direct partitioning was employed instead of Fibonacci search to locate the minimising value of w^2. In either case, we found that the minimum with respect to this parameter was not well determined, frequently lying at either end of the (fairly wide) preassigned maximum interval. The naive 2SLS method also performed poorly. Both methods showed little improvement when the standard deviation of the disturbance to the price adjustment equation was reduced to half its original value. Our results suggest that bias, rather than variance, is the problem with the non-linear least squares technique. This stems from poor location of the variance parameter w^2. They suggest also that methods which perform well for the error-free clearing model may not work well with the more general mechanism.

5.7 Mixed Least-Squares and Likelihood: The Probit Approach

An interesting method applicable in the present context has been described by Lung-Fei Lee [1977]. This involves a combination of Probit analysis with least-squares and can therefore be viewed as a mixture of likelihood and least-squares techniques. As we might expect from the Probit content, the method requires that a sample separation into distinct regimes is available. It is therefore applicable to the EFC model but not to the more general noisy-clearing case, where such a sample separation is not observed.

We shall present first a brief account of the general two-stage Probit method, referring the reader for specific details to Lee [1977]. The model is as follows:

(56)(a) $$y_{1t} = \underset{\sim}{X}'_{1t}\underset{\sim}{\beta}_1 + \varepsilon_{1t} \quad \text{if and only if } \underset{\sim}{Z}'_t\underset{\sim}{\gamma} \geq \varepsilon_t ,$$

(56)(b) $$y_{2t} = \underset{\sim}{X}'_{2t}\underset{\sim}{\beta}_2 + \varepsilon_{2t} \quad \text{if and only if } \underset{\sim}{Z}'_t\underset{\sim}{\gamma} < \varepsilon_t .$$

Here $\underset{\sim}{X}_{1t}$, $\underset{\sim}{X}_{2t}$ and $\underset{\sim}{Z}_t$ are exogenous. The indicator function $\underset{\sim}{Z}'_t\underset{\sim}{\gamma}$ plays the same role in relation to the N(0,1) disturbance ε_t as in Probit analysis (see chapter 2.2.1). If $\underset{\sim}{Z}'_t\underset{\sim}{\gamma} < \varepsilon_t$, the endogenous variable y_{1t} is simply not observed - another variable y_{2t}, with a different expectation, is observed instead. The disturbance terms ε_{1t} and ε_{2t} have standard properties. Note that we cannot simply apply OLS to estimate (56)(a), since $E[\varepsilon_{1t}/\text{regime (a)}] \neq 0$, violating a basic least-squares assumption.

Denote by R_t the sample-separation indicator:[9]

(57) $$R_t = 1 \quad \text{if and only if } \underset{\sim}{Z}'_t\underset{\sim}{\gamma} \geq \varepsilon_t$$
$$= 0 \quad \text{otherwise.}$$

It will be apparent that the restriction of the model to equation (57) defines a standard probit situation. Thus

$$\text{prob}(R_t = 1) = N(\underset{\sim}{Z}'_t\underset{\sim}{\gamma};\, 0,1) .$$

It follows that $\underset{\sim}{\gamma}$ can be consistently and efficiently estimated by standard Probit procedures. Denote by Σ the covariance matrix of the disturbance ε_{1t}, ε_{2t} and ε_t of (56)(a) and (b):

$$\Sigma = \begin{bmatrix} \sigma_1^2 & \sigma_2^2 & \sigma_{1\varepsilon} \\ \sigma_{12} & \sigma_2^2 & \sigma_{2\varepsilon} \\ \sigma_{\varepsilon 1} & \sigma_{\varepsilon 2} & 1 \end{bmatrix}$$

It can be shown that:

$$(58)(a) \quad E(R_t \varepsilon_{1t}) = -\sigma_{1\varepsilon}\, n(\underset{\sim}{Z}_t' \underset{\sim}{\gamma}; 0,1)$$

$$(b) \quad E[(1 - R_t)\varepsilon_{2t}] = \sigma_{2\varepsilon}\, n(\underset{\sim}{Z}_t' \underset{\sim}{\gamma}; 0,1)$$

$$(c) \quad E(R_t \varepsilon_{1t})^2 = \sigma_1^2\, N(\underset{\sim}{Z}_t' \underset{\sim}{\gamma}; 0,1) - \sigma_{1\varepsilon}^2 (\underset{\sim}{Z}_t' \underset{\sim}{\gamma}) n(\underset{\sim}{Z}_t' \underset{\sim}{\gamma}; 0,1)$$

$$(d) \quad E[(1 - R_t)\varepsilon_{2t}]^2 = \sigma_2^2 [1 - N(\underset{\sim}{Z}_t' \underset{\sim}{\gamma})] + \sigma_{2\varepsilon}^2 (\underset{\sim}{Z}_t' \underset{\sim}{\gamma}) n(\underset{\sim}{Z}_t' \underset{\sim}{\gamma}; 0,1) .$$

Using (58)(a) it can now be shown that:

$$E(\varepsilon_{1t} / \underset{\sim}{Z}_t' \underset{\sim}{\gamma} \geq \varepsilon_t) = -\sigma_{1\varepsilon} \cdot \frac{n(\underset{\sim}{Z}_t' \underset{\sim}{\gamma}; 0,1)}{N(\underset{\sim}{Z}_t' \underset{\sim}{\gamma}; 0,1)} .$$

Equation (56)(a) may therefore be represented:

$$(59)(a) \quad y_{1t} = \underset{\sim}{X}_{1t}' \underset{\sim}{\beta}_1 - \sigma_{1\varepsilon} \cdot \frac{n(\underset{\sim}{Z}_t' \underset{\sim}{\gamma}; 0,1)}{N(\underset{\sim}{Z}_t' \underset{\sim}{\gamma}; 0,1)} + \zeta_{1t} ,$$

with $E(\zeta_{1t}/R_t = 1) = 0$. This is a standard OLS situation for the restriction of the available observations to regime (a). One substitutes $\underset{\sim}{\gamma}$ obtained from the Probit estimation into (59)(a). Ordinary least squares in stage two will yield consistent estimates of β_1 and $\sigma_{1\varepsilon}$. Using equation (58)(c), we may write:

$$E(\varepsilon_{1t}^2 / R_t = 1) = \sigma_1^2 - \sigma_{1\varepsilon}^2 (\underset{\sim}{Z}_t' \underset{\sim}{\gamma}) \cdot \frac{n(\underset{\sim}{Z}_t' \underset{\sim}{\gamma}; 0,1)}{N(\underset{\sim}{Z}_t' \underset{\sim}{\gamma}; 0,1)} .$$

An estimate of σ_1^2 may therefore be obtained by regressing the squared computed residuals from stage two upon the variable $(\underset{\sim}{Z}'_t\hat{\underset{\sim}{\gamma}})\dfrac{n(\underset{\sim}{Z}'_t\hat{\underset{\sim}{\gamma}};0,1)}{N(\underset{\sim}{Z}'_t\hat{\underset{\sim}{\gamma}};0,1)}$.

Similar procedures hold, *mutatis mutandis* for equation (56)(b). It can be shown that the resulting estimates are strongly consistent and asymptotically Normal. However the asymptotic covariance matrix is not given by Lee.

Application of the foregoing technique to the EFC model proceeds via the reduced-form of the latter. We observe in respect of the EFC model that regime (a) holds if $p_t < p_{t-1}$. From equation (39), this will be so iff:

$$(\mu-1)p_{t-1} + \frac{1-\mu}{\alpha_1-\alpha_2}(\underset{\sim}{X}'_{2t}\underset{\sim}{\beta}_2 - \underset{\sim}{X}'_{1t}\underset{\sim}{\beta}_1) + \frac{1-\mu}{\alpha_1-\alpha_2}(u_{2t}-u_{1t}) < 0 .$$

Write $\sigma^2 = \mathrm{Var}(u_{2t}-u_{1t})$ and $\varepsilon_t = \dfrac{u_{1t}-u_{2t}}{\sigma}$. The EFC model can be set up in two-stage probit form as:

$$\text{(60)(a)}\quad Q_t = \pi_1^a p_{t-1} + \underset{\sim}{X}'_{1t}\underset{\sim}{\pi}_2^a + \underset{\sim}{X}'_{2t}\underset{\sim}{\pi}_3^a + \varepsilon_{1t}$$

$$\text{iff.}\quad \frac{\alpha_2-\alpha_1}{\sigma}p_{t-1} + \underset{\sim}{X}'_{1t}\left(\frac{-\underset{\sim}{\beta}_1}{\sigma}\right) + \underset{\sim}{X}'_{2t}\left(\frac{\underset{\sim}{\beta}_2}{\sigma}\right) \geq \varepsilon_t$$

$$\text{(60)(b)}\quad Q_t = \pi_1^b p_{t-1} + \underset{\sim}{X}'_{1t}\underset{\sim}{\pi}_2^b + \underset{\sim}{X}'_{2t}\underset{\sim}{\pi}_3^b + \varepsilon_{2t}, \text{ otherwise.}$$

Here:

$$\pi_1^a = \mu\alpha_1,\quad \underset{\sim}{\pi}_2^a = \left(\frac{\mu\alpha_1-\alpha_2}{\alpha_1-\alpha_2}\right)\underset{\sim}{\beta}_1,\quad \underset{\sim}{\pi}_3^a = \left(\frac{\alpha_1(1-\mu)}{\alpha_1-\alpha_2}\right)\underset{\sim}{\beta}_2$$

$$\pi_1^b = \mu\alpha_2,\quad \underset{\sim}{\pi}_2^b = \left(\frac{-\alpha_2(1-\mu)}{\alpha_1-\alpha_2}\right)\underset{\sim}{\beta}_1,\quad \underset{\sim}{\pi}_3^b = \left(\frac{\alpha_1-\mu\alpha_2}{\alpha_1-\alpha_2}\right)\underset{\sim}{\beta}_2 .$$

Also:

$$\varepsilon_{1t} = \frac{\alpha_1(1-\mu)}{\alpha_1-\alpha_2}(u_{2t}-u_{1t}) + u_{1t}$$

$$\varepsilon_{2t} = \frac{\alpha_2(1-\mu)}{\alpha_1-\alpha_2}(u_{2t}-u_{1t}) + u_{2t} .$$

Estimates of the coefficients $\pi_i^{a,b}$ may now be derived as for the standard two-stage probit model. From these and the parameter relationships exhibited in equations (60)(a) and (b), estimates of the desired parameters α_i, β_i and μ are to be obtained. Although this may certainly be done, it will be apparent that there will be multiple solutions for the structural parameters. The two-stage probit calculation can indeed be regarded as establishing the reduced-form of the EFC model. As for the general linear model, problems of overidentification may appear. In the present context, the two-stage probit method does not appear to have the operational advantages of 2SLS methods. However in applications where the reduced-form is of primary interest, such as the nonlinear excess demand problem of chapter 6.1.1, this method should have favourable sampling properties and is obviously worthy of consideration.

5.8 Ancillary Topics

Up to this point we have considered the problem of estimating the parameters of the models. We turn now to an alternative basis of inference, concerned with judgement about the state of the system at any point in time. Two problems are considered. The first is the problem of deciding when the market is in a state of excess demand, and when it is in a state of excess supply. The second is the problem, originally broached in the context of the excess-demand model (chapter 3.7), of deriving point estimates of the equilibrium value p_t^*.

5.8.1 Discriminant Analysis. Where the sample separation is unknown, the problem arises as to whether a given observation belongs in the regime of excess demand or of excess supply. The application of some policy measure may depend on such a judgement. The general statistical problem is that of defining a discriminant function which will partition (p,Q)-space(R) into two regions $R = R_a + R_b$. If a given point (p,Q) falls in R_a we accept that regime (a) applies; otherwise regime (b) is apposite. Since we are going to assume Normal disturbances the probability structure of section 5.4.1 is applicable.

Accordingly, let us define for a given observation (p,Q), prob(a/p,Q) as the probability that regime (a) is holding and prob(b/p,Q) as the probability that the given observation is in (b). Then

$$\text{prob}(a/p,Q) = \frac{\text{prob}(p,Q \text{ and } a)}{\text{prob}(p,Q)},$$

$$= \frac{\int_{-\infty}^{p} f^a(p,Q,p^*)\,dp^*}{\text{prob}(p,Q)},$$

$$= \frac{(2\Pi)^{-1}|\Omega_{11}^{a}|^{-1} \exp\left(-\frac{1}{2}\, \underset{\sim}{y}_a' \Omega_{11}^{a^{-1}} \underset{\sim}{y}_a\right) N\left[\frac{1}{d_a^{\frac{1}{2}}}(p-\mu_3^a-\underset{\sim}{y}_a'\underset{\sim}{\beta}_a);\ 0,1\right]}{\text{prob}(p,Q)},$$

where prob(p,Q) is defined by equation (31) above. Similarly for regime (b). Now introduce constant costs of misclassification. Define $c_{a/b}$ as the cost of classifying an observation as for regime (a) when in fact it comes from regime (b). Likewise $c_{b/a}$ is the cost of classifying as regime (b) when in fact the observation is from regime (a). The expected cost of misclassification is then

$$c_{b/a} \int_{R_b} \text{prob}(a/p,Q)\,dpdQ + c_{a/b} \int_{R_a} \text{prob}(b/p,Q)\,dpdQ \ .$$

It is easy to show[10] that R_a which minimises the above expected cost is defined by:

$$c_{b/a}\ \text{prob}(a/p,Q) > c_{a/b}\ \text{prob}(b/p,Q) \ ,$$

i.e. $$\frac{\text{prob}(a/p,Q)}{\text{prob}(b/p,Q)} > k = \frac{c_{a/b}}{c_{b/a}} \ .$$

In the particular case where the costs are assumed equal, the rule is that (p,Q) is judged to belong to regime (a) if prob(a/p,Q) > prob(b/p,Q). In the case of equality, no decision may be made. Returning to the general case, R_a is then defined by

$$(61) \qquad \frac{(2\Pi)^{-1}|\Omega_{11}^{a}|^{-1} \exp(-\frac{1}{2}\, \underset{\sim}{v}_a' \Omega_{11}^{a^{-1}} \underset{\sim}{v}_a)}{(2\Pi)^{-1}|\Omega_{11}^{b}|^{-1} \exp(-\frac{1}{2}\, \underset{\sim}{v}_b' \Omega_{11}^{b^{-1}} \underset{\sim}{v}_b)} > k \, \frac{N\left[\frac{-1}{d_b^{\frac{1}{2}}}(p-\mu_3^b-\underset{\sim}{v}_b'\underset{\sim}{\beta}_b);\ 0,1\right]}{N\left[\frac{1}{d_a^{\frac{1}{2}}}(p-\mu_3^a-\underset{\sim}{v}_a'\underset{\sim}{\beta}_a);\ 0,1\right]} \ .$$

It is interesting to contrast the region so defined with a "naive region" defined in terms of merely applying the reduced-form likelihood function for each regime:

$$(61)' \qquad \frac{(2\Pi)^{-1}|\Omega_{11}^{a}|^{-1} \exp(-\frac{1}{2}\, \underset{\sim}{v}_a' \Omega_{11}^{a^{-1}} \underset{\sim}{v}_a)}{(2\Pi)^{-1}|\Omega_{11}^{b}|^{-1} \exp(-\frac{1}{2}\, \underset{\sim}{v}_b' \Omega_{11}^{b^{-1}} \underset{\sim}{v}_b)} > k \ .$$

If both $p - \mu_3^b - \underset{\sim}{y}_b' \underset{\sim}{\beta}_b$ and $p - \mu_3^a - \underset{\sim}{y}_a' \underset{\sim}{\beta}_a$ were large, we might justifiably assume that $p - p > 0$, so that regime (a) is more likely to apply. Hence the ratio on the R.H.S. of (61) is small. It is evident that R_a as defined by the naive condition (61)' will be much too small, and the probability of wrongly classifying into regime (b) will be substantial.

From the operational point of view, the task is first to consistently estimate the parameters involved in equation (61). The observed point (p,Q) is then tested by the application of that equation. Since estimates, rather than actual values, are employed in deriving the regions R_a and R_b, any classification based on such regions will be subject to sampling error. We have not investigated the effect of error of this kind.

5.8.2 Estimation of the Equilibrium Price. To complete our analysis of the probability structure of the noisy-clearing model, we shall consider the problem of deriving a point estimate of the imputed equilibrium value p_t^*, given observations on p_t and Q_t. We assume, as before, that all parameters are known. We may write:

$$\begin{aligned} \text{prob}(p^*/p,Q) &= \text{prob}\left[(p^*/p,Q)/p^* < p\right] \times \text{prob}(p^* < p) \\ &\quad + \text{prob}\left[(p^*/p,Q)/p^* \geq p\right] \times \text{prob}(p^* \geq p) \\ &= \text{prob}^{(a)}(p^*/p,Q) + \text{prob}^{(b)}(p^*/p,Q) , \end{aligned}$$

where the superscripts $^{(a)},^{(b)}$ indicate that we are considering the conditional densities confined to regimes (a) and (b) respectively. Therefore,

(62) $$E(p^*/p,Q) = \int_{-\infty}^{p} p^* \,\text{prob}^{(a)}(p^*/p,Q)\,dp^* + \int_{p}^{\infty} p^* \,\text{prob}^{(b)}(p^*/p,Q)\,dp^* .$$

Now the conditional densities concerned have already been obtained for the factorisation of section 5.4.1. We write, for instance,

(63) $$\mathrm{prob}^{(a)}(p^*/p,Q) = \frac{1}{\sqrt{2\pi d_a}} \exp\left[-\frac{1}{2d_a}\left(p^* - \mu_3^a - \underset{\sim}{y}_a' \Omega_{11}^{a^{-1}} \underset{\sim}{\phi}_a\right)\right]^2 .$$

with a similar formulation for regime (b). We may now evaluate the RHS of (62) by using integration formulae similar to those employed to obtain equation (42) of section 5.6.1 (see especially footnote 5). After suitable transformations, the integrals involved may be evaluated in terms of the appropriate cumulative distribution functions. Assuming (63), that is to say parent Normal densities for the disturbance terms, we obtain:

(64) $$E(p^*/p,Q) = m_b + m_a N\left(\frac{p - m_a}{d_a^{\frac{1}{2}}}; 0,1\right) - m_b N\left(\frac{p - m_b}{d_b^{\frac{1}{2}}}; 0,1\right)$$
$$+ d_b^{\frac{1}{2}} \exp\left[-\tfrac{1}{2}\left(\frac{p - m_b}{d_b^{\frac{1}{2}}}\right)^2\right] - d_a^{\frac{1}{2}} \exp\left[-\tfrac{1}{2}\left(\frac{p - m_a}{d_a^{\frac{1}{2}}}\right)^2\right] ,$$

where $m_a = m_a(p,Q) = \mu_3^a + \underset{\sim}{y}_a' \Omega_{11}^{a^{-1}} \underset{\sim}{\phi}_a$ (with a corresponding definition for m_b) denotes the formal conditional mean of p^* in regime (a). We take the RHS of (64) as our estimate of p^* given (p,Q). Such a point estimate could also be used for the purposes of deciding which regime a given observation belongs to, with the discriminant formed as $E(p^*/p,Q) - p$. The implied loss function, however, is not attractive.

5.9 Summary

It may be useful to review the estimation properties of the short-side model. We have seen that these depend crucially upon whether or not sample separation is observed, i.e. some indicator is available to distinguish any observation as belonging to regimes of excess demand or excess supply. With regard to the truly simultaneous models, the error-free clearing model belongs in this category. We described methods based on maximum likelihood, two-stage least squares and instrumental variables, and two-stage probit procedures. This is a regular maximum-likelihood situation. Of the limited-information procedures the 2SLS techniques are most promising, since they are computationally undemanding and do not suffer from overidentification problems. We saw that a procedure known to be inconsistent (the "naive 2SLS" technique) exhibited favourable simulation results.

If sample separation is not observed, things are more difficult. In the case of the simultaneous model, the likelihood function is unbounded for a suitable choice of parameter values, leading to inconsistency. We exhibited a procedure based on non-linear least squares, and conjectured its consistency. However its sampling results were poor. Development of an accurate estimation technique for this model remains an unsettled matter. In the course of describing the probability structure of the short-side model we considered problems associated with estimating the equilibrium price. A convenient point estimate may be derived as a weighted average of the formal conditional means of this variable in each regime. We described a solution to the discrimination problem of deciding whether a given period belongs to excess demand or excess supply regimes. The application of these results must wait upon further development of estimation techniques for the parameters of the noisy-clearing model.

The "short-side" or "Fair-Jaffee" model has received much attention in recent years, as a well-defined and recognisable paradigm of quantity adjustment. We have found that the description of its probabilistic character and estimation possibilities has been considerably facilitated by the use of the PAMEQ specification. The difference $p_t - p_t^*$ provides a simple switch between periods of excess demand and excess supply. Although the nonlinearities implicit in the model at first sight appear formidable, the use of this device in conjunction with the ramp function $R(\cdot)$ leads to the application of standard techniques of estimation.

Our survey of estimation methods has been confined to a consideration of white-noise structural disturbances. The prospects for relaxing this assumption are not promising so far as maximum-likelihood methods are concerned. We have already observed the non-applicability of this method to the noisy-clearing model; we should not feel sanguine that this shortcoming will vanish with serially correlated disturbances. With respect to the EFC model, the likelihood function may be derived for the case of a first-order Markov process for (u_{1t},u_{2t}), but is computationally intractable. Prospects are a little better for the limited-information methods. If (u_{1t},u_{2t}) in the EFC model obey a first-order Markov process standard techniques for 2SLS in the presence of such disturbances will apply. These involve initial 2SLS estimates of the structural parameters, followed by computation of the Markov parameters from the estimated residuals. These are then employed to create quasi-differences of the dependent and independent variables, in familiar fashion. A second application of 2SLS to the transformed variables follows. Apart from straight-forward extensions of this kind, however, the handling of general schemes for serially correlated residuals is a topic that warrants further investigation.

Footnotes to Chapter 5

[1]Sections 5.2 and 5.6 are based on Bowden [1978b]. I should like to thank the editor and publishers of the *International Economic Review* for permission to reproduce material from this paper.
The basic "short-side" model was introduced to the econometric literature by R.C. Fair and D.M. Jaffee [1972].

[2]The correct formulation of the likelihood function of these models is due to T. Amemiya [1974] and G.S. Maddala and F.D. Nelson [1974]. M.J. Hartley and P. Mallela [1977] pointed out the observable variable Q is the first order-statistic from the distribution of D and S (see below).

[3]In general if $\Sigma = \begin{bmatrix} \Sigma_{11} & \Sigma_{12} \\ \Sigma_{21} & \Sigma_{22} \end{bmatrix}$ is a positive definite matrix, then

$|\Sigma| = |\Sigma_{11} - \Sigma_{12}\Sigma_{22}^{-1}\Sigma_{21}| \cdot |\Sigma_{22}|$ (T.W. Anderson [1958] A1.3, Theorem 5)

Renumbering rows and columns we have equation (30).

[4]The formal equivalence of the foregoing to the derivation of a trivariate density as a product of the marginal density of two variables with the conditional density of the third given the first two will not have escaped the reader. However since such probabilistic concepts are formal rather than actual in this case, to avoid confusion we have presented all operations in a mechanical fashion rather than using probabilistic arguments directly.

[5]The proof of this result follows by simple substitution in the required integral. Putting $z = \frac{x - m}{\sigma}$, the integral becomes $\frac{\sigma}{\sqrt{2\pi}} \int_{-\infty}^{-m/\sigma} z e^{-\frac{1}{2}z^2} dz$.

Now put $y = e^{-\frac{1}{2}z^2}$, to yield a constant integrand.

[6]We used in our work NDTR from the SSP package.

[7]The particular parameters were chosen to correspond, apart from scaling, with Model I of the Meat Market in G. Tintner [1963, pp.168-172]. We added the clearing equation to convert it to a disequilibrium model. Our motive in doing so was merely to obtain a realistic pair of equations; we do not wish to imply that Tintner's original model is better specified as a disequilibrium one.

[8]A sketch of the proof is as follows. To avoid cumbersome notation we treat θ as scalar.

Expanding q in Taylor series, about the true value θ_o, we have:

$$q(p_{t-1}, x_t, \hat{\theta}_T, \gamma) = q_t(\gamma) + (\hat{\theta}_T - \theta_o)q^*_{1t}(\gamma) ,$$

where $$q_t(\gamma) = q(p_{t-1}, x_t, \theta_o, \gamma) \text{ and}$$

$$q^*_{1t}(\gamma) = \frac{\partial}{\partial\theta}(p_{t-1}, x_t, \theta^*, \gamma)$$

with θ^* between $\hat{\theta}_T$ and θ_o. We may now write $\frac{1}{T}\times$ the sum of squares to be minimised (in a single-equation approach) in stage two as:

$$\frac{1}{T}\sum_t[Q_t - q(p_{t-1},x_t,\hat{\theta}_T,\gamma)]^2 = \frac{1}{T}\Sigma\,\zeta_t^2 - \frac{1}{T}\Sigma\,\zeta_t[q_t(\gamma) - q_t(\gamma_o)]$$

$$- (\hat{\theta}_T - \theta_o)\,\frac{1}{T}\Sigma\zeta_t q^*_{1t} + \frac{1}{T}\Sigma[q_t(\gamma) - q_t(\gamma_o)]^2$$

$$+ (\hat{\theta}_T - \theta_o)\,\frac{1}{T}\Sigma\,q^*_{1t}(q_t(\gamma) - q_t(\gamma_o)) + (\hat{\theta}_T - \theta_o)^2\,\frac{1}{T}\Sigma\,q^*_{1t}$$

To avoid troubles with the existence of the derivatives q^*_{1t}, we shall assume that the domain of consideration of w^2 is bounded away from zero. The rest of the demonstration consists in using the strong consistency of the OLS estimator $\hat{\theta}_T$ and the strong law of large numbers to show that all terms on the RHS save the first and fourth tend a.e. to zero.

[9] In chapter 2.2.1 we employed y_t as this indicator, in keeping with the notation of that chapter. For present purposes it is more convenient to maintain the notation of this chapter by using R_t for the switch variable.

[10] The proof is standard. Write $R = R_a + R_b$. Then the expected loss is

$$c_{b/a}\int_{R-R_a} \text{prob}(a/p,Q)\,dpdQ + c_{a/b}\int_{R_a} \text{prob}(b/p,Q)\,dpdQ$$

$$= c_{b/a}\int_{R} \text{prob}(a/p,Q)\,dpdQ + \int_{R_a} [c_{a/b}\,\text{prob}(b/p,Q) - c_{b/a}\,\text{prob}(a/p,Q)]\,dpdQ\,.$$

The first term is a given number. The second is minimised by choosing R_a so that it includes the points for which $c_{a/b}$ prob$(b/p,Q)$ - $c_{b/c}$ prob$(a/p,Q) < 0$, and excludes the points for which this expression is positive.

CHAPTER SIX

EXTENSIONS AND APPLICATIONS

In this chapter we consider relaxing some of the assumptions hitherto made about the process of market clearing. The short-side model discussed in the preceding chapter is in many ways a rather extreme construction. Accordingly we shall start by surveying several different dimensions, as it were, in which this model may be relaxed. We move on from this to consider what happens in a multi-good, many-agent setting. The chapter is continued with an application of the spillover coefficients derived from this discussion, with methods utilising also the results of chapter 5. We conclude with a survey of two studies of disequilibrium in the market for commercial bank loans.

6.1 Unequal Price Adjustment Parameters

In chapter 1.1 it was pointed out that there could be no general presumption that prices adjusted equally quickly in either direction. We remarked that the labour market was an example to the contrary where wages might in fact be very slow (perhaps infinitely slow) to adjust downwards. To take another perhaps less extreme example, J-J. Laffont and R. Garcia [1977] in their study of the Canadian market for commercial bank loans found that interest rates adjusted upwards rather more quickly than downwards.

Such unequal adjustment speeds may be handled within the PAMEQ framework by setting $\mu = \mu_a$ if and only if $p_t > p_t^*$ and $\mu = \mu_b$ otherwise, $\mu_a \neq \mu_b$. In the present section we shall indicate briefly how the analysis in two of the standard paradigms discussed in this study must be modified to handle such a contingency.

6.1.1 The Excess Demand Model. We consider first the excess demand problem as defined in chapter 3. It will be apparent that, if the adjustment parameter is to change in magnitude every time a market switches from excess demand to excess supply, handling a multi-good system will pose formidable problems. Accordingly we shall consider only a single market. Following the notation of chapter 3, the excess demand problem for a single good can be written:

$$(1) \quad \begin{cases} p_t = \mu_a p_{t-1} + (1-\mu_a)p_t^* + u_{3t}, & \text{iff } p_t > p_t^* \\ p_t = \mu_b p_{t-1} + (1-\mu_b)p_t^* + u_{3t}, & \text{iff } p_t < p_t^* . \end{cases}$$

$$\alpha p_t^* = \underset{\sim}{\beta}' \underset{\sim}{z}_t + v_t$$

where it will be recalled that u_{3t}[1] and v_t are disturbance terms.

It turns out that the likelihood function for the noisy clearing mechanisms suffers from the same kind of irregular behaviour as that for the short-side model in chapter 5.4.1. As for that model no estimation method which is both practical and consistent is yet available. In the remainder of this discussion we shall therefore drop the disturbance term u_{3t} and consider the problem with error-free market clearing. The EFC likelihood function is derived using arguments presented in chapter 5 in respect of the short-side model. In regime (a) (excess supply) p_t has, assuming Normality of v_t, the formal density

$$f^a(p_t) = n\left(p_t;\ \mu_a p_{t-1} + \left(\frac{1-\mu_a}{\alpha}\right)\underset{\sim}{\beta}'\underset{\sim}{z}_t,\ \left(\frac{1-\mu_a}{\alpha}\right)^2 \sigma_v^2\right)$$

where $\sigma_v^2 = \text{Var } v_t$. Similarly for regime (b).

The likelihood function, under the available sample separation is

$$L(p_1 \ldots p_T,\ R_1 \ldots R_T) = \prod_{t\epsilon\psi_a} f^a(p_t) \prod_{t\epsilon\psi_b} f^b(p_t)\ .$$

The log-likelihood ratio can now be written as:

$$\begin{aligned}\log L = &-\frac{T}{2}\log 2\pi - \frac{T}{2}\log \sigma^2 + \frac{T}{2}\log \alpha^2 \\ &- T_a \log(1-\mu_a) - \sum_{t\epsilon\psi_a}\left(p_t - \mu_a p_{t-1} - \left(\frac{1-\mu_a}{\alpha}\right)\underset{\sim}{\beta}'\underset{\sim}{z}_t\right)^2 \\ &- T_b \log(1-\mu_b) - \sum_{t\epsilon\psi_b}\left(p_t - \mu_b p_{t-1} - \left(\frac{1-\mu_b}{\alpha}\right)\underset{\sim}{\beta}'\underset{\sim}{z}_t\right)^2 .\end{aligned}$$

The form of this likelihood function makes it clear that maximisation cannot be carried out in the two regimes independently because of the presence of common factors $\underset{\sim}{\beta}$ and α. The problem is, however, partly decomposable in respect of μ_a and μ_b, suggesting a step-wise computational algorithm (see Laffont and Garcia [1977], p.1201).

Turning now to limited-information methods, techniques based on linear least squares are no longer available. We might consider, for instance applying the methods of chapter 3 to one regime at a time. Consider the probability density of the observations known to come from regime (a). We write

$$\text{prob}(p_t/R_t = 1) = \frac{f^a(p_t)}{\text{prob}(p_t^* < p_{t-1})}$$

the denominator being the same as $\text{prob}(p_t > p_t^*)$. From this it follows that

$$(2) \qquad E(p_t/R_t = 1) = \frac{\mu_a p_{t-1} + \left(\frac{1-\mu_a}{\alpha}\right)\underset{\sim}{\beta}' \underset{\sim}{z}_t}{N[\alpha p_{t-1} - \underset{\sim}{\beta}' \underset{\sim}{z}_t; 0, \sigma_v^2]},$$

where as usual N denotes the cumulative Normal distribution function. From (2) it follows that regressing p_t on p_{t-1} and $\underset{\sim}{z}_t$ for observations known to come from regime (a) will yield biased results. The regression constructed from (2) is badly nonlinear.

However, the EFC system based on the system (1) may be cast in the following terms:

$$p_t = \mu_a p_{t-1} + (1-\mu_a)\frac{\underset{\sim}{\beta}'}{\alpha}\underset{\sim}{z}_t + \left(\frac{1-\mu_a}{\alpha}\right)v_t, \quad \text{iff } \frac{\alpha}{\sigma_v} p_{t-1} - \frac{\underset{\sim}{\beta}'}{\sigma_v}\underset{\sim}{z}_t \geq \frac{v_t}{\sigma_v}$$

$$p_t = \mu_b p_{t-1} + (1-\mu_b)\frac{\underset{\sim}{\beta}'}{\alpha}\underset{\sim}{z}_t + \left(\frac{1-\mu_b}{\alpha}\right)v_t, \quad \text{iff } \frac{\alpha}{\sigma_v} p_{t-1} - \frac{\underset{\sim}{\beta}'}{\sigma_v}\underset{\sim}{z}_t < \frac{v_t}{\sigma_v}.$$

This is a two-stage Probit model directly comparable with e.g. equations (60)(a) and (b) of chapter 5.7. Since the excess demand problem involves the estimation of a reduced-form to begin with, the overidentification difficulties mentioned in §5.7 do not apply. We note that estimates of α may be obtained from examination of the residual sums of squares of the model (3). All parameters of (3) are therefore consistently estimable by the two-stage Probit technique.

6.1.2 <u>The Short-side Problem</u>. We consider again the EFC version. Corresponding to equations (39), (40)(a) and (b) of chapter 5.6.1 we have

$$(4) \qquad p_t = R(p_{t-1} - p_t)\left[\mu_a p_{t-1} + \frac{1-\mu_a}{\alpha_1 - \alpha_2}(\underset{\sim}{X}_{2t}'\underset{\sim}{\beta}_2 - \underset{\sim}{X}_{1t}'\underset{\sim}{\beta}_1)\right] +$$
$$(1 - R(p_{t-1} - p_t)\left[\mu_b p_{t-1} + \frac{1-\mu_b}{\alpha_1 - \alpha_2}(\underset{\sim}{X}_{2t}'\underset{\sim}{\beta}_2 - \underset{\sim}{X}_{1t}'\underset{\sim}{\beta}_1)\right] + v_t,$$

$$\text{where } v_t = R(p_{t-1} - p_t)\frac{1-\mu_a}{\alpha_1 - \alpha_2}(u_{2t} - u_{1t}) + (1 - R(p_{t-1} - p_t))\frac{1-\mu_b}{\alpha_1 - \alpha_2}(u_{2t} - u_{1t}) .$$

$$(5)\ (a) \quad Q_t = \underset{\sim}{X}'_{1t}\,\underset{\sim}{\beta}_1 + \alpha_1 p_t - \frac{\mu_a(\alpha_2 - \alpha_1)}{1-\mu_a}(p_t - p_{t-1})(1 - R(p_{t-1} - p_t) + u_{1t}$$

$$(b) \quad Q_t = \underset{\sim}{X}'_{2t}\,\underset{\sim}{\beta}_2 + \alpha_2 p_t + \frac{\mu_b(\alpha_2 - \alpha_1)}{1-\mu_b}(p_t - p_{t-1})R(p_{t-1} - p_t) + u_{2t} .$$

We note first the nonlinear character of (4), with the endogenous variable p_t on the RHS. This means that we cannot obtain estimates of the expectations of the nonlinear terms in (5) (a) and (b). Indeed we note in respect of (4) that $E\,v_t \neq 0$ unless $\mu_a = \mu_b$. There are several alternative possibilities open to us. One is simply to regard $(p_t - p_{t-1})R(p_{t-1} - p_t)$ as a variable, regressing it upon all the exogenous variables after the fashion described in chapter 2.6.2. This procedure is followed by Laffont and Garcia. Possibly a more efficient procedure is to exploit the dependence of $E\,v_t$ on the predetermined variables by regressing p_t on p_{t-1}, $\underset{\sim}{X}_{1t}$, $\underset{\sim}{X}_{2t}$ to obtain $\hat{p}_t$. In the second stage, $(\hat{p}_t - p_{t-1})R(p_{t-1} - \hat{p}_t)$ is used in equations (5) as an instrument for the nonlinear variable. Such a procedure will be consistent (see chapter 2.5).

In summary, it will be apparent that postulating unequal reaction speeds for price, according to whether the system is in excess demand or excess supply, does materially complicate estimation procedures. In some circumstances however, the gain in veracity may be worth the extra effort.

6.2 Relaxing the Strict Short-side Model

In chapter 1.2.2 we relaxed the simple-market short-side model to encompass a continuous clearing path for quantities lying inside, and asymptotic to, the short arms of the demand and supply schedules. We mentioned there that a construction of this type had been employed in the literature to derive a Phillips curve, relating the % rate of wage changes to the rate of unemployment. We first take up this suggestion in more detail, expressing the Phillips curve in terms of a PAMEQ specification. We are able by using this device to solve some puzzles concerning the relationship of Phillips-curve analysis to Walrasian demand and supply theory. Following this discussion we shall consider two further possibilities for a clearing mechanism for quantities. In doing so, however, we shall not step outside the confines of the perishable good model, so that inventories are not imagined to exist. Models for a durable good are not considered until chapters seven and eight.

6.2.1 The Phillips Curve. We shall assume as a basis the Phillips curve discussion of chapter 1.2.2. It will be recalled that where excess demand for labour is zero there will nevertheless be a certain amount of "frictional" unemployment U^* and vacancies V^*. Denote by W^* the equilibrium wage rate at any point in time, and let the corresponding equilibrium labour force be L^*. Write $U^* = \alpha^* L^*$, $0 < \alpha^* < 1$. The coefficient α^* is one measure of the extent of "frictional" unemployment, and will presumably depend upon such factors as the mobility of the work force and information arrangements as to the notification of available jobs and workers.

Let us write our wage-adjustment equation as (cf. equation (4) of §1.2.2):

$$(6) \qquad d\left(\frac{W}{W^*}\right) = \phi\left(\frac{V-U}{L^*}, \frac{\dot{(V-U)}}{L^*}\right), \qquad \phi_1 \geq 0, \ \phi_2 \geq 0 .$$

We have simply normalised the excess demand by dividing by the equilibrium labour force. Define $w = \frac{W}{W^*} - 1$, i.e. the proportional deviation of the wage rate from its moving equilibrium level. Likewise let $u = \frac{U}{U^*} - 1$. It will be recalled from chapter 1.2.2 (equation (3)) that we could specify:

$$V - U = h(U) ,$$

with $h(U^*) = 0$. To a first approximation we may write

$$\text{(7)} \qquad \frac{V-U}{U^*} = h'_*\left(\frac{U-U^*}{U^*}\right) ,$$

where h'_* denotes the derivative evaluated at the equilibrium point. Let us assume that both α^* and h'_* are constant over time. Combining (6) and (7) and expanding in Taylor series to terms of first order we obtain

$$\text{(8)} \qquad \dot{w} = \beta_1 u + \beta_2 \dot{u} \; ; \; \beta_1 = \phi_1^* \alpha^* h'_* < 0 , \quad \beta_2 = \phi_2^* \alpha^* h'_* < 0 .$$

Equation (8) can be expressed in terms of the observed proportionate wage increases $\frac{\dot{W}}{W}$ as follows. Note that $\dot{w} = \frac{d}{dt}\left(\frac{W}{W^*}\right) = \frac{W}{W^*}\left(\frac{\dot{W}}{W} - \frac{\dot{W}^*}{W^*}\right)$. Hence from (8)

$$\text{(9)} \qquad \frac{\dot{W}}{W} = \beta_1 . \frac{W^*}{W} . u + \beta_2 . \frac{W^*}{W} . \dot{u} + \frac{\dot{W}^*}{W^*} .$$

We recall that $V - U = L^d(w) - L^s(w)$ where L^d and L^s are the demand and supply functions of labour. Denote by ε_* the excess demand elasticity, evaluated at the moving equilibrium *, namely $W^* . \frac{L_*^{d'} - L_*^{s'}}{L^*}$. Again we shall assume that this is approximately constant over the range of disequilibrium situations considered. Hence in the neighbourhood of equilibrium,

$$h'_* \frac{U - U^*}{U^*} = \varepsilon_* \frac{W - W^*}{W^*} ,$$

so that

$$\frac{W^*}{W} = \frac{1}{1 + \theta u} , \qquad \text{where } \theta = \frac{h'_*}{\varepsilon_*} .$$

It follows also that $\dot{u} = \frac{1}{\theta}\frac{W}{W^*}\left[\frac{\dot{W}}{W} - \frac{\dot{W}^*}{W}\right]$. Substituting for $\dot{u}$ in (9) and simplifying, we obtain

$$(10) \qquad \frac{\dot{W}}{W} = \frac{\beta_1\theta}{\theta - \beta_2}\left(1 - \frac{1}{1+\theta u}\right) + \frac{\dot{W}^*}{W^*} .$$

By writing $\frac{1}{1+\theta u} \simeq 1 - \theta u$ equation (10) can be rewritten:

$$(11) \qquad \frac{\dot{W}}{W} = \gamma_o - \gamma_1 \frac{U}{L^*} + \frac{\dot{W}^*}{W^*} ,$$

where $\gamma_o = \frac{\phi_1^* \alpha^* h_*'^2}{\varepsilon_*(1 - \phi_2^* \alpha^* \varepsilon_*)}$ and $\gamma_1 = \gamma_o/\alpha^*$. We verify that (11) has stationary solution $U = \alpha^* L^* = U^*$ as required by the original model.

Equation (11) is a Phillips curve in the rate of unemployment as defined by $\frac{U}{L^*}$, i.e. actual unemployment as a proportion of the equilibrium labour force. Alternative measures of unemployment are $\frac{U}{L^s}$ and $\frac{U}{L}$. The former measures unemployment in terms of those who wish to be employed, at the going wage rate - this is perhaps the theoretically appropriate measure. The term $\frac{U}{L}$ measures unemployment as a proportion of those currently employed and has the advantage of being more easily measured. Locally, the various measures of unemployment tend to move together, in the sense that movements in any one measure approximate fairly closely movements in another.[2]

Let us turn now to the implications of our Phillips curve for the secular and cyclical behaviour of rates of change in money wages. In the first place, we have shown that the incorporation in the wage adjustment equation of changes in the pressure of excess demand will not necessarily lead to the appearance in the Phillips curve of the rate of change in unemployment rates. This is in contrast with the assertion e.g. of Hines [1971]. Hence observed counter-clockwise movements in wage rates (in the Phillips plane) cannot rely on this effect. There are, in fact, several alternative explanations for these loops. R.G. Lipsey's hypothesis [1960] in terms of the distribution and timing of wage changes between different sectors is well known. Our specification yields an alternative. We need only assume that with the upswing of the business cycle the rate of change of the imputed equilibrium wage rate $\frac{\dot{W}^*}{W^*}$ is positive with increasing demand for labour. At the same time, or more accurately with a slight lag, the rate of unemployment will be decreasing as workers are taken up. Hence for a given level of unemployment, $\frac{\dot{W}}{W}$ will be higher when unemployment is falling, with a slight lead. This is the essence of the famous anticlockwise loops.

The PAMEQ specification solves also the puzzle referred to above, concerning the inclusion of the expected rate of inflation in the Phillips curve. For the term $\frac{\dot{W}^*}{W^*}$ may depend upon anticipated inflation rates. We need only specify that the expected rate of change of prices is built into the supply and demand functions for labour. This may be the case either through the operation of formal industrial agreements or because of the expectations of individual agents in more perfect markets. But even if unions try to claim anticipated price increases as compensation from employers, the demand function of labour may not have shifted proportionately to the right. In such circumstances, the coefficient of the expected inflation rate, as it enters into $\frac{\dot{W}^*}{W^*}$ may be less than unity. Thus the debate about the magnitude of the coefficient in question can be related to Marshallian demand and supply functions in quite a simple way. More generally, we see also that the relationship between $\frac{\dot{W}}{W}$ and the rate of unemployment is a matter also of secular changes in equilibrium wage rates. In particular, ongoing long-term changes in the distribution of national income between labour and capital may be expected to show up as a vertical shifting of the Phillips curve.

Viewed as a problem in disequilibrium estimation, we see how unambitious Phillips curve analysis is. No attempt is made to estimate the parameters of the underlying labour demand and supply schedules. Nor, indeed, should we be sanguine about the possibility of doing so on the basis of observations on wage rates and unemployment. The curve, in short, is very much a "reduced form" kind of relationship.

6.2.2 A PAMEQ Specification for Q? If we assume that a PAMEQ adjustment mechanism holds in respect of prices, a natural question is whether relaxation of the strict short-side model can lead, at least locally, to a corresponding expression for quantities. Let us write a local version of the general clearing path in figure 6.1 as:

$$(12) \qquad Q_t = Q_t^* + \beta_t(p_t - p_t^*) ,$$

where $Q_t = Q(p_t^*)$. Here β_t is itself a function $\beta(p_t - p_t^*)$ of the price discrepancy indicated. A leading possibility is:

$$\begin{aligned} \beta_t &= \beta_a < 0 \qquad \text{if } p_t \geq p_t^* \\ &= \beta_b > 0 \qquad \text{if } p_t < p_t^* , \end{aligned}$$

which ensures that $Q_t < Q_t^*$ always. A similar property would result from $\beta_t = -\beta(p_t - p_t^*)$, $\beta > 0$. On the other hand, the condition $Q_t < Q_t^*$ is by no means to be regarded as a necessary one. Indeed it is worth remarking that the linearisations employed in the Phillips curve analysis of §6.2.1 assume implicitly that such a condition does not hold in a small neighbourhood of Q^* .

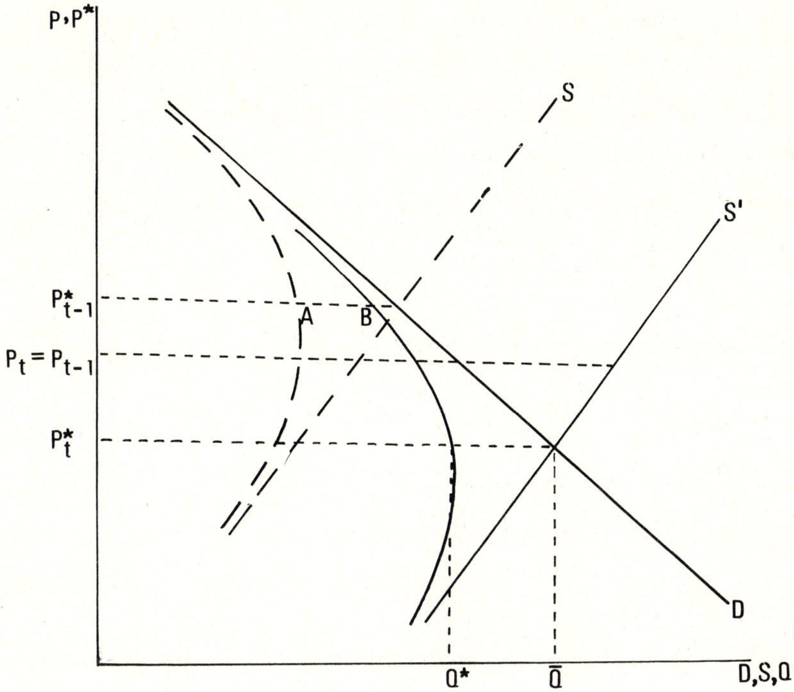

Figure 6.1

Write $\bar{Q} = D(p^*) = S(p^*)$ as the quantity abscissa of the intersection of the demand and supply curves. Define (as in §6.2.1) $\alpha^* = \frac{\bar{Q} - Q^*}{\bar{Q}}$ as the equilibrium degree of friction. Thus $Q^*_t = (1-\alpha^*)\bar{Q}_t = (1-\alpha^*)S(p^*_t)$. It follows that approximately,

(13) $$Q^*_t - Q^*_{t-1} \simeq (1-\alpha^*)\gamma^*(p^*_t - p^*_{t-1}) ,$$

where γ^* denotes the derivative of S evaluated at some constant such as the average of p^*_t over the period of consideration. Assuming for simplicity the EFC model for prices:

(14) $$p_t = \mu p_{t-1} + (1-\mu)p^*_t ,$$

we derive

(15) $$p_t - p^*_t = \mu(p_{t-1} - p^*_{t-1}) - \mu(p^*_t - p^*_{t-1}) .$$

Combining this with (12) and (13) we obtain:

$$(16) \qquad Q_t = \mu_t Q_{t-1} + (1-\mu_t)Q_t^* + \mu_t\left(1 - \frac{\beta_{t-1}}{\gamma^*(1-\alpha^*)}\right)(Q_t^* - Q_{t-1}^*) ,$$

where $\mu_t = \mu\beta_t/\beta_{t-1}$.

In the first place, even if $\beta_t = \beta_{t-1}$ so that $\mu_t = \mu$, we see that (16) is not on all fours with the PAMEQ specification (14). The reason for the extra term in $Q_t^* - Q_{t-1}^*$ can be illustrated with reference to figure 6.1. Suppose that $\mu = 1$ so that $p_t = p_{t-1}$ always. If equilibrium price changes from p_{t-1}^* to p_t^* because of a rightward shift of the supply curve (S to S'), the quantity transacted will nevertheless change from A to B. In this case $Q_t \neq Q_{t-1}$ for an extra term must be added which is related to the change in the equilibrium transacted quantity. Similar reasoning will hold for the more general case where $\mu \neq 1$.

In the second place, the adjustment parameters μ_t of (16) are functions of time and indeed may change sign. Suppose for example that $\beta_t = -\beta(p_t - p_t^*)$. From equation (15),

$$\frac{\beta_t}{\beta_{t-1}} = \frac{p_t - p_t^*}{p_{t-1} - p_{t-1}^*} = \mu\left(1 - \frac{\Delta p_t^*}{p_{t-1} - p_{t-1}^*}\right) .$$

It may be that a disequilibrium state of excess demand is suddenly converted to a state of excess supply, as in the arrival of a boat-load of fallen women in Botany Bay.[3] In such circumstances we could have $\dfrac{\Delta p_t^*}{p_{t-1} - p_{t-1}^*} > 1$ so that $\mu_t = \dfrac{\mu\beta_t}{\beta_{t-1}} < 0$. The adjustment parameters μ_t are therefore not even locally constant. On the other hand if Q_t can be locally expressed as $Q_t = Q_t^* - \beta(p_t - p_t^*)$ for constant β , then we can write $\mu_t = \mu$ and the adjustment parameter is stable.

In general however, a stable PAMEQ relationship of the kind described in chapter 3 will not exist, even locally, for quantities.

The decomposition (16) has nevertheless some points of interest and we shall return to it in the next subsection.

6.2.3 Stochastic Coefficients. Let us return to consider a very simple kind of nonsimultaneous short-side model such as that of chapter 5.1.1:

$$
\begin{aligned}
(17)\qquad D_t &= \underset{\sim}{X}'_{1t}\underset{\sim}{\beta}_1 + u_{1t} \\
S_t &= \underset{\sim}{X}'_{2t}\underset{\sim}{\beta}_2 + u_{2t} \\
Q_t &= \min(D_t, S_t) .
\end{aligned}
$$

Combine $\underset{\sim}{X}_{1t}$ and $\underset{\sim}{X}_{2t}$ into a vector $\underset{\sim}{Z}_t$. The first two equations may thus be represented

$$
\begin{aligned}
Q_t &= \underset{\sim}{Z}'_t\underset{\sim}{\gamma}_1 + u_{1t} \\
Q_t &= \underset{\sim}{Z}'_t\underset{\sim}{\gamma}_2 + u_{2t} ,
\end{aligned}
$$

with $\underset{\sim}{\gamma}_1$ and $\underset{\sim}{\gamma}_2$ appropriately partitioned into zero and non-zero elements. Introducing the (0,1)-ramp function R, the system may be written

$$(18)\qquad Q_t = \underset{\sim}{Z}'_t\underset{\sim}{\gamma}_t + \zeta_t ,$$

with $\gamma_t = \gamma_1 R_t + \gamma_2(1 - R_t)$, $\zeta_t = u_{1t} R_t + u_{2t}(1 - R_t)$, and $R_t = R(S_t - D_t)$.

The parameter $\underset{\sim}{\gamma}_t$ of (18) is random. Its distribution is evidently a rather special one, since it has just two values - $\underset{\sim}{\gamma}_1$ or $\underset{\sim}{\gamma}_2$ - with probabilities which are themselves functions of the disturbance terms and therefore ζ_t. Noting the stochastic character of $\underset{\sim}{\gamma}_t$, Swamy and Mehta [1975] have suggested carrying the interpretation further. They propose to drop the special distributional properties of $\underset{\sim}{\gamma}_t$ in equation (18) above, and assume instead that $\underset{\sim}{\gamma}_t$ can be regarded as a random drawing from a parent "population" with mean $\underset{\sim}{\gamma}_o$ and covariance matrix Σ_γ, constant. A similar property is assumed to be true of the disturbance ζ_t, which is indeed absorbed into the stochastic intercept term in $\underset{\sim}{\gamma}$. Swamy and Mehta are then able to apply estimation techniques designed for random parameter models and in particular to derive a Bayesian posterior.

It is hard to see that such a specification captures the essential features of any disequilibrium process that is at all similar to the system (18). In particular, a realisation of the random variable $\underset{\sim}{\gamma}_t$ must depend upon the particular values of the predetermined variables that are currently holding. For these will help to determine supply and demand pressures and hence the quantities actually transacted. Even if we assumed that the exogenous variables were themselves randomly generated, the likelihood function should record in some way the dependence of the distribution of $\underset{\sim}{\gamma}_t$ upon the exogenous variables. On the other hand such strictures may not apply with equal force to adjustment parameters in a state of disequilibrium. Equation (16) of the previous subsection is a case in point. It may not do too much violence to the dynamics of the adjustment process for quantities to represent the μ_t as stationary random variables after the fashion suggested by Swamy and Mehta. It might, however make more sense in terms of the discussion of (16) to represent the μ_t as a Markov process. Such representations, and their efficacy for the task in hand, must await future developments.

6.3 Many Goods

Until now the discussion of quantity adjustment has been confined to a single market. Many problems of empirical analysis involve the effect of constraints imposed by disequilibrium in one market upon the actions of economic agents with regard to others. As pointed out in chapter 1, much of the wider significance and motivation for the study of disequilibrium econometrics arises from presumed effects of this kind in macroeconomic dynamics. Thus if individuals are prevented from supplying all the labour they require, at going wage rates, their consumption behaviour or asset preferences may be affected. Similar problems arise in respect of the rationing of mortgage credit - individuals may react by putting more of their own equity into the purchase (see chapter 7). While it is possible to multiply instances of this kind, it is better to let the applications speak for themselves. At this point it may be useful to distill one or two of the general features of such problems.

6.3.1 Spillover Coefficients. To investigate the effect of disequilibrium of individual demand and supply schedules, it will be useful to start at the level of the individual choice problem. To fix ideas, we shall employ a simple static model of an individual, facing a continuous possibility set or feasible region of choice. The objects of choice may be either goods, treated as flow quantities, or services of labour. We shall make no formal distinction between demand (as for goods) or supply (as for labour) referring to both as "demand" or "goods" with the understanding that some demands may be negative. Although we illustrate with a flow problem, the same sort of precepts will be applicable to problems with a stock dimension such as the choice among competing assets.

Let us assume initially that the individual is constrained in his demand or supply choices by a quantity restriction on just one good. His decision problem may be represented in standard form as:

(19) $\max u(x_1 \ldots x_n)$

subject to: $\Sigma p_i x_i = M$

$x_1 \leq \bar{x}_1$.

Here u is a twice-differentiable concave utility function, x_i are the quantities, M denotes a fixed endowment of some kind, and $\bar{x}_1$ is his perceived constraint in the demand or supply of good 1. Form the Lagrangian

(20) $L = u - \lambda(\Sigma p_i x_i - M) - \mu_1(x_1 - \bar{x}_1)$,

where λ and μ_1 are Lagrange multipliers. Let us assume that the constraint is actually binding in the optimal solution. The first-order stationary conditions are:

(21) $u_1 = \lambda p_1 + \mu_1$

$u_i = \lambda p_i$, $i=2 \ldots n$.

Solving for $x_1 \ldots x_n$, we obtain:

(22) $x_i = x_i(p_1 \ldots p_n, \lambda, \mu_1)$ $i=1 \ldots n$.

Imposing the constraints yields solution for λ and μ_1 . We end up writing explicit demand functions as:

$x_1 = \bar{x}_1$

$x_i = x_i(p_1 \ldots p_n, M, \bar{x}_1)$, $i=2 \ldots n$.

As mentioned in chapter 1, demand functions of this form have been used to justify the appearance of an income variable in the consumption equation for commodities. In this case $\bar{x}_1 = I = \frac{y}{w}$, where I is a constraint on the supply of labour and y is salary and wage income (or together with M can be construed in the aggregate as total income).

However, it will be useful for our purposes to derive a rather more informative version of the constrained demand functions.

To do this, we return to the original decision problem. Kuhn-Tucker analysis tells us that $\mu_1(x_1 - \bar{x}_1) = 0$. In fact if the constraint on good 1 is binding, then $\mu_1 > 0$, and measures the utility value of relaxing the constraint. If the constraint is not binding, $\mu_1 = 0$ and we may solve the first-order conditions (21) with this substitution. Accordingly, let us compare two situations, in one of which the constraint is of such a magnitude as to be binding while in the other it is not. In the latter case, we may write

$$x_i^* = x_i^*(p_1 \ldots p_n, \lambda^*) \ .$$

From the way we have set up the comparison we must indeed have from (22) when the constraint is not binding,

$$x_i^* = x_i(p_1 \ldots p_n, \lambda^*, 0) \ ,$$

assuming that the functions x_i are continuous in μ_1 . Let us expand (22) in Taylor series about the point $(\lambda^*, 0)$. Truncating after terms of the first order we may write approximately,

$$(23) \qquad \begin{aligned} x_1 &\simeq x_1^* + (\lambda - \lambda^*)x_{1*}^{(\lambda)} + \mu_1 x_{1*}^{(\mu_1)} \\ &\vdots \\ x_n &\simeq x_n^* + (\lambda - \lambda^*)x_{n*}^{(\lambda)} + \mu_1 x_{n*}^{(\mu_1)} \ . \end{aligned}$$

Here $x_{i*}^{(\lambda,\mu_1)}$ denotes the derivative of the ith demand function, cast as (22), with respect to either λ or μ_1 , evaluated at * . Now impose on the approximations (23) the demand constraint $x_1 = \bar{x}_1$. Impose also the endowment (M) constraint on both x_i and x_i^* , i=1...n . We obtain, respectively,

$$(24) \qquad \begin{aligned} \bar{x}_1 &= x_1^* + (\lambda - \lambda^*)x_{1*}^{(\lambda)} + \mu_1 x_{1*}^{(\mu_1)} \\ 0 &= (\lambda - \lambda^*) \sum_i x_{i*}^{(\lambda)} p_i + \mu_1 \sum_i x_{i*}^{(\mu_1)} p_i \ . \end{aligned}$$

Define the following quantities:

(25) $$\varepsilon_{1*} = \frac{\sum_i x_{i*}^{(\mu_1)} p_i}{\sum_i x_{i*}^{(\lambda)} p_i}$$

$$-\alpha_{1i}^* = \frac{x_{i*}^{(\mu_1)} - \varepsilon_{1*} x_{i*}^{(\lambda)}}{x_{1*}^{(\mu_1)} - \varepsilon_{1*} x_{1*}^{(\lambda)}} .$$

Solving (24) we may write

(26) $$x_i = x_i^* + \alpha_{1i}^*(x_1^* - \bar{x}_1) , \qquad i=1....n .$$

From (25), we note that $\alpha_{11}^* = -1$ so that $x_1 = \bar{x}_1$ as is obviously desirable. Equation (26) will be approximately true where the constraint $\bar{x}_1$ is binding but is in the neighbourhood of the unconstrained value. We can write more generally,

(27) $$x_i = x_i^* + \alpha_{1i}^*(x_1^* - \bar{x}_1)R(x_1^* - \bar{x}_1) , \qquad i=1....n ,$$

to refer to both constrained and unconstrained situations. In value terms we may define

$$a_{1i}^* = \frac{p_i \alpha_{1i}^*}{p_1} .$$

Corresponding to equations (27) we may write

(28) $$x_i = x_i^* + a_{1i}^* \left(\frac{p_1 x_1^* - p_1 \bar{x}_1}{p_i} \right) R(x_1^* - \bar{x}_1) , \qquad i=1....n$$

with the implied restriction

$$\sum_i a_{1i}^* = 0 .$$

In equation (28) the term $p_1 x_1^* - p_1 \bar{x}_1$ represents the frustrated expenditure on good 1, now available for spending on all other goods. The quantities a_{1i}^* direct this frustrated expenditure into the various goods. In recognition of this, they deserve the name "spillover coefficients". They may be of either sign, reflecting the substitution or complementarity relationships of the goods with good 1. They will also themselves be functions of prices and of M, the endowment. For a more rigorous treatment of such forced substitution, although not invoking spillover coefficients, we refer the reader to D.H. Howard [1977].

The above development can be generalised to a comparison of the notional demands to the case where k designated constraints are known to hold, say the first k. Corresponding to equations (22) we have

$$x_i = x_i(p_1 \dots p_n, \mu_1 \dots \mu_k, \lambda), \qquad i=1\dots n .$$

By arguments similar to those of the univariate case, it follows that the vector of constrained demand functions $\underset{\sim}{x}$ is, in a neighbourhood of the unconstrained position, given by:

$$(29) \quad \underset{\sim}{x} = \underset{\sim}{x}^* + \begin{bmatrix} x_{1*}^{(\mu_1)} \dots & x_{1*}^{(\mu_k)} & x_{1*}^{(\lambda)} \\ \vdots & & \vdots \\ x_{n*}^{(\mu_1)} \dots & x_{n*}^{(\mu_k)} & x_{n*}^{(\lambda)} \end{bmatrix} \begin{bmatrix} x_{1*}^{(\mu_1)} \dots & x_{1*}^{(\mu_k)} & x_{1*}^{(\lambda)} \\ \vdots & & \vdots \\ x_{k*}^{(\mu_1)} \dots & x_{k*}^{(\mu_k)} & x_{k*}^{(\lambda)} \\ \beta^{(1)} \dots & \beta^{(k)} & \sum_i x_{1*}^{(\lambda)} p_i \end{bmatrix}^{-1} \begin{bmatrix} \bar{x}_1 - x_1^* \\ \bar{x}_2 - x_2^* \\ \vdots \\ \bar{x}_k - x_k^* \\ \underset{\sim}{0} \end{bmatrix},$$

where $\beta^{(j)} = \sum_i x_{i*}^{(\mu_j)} p_i , \quad j=1\dots k .$

By use of the partitioned inverse on the RHS of (29), we can write

$$(30) \qquad \underset{\sim}{x} = \underset{\sim}{x}^* + \begin{bmatrix} I_{kk} & 0_{n-k,n-k} \\ & \\ -A_{21}^* & -A_{22}^* \end{bmatrix} \begin{bmatrix} \bar{x}_1 - x_1^* \\ \vdots \\ \bar{x}_k - x_k^* \\ \underset{\sim}{0} \end{bmatrix} .$$

Here A_{21}^*, of order (n-k,k), and A_{22}^*, of order (n-k,n-k), are the generalisation of the physical spillover coefficients (e.g. α_{1i}^*) of the univariate case. We can similarly recast (30) into value terms by defining value spillover coefficients

$$a^*_{ij} = \frac{p_j}{p_i} \alpha^*_{ij} \; ; \qquad i=1...k, \; j=(k+1)...n \; .$$

It must then follow that $\sum_j a^*_{ij} = 1$.

The above generalisation of the case of one constraint presupposes a given set of k constraints known to be binding. Suppose that a different set of constraints were known to be binding. It will be apparent from the form of (30) that spillover coefficients will not be stable in such a contingency, even for those variables which are themselves never binding. Hence no universal representation like (28) exists. The practical implication of this is that application of models incorporating spillover coefficients may be limited to cases where only a few constraints are known to be binding at any time.

So far we have confined our discussion to the problem of deriving a set of demand functions subject to externally imposed constraints. Let us consider now an interdependent set of markets with both buyers and sellers of each type of good. We may now interpret the constraints ($\bar{x}_i$ above) facing demanders of good i as representing the available supplies of this good at prices currently ruling. If these constraints are binding, then the $\bar{x}_i$ are identical with the quantities actually transacted, which we write as q_i . Likewise, from the point of view of suppliers, constraints on their supply may be imposed by the quantities demanded. As before, the ultimate expressions of binding constraints, under the short-side clearing rule, are the quantities actually transacted. From this fact we may obtain equations relating observed quantities (q_i) to the notional demand and supply schedules. Such equations may be regarded as the generalisation of the single market short-side model.

Accordingly, let us suppose that at current prices, the first k goods are supply determined, in the sense that demanders of these goods feel constrained as to their purchases. Denote by q_i, $i=1\ldots n$, the quantities transacted of all goods. Also let x_i^{s*} denote the notional, or unconstrained, supply of good i, and x_i^{d*} the notional demand. Given that the first k goods are supply determined we may write (cf. equation (30) above);

$$(31)\quad \begin{bmatrix} q_{k+1} \\ \vdots \\ q_n \end{bmatrix} = \begin{bmatrix} x_{k+1}^{d*} \\ \vdots \\ x_n^{d*} \end{bmatrix} - A_{21}^{d*} \begin{bmatrix} q_1 - x_1^{d*} \\ \vdots \\ q_k - x_k^{d*} \end{bmatrix} .$$

(It will be noted that the spillover coefficient matrix A_{21}^* of equation (30) has acquired a superscript d, to refer to the demand system.) Transactions in the last (n-k) goods are demand determined, amounting to the notional demand curves corrected for spillover effects from the first k markets, where transacted quantities constitute a constraint upon demanders. We may write equations corresponding to (31) for suppliers. In this case, the last (n-k) goods are demand determined and we can write:

$$(32)\quad \begin{bmatrix} q_1 \\ \vdots \\ q_k \end{bmatrix} = \begin{bmatrix} x_1^{s*} \\ \vdots \\ x_k^{s*} \end{bmatrix} - A_{12}^{s*} \begin{bmatrix} q_{k+1} - x_{k+1}^{s*} \\ \vdots \\ q_n - x_n^{s*} \end{bmatrix} ,$$

where A_{12}^{s*} is a $k \times (n-k)$ matrix of spillover coefficients.

Equation systems (31) and (32) constitute a joint system in the transacted quantities $q_1 \ldots q_n$. We may solve for $q_1 \ldots q_k$ as:

$$(33)\quad \begin{bmatrix} q_1 \\ \vdots \\ q_k \end{bmatrix} = \begin{bmatrix} x_1^{s*} \\ \vdots \\ x_k^{s*} \end{bmatrix} + [I - A_{12}^{s*}A_{21}^{d*}]^{-1} A_{12}^{s*} \left\{ \begin{bmatrix} x_{k+1}^{s*} - x_{k+1}^{d*} \\ \vdots \\ x_n^{s*} - x_n^{d*} \end{bmatrix} - A_{21}^{d*} \begin{bmatrix} x_1^{d*} - x_1^{s*} \\ \vdots \\ x_k^{d*} - x_k^{s*} \end{bmatrix} \right\} .$$

A corresponding equation system exists for the complementary set $q_{k+1} \ldots q_n$.

Equations (33) tell us that although we are in a state of excess demand for the goods in question (1...k), the quantities transacted are not those given by the notional supply schedules (x_i^{s*}). In this respect, the multimarket setting is quite different from the single-market models of chapter 5, where in a state of excess demand transactions are determined by a stable supply schedule. Instead, observed quantities are related to the notional excess demands or supplies for all markets, as well as to the specific notional supply schedule. Each notional supply schedule in (33) must be corrected: (i) For excess supply in the complementary set of goods (here (k+1)...n). This means that more of goods 1...k will now be offered. (ii) For the indirect effect of excess demand in the subset under consideration. At first sight it looks odd that such excess demands should affect actual supplies, the short side. However, the frustrated demand will affect demands for the complementary set (k+1)...n and hence the excess supply of these goods. As pointed out in (i) above, this will in turn react on supplies in markets 1...n, and hence transacted quantities.

Such insights are useful, but we are still some distance from an estimable representation of a multimarket system. We have assumed, for instance, that it is known that the first k (or more generally a designated set) of markets are in a state of excess demand, the remainder in excess supply. If such observable switches are not available, there is as yet no universal representation available. Moreover, every time some market changes from excess demand to excess supply, the reduced-form spillover coefficients of equations like (33) will change. Evidently, much has still to be resolved in the difficult area of the representation and estimation of multimarket disequilibrium models, and we may in the interim have to restrict ourselves to much simpler structures.

In many practical applications there may indeed be only one or at most a few goods which are considered as sometimes binding. There is, for a start, no virtue in applying this sort of calculus to constraints which are always binding. As decision-makers we are bounded in a nutshell, and many such constraints are simply taken for granted as part of the economic environment in which we live. If a constraint is always binding we simply incorporate it, or its numerical value, as a datum or parameter of the demand functions for the goods being studied. Such demand functions correspond to the idea of the "conditional demand function" which has been studied by R. Pollak [1969]. It is worth remarking also that there is a time dimension involved. Some constraints, such as those arising from our educational qualifications, we can do little about in the short run but may be able to overcome in the longer run. But in making up our mind as between bananas and oranges, our educational qualifications, or the income therefrom, is a given datum.

In practice, then, we may find that in discussing the demand for any one good or asset, the number of constraints we have to consider as sometimes binding, sometimes not, is limited in number. When considering an individual's demand for housing, we shall later take as a given parameter (so to speak) his income. Mortgage restraints, however, are in a different category and explicit consideration of spillovers from this source will become necessary. In section 6.4.1 of the present chapter we shall also employ the notion of a spillover coefficient developed in connection with just a single possible constraint.

6.3.2 Aggregation. In §6.3.1 we considered the problem of constrained demand and supply on an individual level. The aggregation process may be subject to several difficulties. In the first place, with regard to the notional demands x_i^* there are the usual problems of obtaining a stable function of prices or other arguments, problems which are common to all aggregation processes. These problems are compounded by a new one, which will be the subject of subsequent discussion. Since the constraints facing each individual will differ, we have the problem of what happens in the aggregate to equations like (28) when the threshold level ($\bar{x}_1$) varies from person to person. Indeed if our context is one of disequilibrium in which the good in question may be exchanged, the list of constraints will differ from agent to agent, and differ over time. However where the aggregation involves two economically quite distinct sorts of agent, the constraints faced by one group may be well preserved in the aggregate. In the case of mortgage rationing for instance, mortgagees and mortgagors are quite distinct and identifiable groups. Aggregation over those who demand mortgages might expect to exhibit the effects of mortgage rationing, if it exists.

Some of the effects of aggregation over differing individual constraints can be seen by considering its effects on the simple constrained demand function (26). Suppose that we have a collection of agents identical in their notional demands for a good (x*). However the constraints they face differ, for reasons which may have nothing to do with their individual demands. (One might think for instance of mortgage institutions viewing individuals as different risks and varying the funds available to each on this basis.) Thus the demand curve facing the individual is:

$$(34) \qquad x = x^* + \alpha_1^*(x_1^* - \bar{x}_1)R(x_1^* - \bar{x}_1) \ ,$$

where the constraint $\bar{x}_1$ on good 1 (say) can be regarded as a random variable over different consumers. We shall imagine that $\bar{x}_1$ is Normal, with mean μ_1 and variance σ_1^2.

Let us consider the expectation of x - this will correspond statistically to the aggregation of a large number of such consumers. In view of the definition of the (0,1)-ramp function R ,

$$\mu_x = E(x) = x^* + \alpha_1^* \int_{-\infty}^{x_1^*} (x_1^* - \bar{x}_1) n(\bar{x}_1; \mu_1, \sigma_1^2) d\bar{x}_1 \, .$$

Using result (42) of chapter 5.6.1, this can be written as

$$(35) \qquad \mu_x = x^* + \alpha_1^*(x_1^* - \mu_1) N(x_1^*; \mu_1, \sigma_1^2) + \frac{\alpha_1^* \sigma_1}{\sqrt{2\pi}} \exp\left[-\frac{1}{2\sigma_1^2}(x_1^* - \mu_1)^2\right] .$$

Equation (35) is the aggregate version of (34). The last term in (35) is a "bias" term of small magnitude. We may write approximately,

$$(35)' \qquad \mu_x = x^* + \alpha_1^*(x_1^* - \mu_1) N(x_1^*; \mu_1, \sigma_1^2) \, .$$

In short, if we replace the individual constraints $\bar{x}_1$ by their mean μ_1 - as a measure of the aggregate constraint - the sharp relationship (34) is replaced by the fuzzy one incorporated in equation (35). Instead of the ramp function R of equation (34), we end up with the cumulative Normal function N of (35)'. Figure 6.2 illustrates.

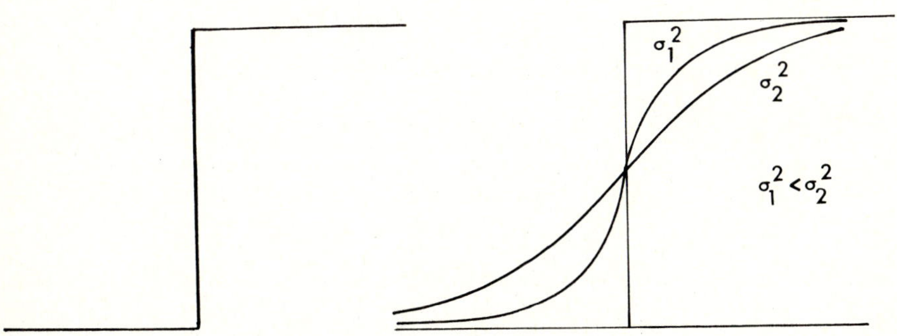

Figure 6.2

As the variance across individuals of the constraint $\sigma_1^2 \to 0$, the individual and aggregate formulations become of the same form. It is interesting to note that fuzzy switches like (b) have been proposed by S. Goldfeld and R.E. Quandt [1972] in other contexts. Suppose in addition that the notional demands, as well as the constraints, vary across individuals. Thus let x* be itself a random variable with mean μ_* (a function of prices and other arguments) and variance σ_* , and is distributed independently of the constraints $\bar{x}_1$. The aggregated version becomes

$$\mu_x = \mu_* + \alpha_1^* E\left[(x_1^* - \mu_1)N(x_1^*; \mu_1, \sigma_1^2)\right] - \frac{\alpha_1^* \sigma_1}{\sqrt{2\pi}} E \exp\left[-\frac{1}{2\sigma_1^2}(x_1^* - \mu_1)^2\right] ,$$

which as a function of μ_* and μ_1 looks even fuzzier, and may indeed involve further bias. In summary, one would expect that the effects of aggregation would be to reduce, perhaps considerably, the sharpness of definition of the constraint involved.

6.4 Application to the Supply Mechanism of Money

The possible role for income Y in addition to the rate of interest as a determinant of the money supply has not been investigated econometrically with the thoroughness which the importance of the point deserves. Discussion has taken place on two possible sources for such an effect. (a) The first is that the public's desired holding of currency (in proportion to demand deposits) may depend on income. It is usually hypothesised that this dependence is negative, on the grounds that people tend to make greater use of cheque accounts with increasing income. On the other hand some empirical evidence suggests the contrary. (b) The second, perhaps more intriguing possibility may operate in the context of the multiple expansion of bank deposits. Textbook accounts suppose that banks are fully loaned up. However it may be that banks are constrained in their supply of loans by a deficient demand for such from the public. A deficiency of this kind has been adduced by N. Kaldor [1970] and others as the reason for the large holdings of excess reserves carried by the banks during the Great Depression. The implication is that such a phenomenon contributes to the variability of the money supply in recent less extreme cycles. Now it if were true that the market for bank loans was always in equilibrium, the supply of money should not depend - point (a) above apart - on income. For the effect of a higher Y should manifest itself in a higher equilibrium interest rate on bank loans. The supply of money would then simply depend upon the (equilibrium) interest rate. But if the market for bank loans were not always in equilibrium, income would exert a direct effect on the supply of money. That is, income as an observed variable would incorporate information about the money supply in addition to interest rates. This we take as the essence of the view of the endogeneity of the money supply referred to above.

We shall examine the second of these possibilities in this section. Let us be more specific. If the rate of interest on bank loans adjusted instantaneously to clear the market, the resulting supply of money would be a function only of the equilibrium rate of interest on bank loans. In other words, determinants of the demand schedules for bank loans would play no role independently of the equilibrium interest rate. Suppose however that bank loan rates were sticky downwards. One can think of several possible reasons why this might be so.

1. In exceptional times (as in the Great Depression?) loan rates may have sunk so low that a further fall would not recoup the risk and administrative cost associated with making new loans.
2. In more normal times there is always a recognition and action lag following, say, a new access of reserves, or changed demand by the public for loans.
3. There may be government or central bank regulations or directions concerning minimum or maximum loan rates.

What is important is the effect of the disequilibria created by this possible stickiness of the bank loan rate. One could argue that any temporary excess reserves created by such a disequilibrium are invested in treasury notes or other short-term marketable assets. Thus even if the composition of bank assets is not continuously an equilibrium one, the net effect is nevertheless that the banking system is always fully loaned up. However if banks do not monitor their reserve positions quite this closely, the banks could hold excess reserves as a result of deficient demand in the market for bank loans. Income levels, as presumed determinants of the demand for bank loans, could then exert an influence on the money supply independently of interest rates. We now develop and test a very simple model of this process.

6.4.1 The Model. Our model is geared towards exhibiting the sort of independent role of income we have just outlined. It is manifestly incomplete as a complete model of the money supply process, for it ignores the role of borrowed reserves, the distinction between time and demand deposits, and a proper demand function for currency. We imagine that reserves R (unborrowed) are available to the banking system. Banks divide their assets between reserves, bonds and bank loans. Given D, demand deposits, the banks' supply of loans is given by the function

(36) $$L^{s*} = \ell(i_\ell,\ i_b,\ k,\ d)D\ ,$$

where: k = required reserve ratio

i_ℓ = rate on bank loans

i_b = rate on bonds

d = Central Bank discount rate.

Its demand for reserves is given by

(37) $$R^{d*} = \phi(i_\ell,\ i_b,\ k,\ d)D\ .$$

Finally leaving aside net worth on the liabilities side of the balance sheet, we suppose that the banks' demand for bonds is given by

(38) $$B^{d*} = b(i_\ell,\ i_b,\ k,\ d)D\ ,\quad \text{where } b = 1 - \ell - \phi.$$

Note that B is in value terms (i.e. the number of bonds divided by the interest rate). The final ingredient of our disequilibrium analysis will be the public's demand function for bank loans $L^d(i_\ell,\ i_b,\ Y)$.

(i) Equilibrium. Before proceeding to disequilibrium aspects a prior task is to verify that the model is properly determined in its equilibrium values. In order to do this, we shall construct a minimal model within which the above schedules and equations may be presumed to be set. Accordingly we designed such a model along lines very similar to the macro-models of part II of D. Patinkin [1965]. There are five objects of study - bonds, loans, demand deposits, hand-to-hand currency and goods. Equilibrium conditions are:

(39) (Loans) $L^{s*}(i_\ell, i_b, k, d, D) = L^d(i_\ell, i_b, Y)$.

(40) (Bonds) $B^{d*}(i_\ell, i_b, k, d, D) = B^{exs}(i_\ell, i_b, Y)$,

where B^{exs} denotes the excess supply function of bonds by the non-bank public together with the government.

(41) (Demand deposits) $D^d(i_\ell, i_b, Y) = D$

(42) (Goods) $Y^d(i_\ell, i_b, Y) = Y$

(43) (Currency) $C_p^d(i_\ell, i_b, Y) = M_o - R^{d*}(i_\ell, i_b, k, d, D)$.

In (43), C_p^d denotes the non-bank demand for hand-to-hand currency. The quantity M_o denotes the stock of outside money, assumed exogenously determined.

In addition to the five equilibrium conditions there are two constraints. First the non-bank private sector's budget constraint:

(44) $D^d + C_p^d + Y^d = (B^{exs} - B) + (L^d - L) + D + Y + C_p$,

where B denotes the value of bonds currently held by the banks. The banks' balance sheet reads:

(45) $L + B + R = D$.

Finally as a matter of definition

(46) $R + C_p = M_o$.

The equilibrium conditions (39)-(43) constitute a set of 5 equations in the 4 endogenous unknowns i_ℓ, i_b, D and Y . However using the constraints (44)-(46) we derive Walras' law for the system as:

(W) $(D^d - D) + (Y^d - Y) = (L^d - L^s) + (B^{exs} - B^d) + (M_o - R^d - C^p_d)$.

It follows that the five equations (39)-(43) are not functionally independent, for by (W) if any four are satisfied so is the fifth. The equilibrium values i_ℓ, i_b, D and Y are therefore - assuming well-behaved supply and demand functions - well determined.

(ii) Disequilibrium. Let us return to the three equations (36)-(38), which are explicit forms for the banks' behavioural functions. Suppose that the banks are not constrained by the public's demand for bank loans. If this is the case, the stationary level of demand deposits D^w (the "warranted" level) is given in terms of R by equality between the demand for reserves as given by (37) and the given available stock R . Thus

(47) $$D^w = \frac{R}{\phi} \ .$$

Suppose however that at the going interest rate, banks are not free to supply all the loans they would like. Our supposition is that interest rates are sticky downwards so that at the existing interest rate $L^d < L^{s*} = \ell D$. Evidently the banks will be left at the instant of decision with an excess of reserves. Some of this quantity will spill over into excess reserves, the rest will be reallocated to bonds. We introduce a spillover coefficient ε_{LR} , which indicates the propensity for banks to divert funds originally intended for loans to excess reserves. Thus an amount ℓD was originally intended for bank loans. The short-fall is $\ell D - L^d$. A proportion ε_{LR} of this is added to the unconstrained demand ϕD to give the constrained demand for reserves.

(48) $$R^{d'} = \phi D + \varepsilon_{LR}(\ell D - L^d) \ .$$

Write $\mu = \mu(i_\ell, i_b, d, k) = \frac{\ell}{\phi}\varepsilon_{LR}$. Equating the constrained demand (48) for reserves with the existing stock R , it follows that when deficient demand for bank loans exists, demand deposits are given by

$$D = \frac{\mu}{1+\mu}\frac{L^d}{\ell} + \frac{1}{1+\mu} D^w ,$$

where D^w was defined above as $\frac{R}{\phi}$. Write $\lambda = \frac{\mu}{1+\mu}$. Thus the (reduced) level of demand deposits is given by

$$D = \lambda\frac{L^d}{\ell} + (1-\lambda)D^w . \tag{49}$$

However, it will be recalled that (49) is applicable only if there is disequilibrium due to deficient demand in the "market" for bank loans. One possible manifestation of this is a falling rate of interest. Recalling the definition of the (0,1)-ramp function R , we can employ $R(i_{\ell t-1} - i_{\ell t})$ as an indicator of disequilibrium deficient demand for bank loans. Hence

$$D = \left[1 - R(i_{\ell t-1} - i_{\ell t})\right]D^w + R(i_{\ell t-1} - i_{\ell t})\left(\lambda\frac{L^d}{\ell} + (1-\lambda)\,D^w\right)$$

$$= (1-\lambda R)D^w + \lambda R\frac{L^d}{\ell} . \tag{50}$$

Equation (50) is our general formula for the expansion of demand deposits. As suggested above, it would be a mistake to take this as the literal basis for a money supply equation; there are some important factors ignored in its derivation. But it does suggest the incorporation of an additional term involving income (via L^d) which comes into play only in times of falling interest rates. It may be too that interest effects on the money supply will differ in such times. But since the sign of expressions like $R\frac{L^d}{\ell}$ is ambiguous with respect to the rate of interest, we have chosen to incorporate only an income effect into our tests.

6.4.2 Empirical Tests.[4] For these tests, we again chose a logarithmic model of the money supply (for similar equations see R. Teigen [1964] and Gibson [1972]). We employed two different interest rates: (i) the banks' prime rate as a direct reflection of loan rates,

(ii) CP, the commercial paper rate as a proxy for bond rates. We found the prime rate to be disappointing, very possibly because of its infrequent changes. On the other hand the rate on 4-6 month commercial paper gave a much more sensible basic supply equation and was accordingly retained for the subsequent testing. We decided to retain just the one rate rather than work with both, retaining the commercial paper rate as the sole interest rate appearing in the supply function for money. Following Teigen and Gibson, we employed as an estimate for k the ratio of required reserves to demand deposits (the "weighted average reserve requirement").

The basic supply equation, fitted by 2SLS for the period 1957 I to 1971 III is:

$$\begin{aligned} \log M_t = {} & \underset{(1.908)}{0.535} + \underset{(6.929)}{0.135} \log CP_t - \underset{(-2.674)}{0.063} \log d_t + \underset{(57.055)}{1.070} \log R_t \\ & - \underset{(-16.312)}{1.215} \log k_t + \underset{(4.458)}{0.016}\, S1_t + \underset{(4.324)}{0.016}\, S2_t \\ & - \underset{(-0.448)}{0.002}\, S3_t \end{aligned}$$

$$s^2 = 0.0012\ , \qquad V.N. = 0.310\ .$$

All coefficients are as expected in sign and significance, but the V.N. ratio is low, suggesting some missing variable(s).

We now introduce[5] our disequilibrium variable $R(CP_{t-1} - CP_t)Y_t$. Since both CP_t and Y_t are endogenous, it would be incorrect merely to add this variable to the list of regressors. Following the discussion of chapter 5, we tried two alternative estimation techniques. In the first, we regarded the term $R_t Y_t$ as a new variable. In stage one this variable is regressed on all the exogenous variables; the fitted value so obtained is employed in stage two in place of $R_t Y_t$. Unfortunately the fit of $R_t Y_t$ to the exogenous variables in stage one is very poor, with $R^2 = 0.478$. The fitted value is therefore a poor instrument for the natural variable. Nevertheless we present the results of this 2SLS procedure.

$$\log M_t = \underset{(2.615)}{0.625} + \underset{(8.043)}{0.133} \log CP_t - \underset{(-3.057)}{0.061} \log d_t + \underset{(67.243)}{1.078} \log R_t$$

$$- \underset{(-19.601)}{1.248} \log k_t + \underset{(5.495)}{0.017}\, S1_t + \underset{(4.415)}{0.014}\, S2_t$$

$$- \underset{(-1.567)}{0.005}\, S3_t - \underset{(-4.509)}{0.002}\, R_t Y_t$$

$$s^2 = 0.0011 , \qquad V.N. = 0.367 .$$

The coefficient of $R_t Y_t$ is perversely negative and significant, and the overall fit has hardly improved.

More sensible results are obtained with a second possible approach to the estimation problem, the "naive 2SLS" method of chapter 5. Instead of regressing the entire variable $R_t Y_T$ on the exogenous variables in the first stage, we regressed first $\hat{CP}_t$ to obtain the fitted value CP_t and also Y_t to obtain $\hat{Y}_t$. In the second stage regression the variable employed was $R(CP_{t-1} - \hat{CP}_t)\hat{Y}_t$. This procedure does in general yield inconsistent estimates. However sampling experiments in chapter 5 suggested that it has favourable M.S.E. properties. The results using this approach to the estimation problem are:

$$\log M_t = \underset{(1.881)}{0.536} + \underset{(5.965)}{0.135} \log CP_t - \underset{(-2.570)}{0.063} \log d_t + \underset{(18.569)}{1.069} \log R_t$$

$$- \underset{(-12.378)}{1.213} \log k_t + \underset{(4.115)}{0.016}\, S1_t + \underset{(4.068)}{0.016}\, S2_t - \underset{(-0.430)}{0.002}\, S3_t$$

$$- \underset{(0.020)}{0.00065}\, R_t Y_t$$

$$s^2 = 0.0011 , \qquad V.N. = 0.352 .$$

The coefficient of $R_t Y_t$ though now of the right sign, is quite insignificant. Our results therefore suggest that over the period considered banks have managed their reserves fairly closely. Consequently there appears to be no independent role for income in the money supply function arising from deficient demand for bank loans. Income appears in the supply function for money directly only through a possible effect from the demand for currency. Apart from this, it should not be inferred that income has no effect. Such effect as it has, however, will operate via the equilibrium rate of interest and will be captured by specifying the supply of money function in terms of the interest rate alone.

6.5 Application to the Commercial Loans Market

The existence of credit rationing by commercial banks at certain times has long featured in the public consciousness of economic processes. There have been several attempts[6] to verify or measure the extent of the rationing of short-term credit by banks. In the present section we shall briefly survey two of these attempts, characterised by a more structured approach to the problem of testing for disequilibrium. Both are studies of the market for short-term commercial or business loans rather than of the entire spectrum of bank lending.

We shall begin with the more recent of the two, the Canadian study by J-J Laffont and R. Garcia mentioned already in section 6.1. They test a variety of disequilibrium structures corresponding to the recursive and truly simultaneous models of the short-side dynamics discussed in chapter 5. As a price variable they employ the banks' prime rate, in the absence of any data on more representative business loans. In the supply equation, this price variable appears as a two-period Almon distributed lag of the prime rate. In the demand equation, the price variable appears as the differential of the prime rate over an index of the price of alternative short-term financing for firms (taken as the 90-day rate on finance company paper). A variety of exogenous variables are employed in both the demand and supply equations. We shall not therefore reproduce these equations in detail, but will confine discussion to a somewhat schematic representation of the essential features of the Laffont/Garcia models. For our purposes, most interest will lie in their "quantitative models" which correspond to the E.F.C. model of chapter 5 of this study. Within this class, they distinguish and test two possibilities. In discussing these, we separate out P to refer here to the prime rate, although as noted above the price variable occurs in different forms as between the demand and supply equations.

(i) The first form corresponds to the truly simultaneous EFC model. Laffont/Garcia call this the "Fair-Jaffee" (F-J) model.

$$\text{(51)(i)} \quad \text{(a)} \quad D_t = \alpha_o X_t + \alpha_1 P_t + u_t$$

$$\text{(b)} \quad S_t = \beta_o Z_t + \beta_1 P_t + v_t \qquad \text{(X,Z exogenous)}$$

$$\text{(c)} \quad Q_t = \min(D_t, S_t)$$

$$\text{(d)} \quad P_t - P_{t-1} = \gamma_1(D_t - S_t) \qquad \text{if } D_t - S_t > 0$$

$$= \gamma_2(D_t - S_t) \qquad \text{if } D_t - S_t < 0 \, ,$$

with $\gamma_1 \neq \gamma_2$ (see section 6.1 of this study).

(ii) The second form respecifies timing relationships. The flavour of this approach may perhaps best be conveyed by recasting the original Laffont/Garcia notation, writing (c), (d) as above but

$$\text{(51)(ii)} \quad \text{(a)} \quad D_t = \alpha_o X_t + \alpha_1 P_{t-1} + u_t$$

$$\text{(b)} \quad S_t = \beta_o Z_t + \beta_1 P_{t-1} + v_t \, .$$

The interpretation is that D and S during period t are supposed to depend upon P as at the end of the previous period. D_t and S_t then help to determine P at the end of period t , as P_t. In the (F-J) specification (i) above D_t and S_t react back to help in forming P_t which is consequently reinterpreted as the price <u>during</u> period t rather than being located at the end of the period. In the L-G version, therefore, P_t, D_t, S_t are not simultaneously determined and this indeed corresponds to the "recursive" model discussed in chapter 5.4.2. It is not clear whether these differences in specification are reflected (as they should be) in differing ways of measuring the observations.

Each of the two possible specifications implies a different observable system. For the F-J version,

$$(52)(i) \quad Q_t = \alpha_o X_t + \alpha_1 P_t - \frac{1}{\gamma_1}(P_t - P_{t-1})R(P_t - P_{t-1}) + u_t$$

$$Q_t = \beta_o Z_t + \beta_1 P_t + \frac{1}{\gamma_2}(P_t - P_{t-1})(1 - R(P_t - P_{t-1})) + v_t ,$$

where R is the (0,1)-ramp function. The L-G model yields

$$(52)(ii) \quad Q_t = \alpha_o X_t + \alpha_1 P_{t-1} - \frac{1}{\gamma_1}(P_t - P_{t-1})R(P_t - P_{t-1}) + u_t$$

$$Q_t = \beta_o Z_t + \beta_1 P_{t-1} + \frac{1}{\gamma_2}(P_t - P_{t-1})(1 - R(P_t - P_{t-1})) + v_t .$$

Laffont and Garcia also set up the model discussed in chapter 5.1.1 where no sample separation of any kind is available. They report very poor results with this model. Better results were obtained from the more informative models (52)(i) and (ii), which were fitted using both 2SLS and maximum-likelihood. The conclusions in respect of the disequilibrium behaviour are similar with both specifications (i) and (ii), although the more essentially simultaneous model (i) performed a little better than (ii). They tested $\frac{1}{\gamma_1} = 0$ and $\frac{1}{\gamma_2} = 0$. The adjustment parameter $\frac{1}{\gamma_2}$ was significantly different from zero, but the hypothesis $\frac{1}{\gamma_1} = 0$ could not be rejected. This suggests that "most of the period corresponds to either equilibrium or excess supply and that the price adjustment process is much faster upward than downward" (p.1197). Earlier (chapter 3) we noted that the test $\frac{1}{\gamma} = 0$ was rather arbitrary and this feature is indeed apparent from Table I of the Laffont-Garcia study. It would be interesting to compute the implied PAMEQ parameters μ_1 and μ_2. This is unfortunately not possible from the form of their results.

The Laffont/Garcia study follows very closely the methodology of the original Fair/Jaffee study and the commentators thereon. An earlier study for the U.S. by D.M. Jaffee [1971] employs a less structured disequilibrium apparatus. Instead of estimating separate demand and supply equations and using the short-side model, Jaffee works with the demand function alone, writing the quantity actually observed as

$$L = L^d(1 - b_3 H) . \tag{53}$$

Here b_3 is a parameter and H is a proxy for the existence of credit rationing. For instance, in terms of the strict short-side model we might write:

$$L = L^d\left(1 - \frac{L^d - L}{L^d} R(L^d - L)\right) ,$$

which has the form of equation (53). However a suitable proxy might not necessitate the rigid short-side clearing pattern. Jaffee uses for H various measures based on the proportion of loans granted to "risk-free" customers, these being in practice defined as the loans made at the prime rate. The idea is that in times of stringent credit availability, banks will ration their credit according to the risk status of customers.

The equation (53) determining loans - with suitable substitutions for L^d - is estimated in conjunction with equations determining the loan rate, r_L. Define the rate r_L^* as the banks' long-run desired level for the commercial loan rate. This is specified as depending on the yield on treasury bills and variables representing the imputed liquidity yield on alternatives to commercial loans. Then

$$\Delta r_L = g + h(r_L^* - r_{L,-1}) , \tag{54}$$

where g and h may be variable, depending upon changes in the Federal Reserve discount rate. The unobservable r_L^* may be eliminated by use of the proxy relationship:

(55) $$H = a_o + a_1(r_L^* - r_L) + \varepsilon .$$

There is a certain resemblance in equations (53)-(55) to the PAMEQ specification working in conjunction with a quantity clearing hypothesis. But there are some differences. The variable r_L^* is not to be interpreted here as an imputed market equilibrium - it represents a "personal equilibrium" in the sense described in chapter 1.4. Note also that in general L never attains L^d. Suppose for instance $H = \frac{L_1}{L_1 + L_2}$, where L_1 = risk-free loans at the prime rate and L_2 denotes the rest. Evidently $h \leq H < 1$, where h denotes the attained minimum of H, certainly greater than zero. Thus from equation (53),

$$L^d(1-b_3) < L \leq L^d(1-h\,b_3) < L^d ,$$

so that L never attains L^d. There is always rationing in some amount, and the influence of the Jaffee/Modigliani concept of "equilibrium rationing" (see our chapter 1.3) is manifest. It is this special feature which enables Jaffee to avoid some of the awkward discontinuities of models like the short-side specification.

In his empirical work, Jaffee found that the credit rationing variable was insignificant in the aggregate equation for loans based on (53), and the interest rate coefficient for loan demand was insignificant. In respect of rationing, this is the same negative conclusion as obtained by Laffont and Garcia with Canadian data. The significance of the interest-rate coefficient, however, differs between the two studies. Jaffee uses ordinary least squares to estimate what is essentially a reduced-form equation for bank loans. It may be that the use of structural-form methods would better identify the interest-rate coefficient in the demand equation. In summary neither of the two studies surveyed in this section supports the existence of credit rationing in the market for existing loans.

This conclusion is somewhat at odds with a variety of more informal or circumstantial evidence in favour of credit rationing. Neither study can be called conclusive and more work in the area would be most welcome.

Footnotes to Chapter 6

[1]Given now that different adjustment parameters apply in each regime it may be unduly restrictive to suppose that the disturbance term has the same variance in either regime.

[2]Consider, for instance the relationship between $\frac{d}{dt}\left(\frac{U}{L}\right)$ and $\frac{d}{dt}\left(\frac{U}{L^*}\right)$. We may write locally

$$\frac{d}{dt}\left(\frac{U}{L}\right) = \frac{d}{dt}\left(\frac{U}{L^*}\right) + \alpha^* \frac{L^*}{L}\left(\frac{\dot{L}^*}{L^*} - \frac{\dot{L}}{L}\right) .$$

The second term of the RHS is small in relation to the first. Hence $\frac{U}{L} \simeq \frac{U}{L^*} + C$ where the constant C can be absorbed into the constant of the Phillips curve.

[3]The deluge of male convicts in the 1820's was a disaster for the ratio of males to females in early Australian settlement. Suffering already from an imbalance of about 1.8 males to 1 female, the ratio soared in 1828 to 3.33 to 1. Emancipated convicts and "merinos" alike were unable to secure wives and promiscuity, prostitution and homosexuality were rife. Most of the early emigration of women and girls was entrusted to John Marshall. When (as usually happened) he was unable to fill his ships with respectable and healthy women, he resorted to the streets and poorhouses of England. According to Governor Arthur of Van Dieman's Land (Tasmania) they were "among the most abandoned creatures that could have disgraced the streets of the metropolis" (quoted in M. Cannon [1971]).

[4]The data sources for this project are as reported for the study of chapter 4, either from the U.S. Commerce Department's Survey of Current Business or else from various issues of the Federal Reserve Bulletin.

[5]According to (45) we should also incorporate the switch R_t into the coefficients of D^W, i.e. into the coefficients of the basic equation like (46). This involves estimation problems, since the list of regressors is thereby doubled. Our feeling was that simply adding the term involving income, namely $R_t Y_t$, as an additional regressor to the basic equation (46) would prove sufficient to test for the presence of the disequilibrium income effect.

[6]See the survey in D.M. Jaffee [1971].

CHAPTER SEVEN

THE HOUSING MARKET

Disequilibrium econometrics has not yet advanced to the stage where a series of interlocking markets can be examined in regard to the effect of disequilibrium in one or more upon the remainder. While we recognise this as a goal, many practical applications will have to remain content with a more *ad-hoc* approach to such problems of interdependence. Typically these approaches involve the use of proxy variables to represent indirectly the impact of disequilibrium in associated markets upon the market actually being studied. But although the *ad-hoc* character of these procedures must be recognised, the econometrics involved may be improved by the insights as to specification and estimation of the kind discussed in chapters five and six. We illustrate some of these considerations in the present chapter.

To give the discussion some unified economic interest, we have chosen to discuss different aspects of the housing market. Substantive interest in this context arises from the possible existence of mortgage rationing and the effect thereof on market dynamics for both new and used housing. In addition, the housing market is a natural place to study certain propositions of capital theory which depend upon the existence of flexible prices. In this way there is a link with the more general body of thought, characteristic of the "Keynesian reinterpretation", which views disequilibrium states as a manifestation of prices which are not in fact flexible. Accordingly our analysis in section 7.2 will be devoted not only to the existence or effect of mortgage rationing, but also to an examination of the relative role of price and quantity adjustments in the housing market.

7.1 New Housing Starts: The Fair Analysis

In their pioneering article on the short-side model, R.C. Fair and D.M. Jaffee [1972] applied a variant of this model in a study of new housing starts in the U.S. The model is simultaneous, but not quite on all fours with those considered in chapter five. For the rationing variable is represented by a proxy, which is nevertheless simultaneously determined with quantities. Similar equations were incorporated by Fair [1971] in his econometric model of the U.S. and we shall follow the exposition in that volume.

The demand HS^d for new housing starts is assumed to be a function of: (i) Population growth and trend income, both of which are approximated by a time trend. (ii) The number of houses in existence or under construction in the previous period. In the regressions, the effect of this stock variable is represented by $\sum_{i=1}^{t-1} HS_i$, the number of actual starts prior to t. The cumulative depreciation or destruction of older houses is absorbed into the trend term. (iii) The mortgage rate[1] lagged two periods, rM_{t-2}. (iv) A variable representing the number of working days per month (W_t). (v) Eleven seasonal dummy variables (DI), the study being on a monthly basis.

The physical supply of new starts is assumed never to be binding. On the other hand, there may be an implied constraint on new starts created by the limited availability of mortgage funds. Denote by HS_t^{FS} the "warranted" level of new starts implied by the current availability of mortgage finance. Write

$$HS_t^{FS} = (a_o + a_1 t)MORT_t^s .$$

This is then approximated as $a_o' + a_1' t + a_2' MORT_t^s$. Here $MORT_t^s$ indicates the availability of new mortgage funds at existing interest rates. It is assumed that the debt:equity composition of investment in housing exhibits a long-term increase. The flow of new mortgage money depends upon: (i) Lagged deposit flows into Savings and Loan Associations (SLA) and Mutual Savings Banks, the principal sources of mortgage finance in the U.S. Best results were achieved using a 6-month moving average of the sum of these two flows, lagged one month (denoted $DSF6_{t-1}$). (ii) Lagged borrowings by the SLA from the Federal Home Loan Bank (DHF). A 3-month moving average lagged two months gave best results (denoted DHF3). (iv) rM_{t-1}. (v) W_t. (vi) The seasonal dummies.

Actual housing starts are, in the Fair analysis, determined as the minimum of demand, and the level warranted by the availability of finance. Thus

$$(1) \qquad HS_t = \min(HS_t^d, HS_t^{FS}) .$$

Finally it is assumed that mortgage interest rates are related to starts by

$$(2) \qquad \Delta rM_t = q(HS_t^d - HS_t^{FS}) .$$

Equations (1) and (2) mean that we can write

$$(3)\ (a) \qquad HS_t = HS_t^d - \frac{1}{q}(\Delta rM_t)R(\Delta rM_t) + \zeta_{1t}$$

$$(b) \qquad HS_t = HS_t^{FS} + \frac{1}{q}(\Delta rM_t)[1 - R(\Delta rM_t)] + \zeta_{2t} ,$$

where as usual R is the (0,1)-ramp function. Equations (3)(a) and (b) are evidently of the same general form as those discussed in chapter five. The simultaneity problem caused by the appearance of rM_t on the RHS of (3), together with (2), should be noted.

In his 1971 treatment, Fair assumes that the errors ζ_{1t} and ζ_{2t} are serially correlated. He estimates equations (3)(a) and (b) taking into account the cross-equation equality restrictions on the coefficients of the nonlinear terms together with the possibility of serial correlation in the residuals. On the other hand the possible simultaneity bias discussed above is noted but not treated. Results for the period June 1959 - December 1969 were:

$$\text{(3) (a)} \quad HS_t = \sum_{I=1}^{11} \hat{d}_I DI_t + \underset{(4.63)}{2.70}\, W_t + \underset{(2.46)}{112.95} - \underset{(-2.27)}{0.0709} \sum_{i=1}^{t-1} HS_i$$

$$+ \underset{(2.31)}{8.84}\, t - \underset{(-1.54)}{0.127}\, rM_{t-2} - \underset{(-2.81)}{0.412}\, \Delta rM_t R(\Delta rM_t) ,$$

$$\hat{\rho} = \underset{(17.54)}{0.841} \qquad s^2 = 8.98 \qquad R_\Delta^2 = 0.790 .$$

$$\text{(b)} \quad HS_t = \sum_{I=1}^{11} \hat{d}'_I DI_t + \underset{(4.42)}{2.84}\, W_t - \underset{(-1.75)}{49.22} - \underset{(-2.63)}{0.164}\, t + \underset{(8.07)}{0.0541}\, DSF6_{t-1}$$

$$+ \underset{(5.27)}{0.0497}\, DHF3_{t-2} + \underset{(2.67)}{0.100}\, RM_{t-1}$$

$$+ 0.412\, \Delta rM_t [1 - R(\Delta rM_t)] ,$$

$$\hat{\rho} = \underset{(6.64)}{0.507} \qquad s^2 = 8.30 \qquad R_\Delta^2 = 0.822 .$$

Here $\hat{\rho}$ denotes the estimate of the first-order serial correlation coefficient, and R_Δ^2 measures the proportion of the variance of changes in HS_t explained by the equation. We do not reproduce the actual seasonal coefficients d and d'. The signs of the mortgage rationing variable are as expected and are significant.

In their 1972 paper, Fair and Jaffee reestimate these equations without the seasonal variables, using standard nonlinear two-stage least squares and ignoring possible serial correlation. They found that the rationing variable was again significant, but since the relevant cross-equation constraint was not taken into account, the coefficient of the rationing variable differed between the two equations. We can take all these results in support of an impact of mortgage rationing on the market for new houses. As a note of caution, however, G.S. Maddala and F.D. Nelson [1974] reworked the same data using maximum-likelihood methods similar to those described for the EFC model in chapter 5. The results were much less favourable to the above conclusion.

7.2 The Market for Existing Houses

To complement the analysis of new housing starts in section 7.1, it is natural to move on to consider the dynamics of the market for existing houses. Quite apart from their intrinsic interest, the movements of house prices are of wider significance because of the light they may throw on the transmission mechanisms of monetary or fiscal policy. Common to both "portfolio" theorists and monetarists has been the view that policy actions affect initially the price of existing financial and durable assets. If the prices of durable assets rise above their physical reproduction cost the result is a stimulus to the output of the construction industries with income- and employment-creating effects becoming pervasive throughout the economy. Suppose, for instance, that there is an open-market purchase by the central bank. Monetarists would claim that the resulting increase in money would in itself raise the price of durable assets. Portfolio theorists, or "post-Keynesians" would claim that the same effect results from the general decrease in interest rates, both as a substitution effect and a wealth effect. This has been expressed by Warren L. Smith:

> "... With the expected yield on a unit of real capital unchanged, the decline in the yields of financial assets and on the more favourable terms on which new debt can be issued, the balance sheets of households and businesses will be thrown out of equilibrium. The adjustment toward a new equilibrium will take the form of a sale of existing financial assets and the issuance of new debt to acquire real capital and claims thereto. This will raise the price of existing units of real capital - or equity claims against these units - relative to the (initially unchanged) cost of producing new units, thereby opening up a gap between desired and actual stocks of capital, a gap that will gradually be closed by the production of new capital goods. This stock adjustment approach is readily applicable, with some variation to suit the circumstances, to the demand for a wide variety of both business and consumer capital - including plant and equipment, inventories, residential construction, and consumer durable goods."
>
> Smith [1969]

Supplementary to the operations of the price mechanism just described, there may be a credit availability effect, reflecting imperfections in the market for funds needed to finance the purchase of existing assets and the construction of new ones. Thus if interest rates do not immediately move to clear the market for funds, an open-market purchase may signal also an increase in the availability of credit and hence have a direct effect on decisions to purchase and invest.

The study of the housing market, in particular, and of the transmission mechanisms just referred to in general, has been hampered by the unavailability of data on the market prices of existing (rather than new) capital goods. Thus students (e.g. R.J. Bowden [1975]). of the dynamics of the housing market have usually relied on casual empiricism as a basis for their model building. Likewise, studies of the transmission of monetary and fiscal impulses have had to treat the prices of existing physical assets as unobservable variables to be eliminated by a process of substitution (e.g. A. Ando [1974]). Because direct tests are not available, the power of such testing procedures is diminished.

For a number of years, the Real Estate Institute of Western Australia (REIWA) has been keeping a monthly record of the prices and numbers of residential properties sold in the Perth urban area through the Institute's multiple listing bureau. The quality of this data has improved through time to the point where it can be utilised for serious econometric work. A more detailed account of its nature and quality is given in the Data Appendix to this chapter. We shall employ this data to tackle the study of the dynamics of the market for existing houses and to test some of the propositions associated with the views of the transmission mechanism outlined above. In connection with the latter, there are two links in the chain connecting changes in policy with resulting effects on construction activity. The first link embodies the effect of arguments such as incomes, rates of interest and monetary variables on the demand for houses and hence on prices and transactions in existing houses. The second link is the effect of the relationship between the price of existing houses and construction costs upon housing starts. The first link is studied in §7.2.1, which presents some basic theory, and §7.2.2, which details empirical results. The second link is explored in §7.2.3. Section 7.2.4 summarises the findings of the study.

7.2.1 Prices and Transactions: The Model. It is useful to start by imagining a representative individual defined, as is often the case, as Collective Man, the distillation of the aggregate effect of the thousands of individual decisions that underlie the market. Write W as his wealth, and H as the part which he is willing to devote to housing, considered as an asset. The yield in owning a house can be considered as having two components. The first is the implicit service yield. Most recent studies on durable goods recognise this as part of the return from holding goods (in the context of the housing market see e.g. J.H. Kalchbrenner [1972]). Write P as the price of a representative house and S as its service price, or the imputed value of its services. The service yield we then write as $\frac{S}{P}$. The service price S can be imagined as moving to clear the "dual" market for housing services (the "dual-market" hypothesis). Thus it will depend upon nominal income Y and upon demographic variables (such as marriages, or the age-structure of the population, or immigration) which bear on the number of heads for which shelter must be found. The second element to the yield on owning a house is the expected rate of inflation of house prices (π). Casual empiricism suggests that the very high rate of increase in house prices in the early 'seventies led to a significant inflow of speculative funds to the market, motivated by the expectation of further increases. Combining the two yield elements, we might write:

$$(4) \qquad H = \Phi(i,\pi,\frac{S}{P}, \ldots)W .$$

Here i represents either or both the yields on alternative assets or the cost of mortgage funds, both elements of the individual's portfolio in addition to housing. Of course, these two yields ought to be separately represented, even though the sign of their partial effects is the same, but both institutional practices and data limitations in the application at hand force the use of just one interest rate.

Given, now, H as determined by the preceding exposition, we can define an equilibrium price for the existing stock (N) of houses as

$$(5) \qquad P^* = \frac{H}{N} .$$

Thus (using lower-case letters for proportional changes),

$$(6) \qquad p^* = \Delta \log P^* = \Delta \log \Phi + \Delta \log W - n ,$$

where $n = \Delta \log N \simeq \frac{N}{N_{-1}} - 1$.

We come now to the proxy for S, the service price of houses, both rented and owner-occupied. We write

$$(7) \qquad \Delta \log S = \gamma_o + \gamma_1 y + \gamma_2 (dv-n) .$$

Here $y = \Delta \log Y$ (incomes) and the variable $dv = \Delta \log DV$, where DV is a demographic variable representing the number of families for whom shelter must be found. The variable DV-N thus represents the supply-demand imbalance in the dual market for housing services, and dv-n its proportional change.

Up until now we have omitted the possible influence of credit rationing, i.e. the influence of a persistent imbalance in the demand and supply of mortgage finance. Let us reconsider the basic equation (4). Write $\Phi = m + e$. Here m represents the mortgage content and e the owners' equity in the desired housing stock. The demand for new mortgages would then be given by:

$$NM^d = mW - M_{-1} ,$$

where M_{-1} denotes the value of mortgages already outstanding. However at current rates of interest, the institutions may not be willing or able to supply NM^d, but a smaller amount NM^s. Naturally such a contingency might be expected to reduce the effective demand for housing (see e.g. D. Tucker [1968], also chapter 8 of this study). However it will also alter the debt:equity ratio for investment in housing. As finance becomes tighter, institutions will usually insist on a higher equity component for a purchase agreement. Thus the effective flow of new demand is not reduced directly in proportion to the shortcoming in available finance. Another way of making the same point is in terms of the spillover coefficients discussed in chapter 6.3.1. Rationing of mortgages may induce a redistribution of notional demand away from other purchases of goods and services (such as motor cars or other durable goods), towards improving the owner's equity in the prospective house purchase. Accordingly we modify equation (4) above to:

$$(8) \qquad H = f(NM^d - NM^s)\phi W ,$$

and assume that f can be locally approximated by:

$$(9) \qquad f(NM^d - NM^s) = \exp(-\lambda(NM^d - NM^s)R(NM^d - NM^s)) ,$$

where R is the (0,1)-ramp function.

Thus when $NM^d < NM^s$, $f(\cdot) = 1$ and the unrestricted equation (4) applies. Where $NM^d > NM^s$, H as defined by (8) will become increasingly restricted by the availability of finance. (Note on the other hand, that the representation will become increasingly poor as $NM^d >> NM^s$, for H can obviously never approach zero; thus in using (9) we implicitly suppose only moderate levels of rationing.) Combining (8) and (9) we can now write

$$(10) \qquad \Delta \log H = -\lambda\Delta(NM^d - NM^s)R(NM^d - NM^s) + \Delta \log \phi + \Delta \log W \; .$$

Being more in the nature of an administered, rather than a demand-determined price, the mortgage rates of the principal lending institutions in W.A. move only sporadically (rather like the U.S. trading bank prime rate). We cannot therefore expect to base a sample separation into regimes of excess demand and excess supply for mortgages on observed movements in interest rates. We have therefore to establish a proxy for the rationing variable $(NM^d - NM^s)R(NM^d - NM^s)$. Most first-mortgage finance in W.A. comes from three sources, the (permanent) building societies, the savings banks, and the insurance companies. Smaller amounts come from such sources as finance companies, the trading banks, from the state-operated Housing Commission, and from private sources. A complete approach might attempt to model the mortgage market together with the market for new and existing houses. An estimate of the excess demand for mortgages at any point in time might then be attempted. Unfortunately such an approach is not feasible with existing data. However, since March 1973, REIWA has kept records of the number of agreements fallen through for lack of finance. The typical pattern for a sale is for agreement to be reached between purchaser and vendor, which allows about 30 days for the purchaser to find mortgage finance. If he does not succeed in doing so, the agreement becomes void and the sale has fallen through. Clearly the percentage of sales falling through at any point in time would be a good index of the excess demand for finance. Although the series itself is not long enough for our regression purposes, the obvious step was to employ it to validate other proposed indices of financial stringency available over a longer period.

The variable we eventually decided to use was the mortgages: free assets ratio of the savings banks (SMFA). If this is very high, the implication is that the margin for writing up new mortgages is small. We found that with the exception of one outlier, there was a general positive relationship between SMFA and the percentage of sales falling through, which was especially marked at high values of both. High values of SMFA would exclude the outlier referred to, and isolate all the high fall-through figures. Although the figure of 90.0 appeared from a visual comparison of the two series to be an appropriate critical point, we decided to try a range of critical values C, namely 0.80, 0.85 and 0.90. That is, the switch variable involved was considered to be SMFA.R(SMFA - C), for various values of C .

In two recent papers (Bowden [1975], [1978] and also chapter 8, below), this author has noted that the market for existing houses is characterised by imperfect information as to ruling prices and the availability of suitable prospects, on the part of both buyers and sellers. This implies that clearing in the market may be less than instantaneous. The problem of representation can be conveniently handled with the PAMEQ approach. Recall that P* was defined as the price level that would equate the demand for houses with the stock (N), given at any point in time. We define our price adjustment mechanism as:

(11) $\log P = \mu \log P_{-1} + (1-\mu) \log P^* .$

In terms of proportional changes,

(12) $p = \mu p_{-1} + (1-\mu)p^*$.

Combining equations (4)-(12), with the specification for the switch variable, yields a single equation derived in terms of a portfolio approach, explaining p, the proportional or percentage change in house prices. The basic form - with lags as yet unspecified - is:

(13) $$p = \beta_o + \beta_1 p_{-1} + \beta_2 \Delta\pi + \beta_3 \Delta i + \beta_4 y + \beta_5 dv + \beta_6 n + \beta_7 \frac{\Delta M3}{PN + M3} + \beta_8 \, \Delta(SMFA\ RF(SMFA - C)) + \text{seasonals} .$$

Equation (13) is cast in terms of percentage changes. The difficulty in obtaining significant coefficients with such a formulation is well known. It is, however, forced on us by the unavailability of wealth figures for W.A. We chose instead to cast the equation in terms of proportionate changes in wealth, for which better proxy variables might be available. In this respect, the variable M3 denotes here a broad definition of liquid assets. The expression $\frac{\Delta M3}{PN + M3}$ can be written $\frac{\Delta M3}{M3} \cdot \frac{M3}{PN + M3}$. The term $\frac{\Delta M3}{M3}$ serves as the basic proxy for proportional changes in wealth. However the effect of this will be larger if $\frac{M3}{PN + M3}$ is larger, that is if the composition of wealth is currently more liquid. The variable $\frac{\Delta M3}{PN + M3}$ therefore reflects both composition and magnitude effects. With regard to the coefficients of (13), *a-priori* considerations suggest that β_o , β_1 could be of either sign[2]; $\beta_2, \beta_4, \beta_5, \beta_7 \geq 0$; and $\beta_3, \beta_6, \beta_8 \leq 0$.

It will be noted that an equation like (13) can have an alternative interpretation in terms of partial adjustment to a desired stock of services from housing. In other words, a stock adjustment mechanism will yield a final estimating equation of rather similar form to that derived above.

Our analysis has so far been confined to the determination of prices. In the absence of a satisfactory theory of transactions, we simply assumed that the determinants of prices are also those of transactions. That this is incomplete as a theory of transactions volume is evident from comparison with the share market, where volume increases may accompany both sharp rises and falls in the market. However the history of price movements in the W.A. real estate market has not included periods of sudden price declines, and the regressions do turn out to yield some rather interesting insights into the question of transactions volume.

7.2.2 Empirical Results. We turn now to the empirical implementation of equation (13). Expectations π are expectations of the percentage change in prices and were generated in terms of static, adaptive and extrapolative mechanisms. As reported earlier we tried several values for the critical point C in the credit-rationing variable. Of the 28 observations available on SMFA, 6 were in the range 90.0 and above, 13 in the range 85 and above; the median value was 82.34. As a general rule concerning lags, we assumed that in defining prices holding during quarter t, wealth measured at the end of period $t-1$ was relevant. Thus π, i and M3 are (unless otherwise stated) dated from or at the end of the preceding quarter. For the price and transaction figures, the average of the three monthly figures for the quarter was taken; quarterly observations were necessary to conform with data for incomes, monetary variables and the rate of interest. For the income variable we employed the official W.A. average weekly earnings index (AWE, or in percentage-change form, awe). Since this reflects movements in awards, rather than actual earnings it may be both an imperfect and lagged indication of the changes in actual incomes. Finally for the demographic variable dv we used the number of people in the 15-24 age group. As (13) indicates, we initially freed this variable from n, since it has only proxy status. Data are as given in the Data Appendix to this chapter.

The first set of experiments related to the entire period for which price observations were available. Since SMFA was not available for such a long period, the credit-rationing variable was simply omitted. The regression spanned 72 observations from the December quarter 1957 to the September quarter 1975. The results were uniformly poor, regardless of which form of expectations was adopted. Equation (14) is a quite representative result.

$$
\begin{aligned}
(14)\quad p_t = {} & \underset{(1.045)}{4.597} - \underset{(-0.911)}{0.422}p_{t-1} + \underset{(.271)}{0.034}\Delta\pi_t + \underset{(0.265)}{0.709}\Delta i_{t-1} \\
& + \underset{(1.048)}{0.312}\frac{\Delta M3_{t-1}}{P_{t-2}N_{t-2}+M3_{t-2}} + \underset{(1.383)}{0.555}awe_{t-2} - \underset{(-0.490)}{.744}dv_{t-1} - \underset{(-0.185)}{.520}n_{t-1} \\
& - \underset{(-0.186)}{0.954}S1_t - \underset{(-0.911)}{5.143}S2_t - \underset{(-0.812)}{4.835}S4_t
\end{aligned}
$$

$D.F. = 61, \quad R^2 = 0.257, \quad D.W. = 2.105.$

Here S1, S2, S4 refer to the seasonal dummies, indexed by the corresponding quarter. The figures in parentheses underneath the estimated coefficients refer to t-values against the null hypothesis of zero effect. The only remotely satisfactory t-value is attached to the change in incomes (significant against the one-tailed "positive effect" alternative at about 8½%). The optimal lag here is 2 periods. R^2 is low, but on the other hand the value of the Durbin-Watson statistic, although possibly biased upwards by the presence of the lagged endogenous variable, suggests that little systematic information about p_t has been omitted.

In the second set of experiments, we introduced the credit-rationing variable. In order to do so, it was necessary to restrict the regressions to the last 26 observations (up to June 1975). With the addition of yet another variable to an already long list of independent regressors, some conservation of degrees of freedom thus became necessary. We decided to define a new yield variable as $(\pi - i)$, i.e. the excess of the expected inflation yield over the interest rate, and to combine dv and n into a single variable (dv-n) representing pressures of population relative to the growth in the stock of housing.

Use of the credit-rationing variable $SMFA_t\ R(SMFA_t - C)$ poses some statistical problems. For this variable to effectively measure financial stringency, it should refer to the same quarter as the dependent variable p_t. But since $SMFA_t$ evidently itself depends upon p_t, there is an element of feedback involved, leading to the possibility of simultaneity bias from the application of ordinary least squares. To overcome this problem, we employed the "naive 2SLS" technique described in chapter 5. Having decided[3] on a set of exogenous variables which might belong to an implicit model jointly generating $SMFA_t$ and p_t, we first projected $SMFA_t$ on this set, as stage one. Having obtained the calculated or fitted value $\widehat{SMFA}$, we employed $\widehat{SMFA}.R(\widehat{SMFA} - C)$, for various values of C, in the second-stage regression.

Again, the results were poor. Whatever the scheme of expectations - static, adaptive or extrapolative - no variable even approached significance. Table 7.1 gives an indication of the results obtained. The credit rationing variable is insignificant, sometimes with the wrong sign.

Let us consider now the effect of replacing percentage price changes with the percentage change in transactions (i.e. in volume of sales)[4] as the dependent variable. To test the impact of mortgage rationing the ideal transactions variable would be net sales, i.e. the agreements successfully consummated with finance. Unfortunately we have available for the required length of time only gross sales, which include those subsequently falling through. However it may be that publicly-known finance conditions affects the decisions of buyers and sellers to enter the pool of active market searchers. Moreover, some buyers will approach lending institutions to check on their mortgage prospects before committing resources of time and energy to the search process. Thus while we might expect a more definite relationship between net sales and a rationing variable, useful information might also result from the use of a gross sales dependent variable.

Table 7.2 presents some results, and is organised in the same manner as Table 7.1. In general these results are, in comparison with the price equation, much better. R^2 is still low but is materially improved in relation to the price equation; we should, indeed, note that such measures of fit are typically rather poor for data in the form of percentage changes. Most of the independent variables have at least the expected sign and improved t-values. Only the negative value for (dv-hn) is hard to explain with any degree of conviction. The most dramatic difference is in the performance of the credit-rationing variable. This is of the right sign just where expected, namely for values of C over 90.0, and has a greatly improved t-value, even if not significant at 95%. It is of interest to note

Table 7.1 : Price Equations

Regressor:	Const.	P_{t-1}	$\Delta(\pi_t - i_{t-1})$	awe_{t-2}	$(dv_{t-2} - n_{t-2})$	$\frac{\Delta M3_{t-1}}{P_{t-2}N_{t-2} + M3_{t-2}}$	$\Delta\hat{SMFA}_t \cdot RF(\hat{SMFA}_t - C)$	$S1_t$	$S2_t$	$S4_t$
Static Expectations										
(a)	C = 0.90 (D.F. = 16, R^2 = 0.090, D.W. = 2.021, $*S^2$ = 43.764)									
	-0.932	-0.011	0.042	0.521	1.405	0.093	-0.004	-0.633	4.142	3.181
t-values*	(-0.141)	(-0.027)	(0.146)	(0.691)	(0.357)	(0.244)	(-0.007)	(-0.121)	(0.429)	(0.581)
(b)	C = 0.85 (D.F. = 16, R^2 = 0.170, D.W. = 2.088, $*S^2$ = 45.615)									
	-2.705	-0.004	0.079	0.769	1.494	0.151	1.008	-0.732	6.691	2.292
t-values*	(-0.398)	(-0.008)	(0.273)	(0.973)	(0.383)	(0.383)	(1.067)	(-0.136)	(0.663)	(0.428)
Adaptive Expectations (parameter LA = 0.6)										
(a)	C = 0.90 (D.F. = 16, R^2 = 0.113, D.W. = 2.073, $*S^2$ = 42.772)									
	-1.094	-0.270	0.792	0.648	1.803	0.094	0.082	-0.576	5.751	3.761
t-values*	(-0.170)	(-0.477)	(0.609)	(0.860)	(0.465)	(0.253)	(0.153)	(-0.111)	(0.594)	(0.687)
(b)	C = 0.85 (D.F. = 16, R^2 = 0.187, D.W. = 2.134, $*S^2$ = 44.807)									
	-2.815	-0.207	0.725	0.866	1.804	0.141	0.973	-0.635	7.848	3.128
t-values*	(-0.427)	(-0.362)	(0.568)	(1.097)	(0.474)	(0.366)	(1.047)	(-0.120)	(0.777)	(0.571)

* The S^2 and t-values are asymptotic, based on the (formal) 2SLS asymptotic variance formulas and error analysis. On the other hand, R^2 and D.W. refer merely to the stage II regression, regarded as O.L.S.

Table 7.2 : Transactions

Regressor:	Const.	P_{t-1}	$\Delta(\pi_t - i_{t-1})$	awe_{t-2}	$(dv_{t-3} - n_{t-3})$	$\frac{\Delta M3_{t-1}}{P_{t-2}N_{t-2}+M3_{t-2}}$	$\Delta\hat{SMFA}_t \cdot RF(\hat{SMFA}_t - C)$	$S1_t$	$S2_t$	$S4_t$
Static Expectations										
(a) C = 0.90	(D.F. = 16, R^2 = 0.376, D.W. = 1.814, $*S^2$ = 302.95)									
	-21.132	-0.305	-0.108	2.393	-17.631	0.517	-1.515	-0.394	12.551	18.995
t-values*	(-1.208)	(-0.305)	(-0.142)	(1.259)	(-1.793)	(0.519)	(-1.116)	(-0.027)	(0.495)	(1.301)
(b) C = 0.85	(D.F. = 16, R^2 = 0.367, D.W. = 1.907, $*S^2$ = 329.846)									
	-19.279	-0.294	0.010	2.511	-12.336	0.727	2.557	0.592	14.105	8.662
t-values*	(-1.063)	(-0.279)	(0.012)	(1.235)	(-1.166)	(0.687)	(0.963)	(0.039)	(0.524)	(0.608)
Adaptive Expectations (Parameter LA = 0.4)										
(a) C = 0.90	(D.F. = 16, R^2 = 0.375, D.W. = 1.812, $*S^2$ = 298.470)									
	-21.422	-0.299	-0.186	2.415	-17.779	0.526	-1.522	-0.384	12.876	19.023
t-values*	(-1.240)	(-0.231)	(-0.098)	(1.252)	(-1.824)	(0.529)	(-1.104)	(-0.027)	(0.505)	(1.302)
(b) C = 0.85	(D.F. = 16, R^2 = 0.368, D.W. = 1.916, $*S^2$ = 329.141)									
	-19.593	-0.381	0.168	2.573	-12.539	0.734	2.548	0.460	14.817	8.849
t-values*	(-1.094)	(-0.281)	(0.086)	(1.250)	(-1.186)	(0.697)	(0.961)	(0.031)	(0.549)	(0.616)

* The S^2 and t-values are asymptotic, based on the (formal) 2SLS asymptotic variance formulas and error analysis. On the other hand, R^2 and D.W. refer merely to the stage II regression, regarded as O.L.S.

that the coefficient of S4 is positive, with a relatively good t-value. This conforms with casual observation of periods of greater activity in the market (in the Southern Hemisphere!).

We shall comment at greater length later on the significance of these results. It may be apposite to mention at this point, that spurred by the poor performance of the price equation we investigated also a monetarist-oriented explanation. Specifically, we considered Koyck-lag schemes in which the forcing factors were the change in the stock of money (various lags thereof), price expectations and the seasonals. Such a specification performed no better than the portfolio-oriented explanation considered above.

7.2.3 The Link With New Construction. According to the view of the transmission process outlined in the introduction to this section, new construction activity is stimulated when the price of existing durable assets rises above their physical replacement cost. We can employ our price series to test this idea. To proxy the construction cost of new houses we employed the W.A. Bureau of Statistics index of the cost of housing materials. This series unfortunately excludes an index of the cost of labour, which is not available. Since the replacement cost includes also the cost of land, the construction cost cannot be regarded as a complete index for the replacement cost.

Equations (15) and (16) for approvals (AP) and commencements (COM) employ a Koyck-type exponential lag scheme with forcing factor $\left(\frac{P}{PC}\right)_t$, where PC is the index of construction costs.

(15) $$AP_t = \underset{(0.120)}{1.504} + \underset{(5.432)}{0.717}AP_{t-1} + \underset{(0.760)}{0.834}\left(\frac{P}{PC}\right)_t$$

D.F. = 34, R^2 = 0.593, D.W. = 1.790.

(16) $$COM_t = \underset{(-0.218)}{-2.348} + \underset{(4.521)}{0.650}COM_{t-1} + \underset{(1.323)}{1.280}\left(\frac{P}{PC}\right)_t$$

D.F. = 34, R^2 = 0.560, D.W. = 1.792.

In neither case is the forcing term significant at 95%, although signs are as expected. R^2 is relatively low for levels data. The implied mean lag for approvals is 2.53 quarters, while that for commencements is 1.86 quarters. (It seems a little odd that approvals should exhibit a longer mean lag than starts, but the difference is quite within the bounds of sampling error.) The general order of the lag involved (6-8 months) seems intuitively quite plausible.

In summary, although link two in our transmission mechanism looks a little better than link one, it cannot be said that the data offers unequivocal support. In assessing our results we must bear in mind the "variation due to circumstances" of the quotation from W. Smith referred to above. Thus one might argue that existing houses are not perfect substitutes for new houses, so that the kind of arbitrage we have been investigating operates imperfectly. We may refer in this context to some unpublished results obtained by J. Ellis, and quoted here with his kind permission. In investigating the determinants of new housing starts he finds good statistical significance for levels of the rate of interest, on income lagged two periods and possibly (some interpretive doubt is attached) to age group changes. These results indicate, by comparison with our own, that the market for new houses cannot be considered to be on all fours with the market for existing houses.

7.2.4 Summary. Let us now sum up the results of this empirical study of the market for existing houses. The first point of interest in the results of this data is perhaps the large amount of "noise", or unexplained variation, in the price changes in the market for existing houses. It is unlikely that this is wholly due to the sampling procedure employed, or to the acknowledged limitations of the data on independent variables. Indeed results of official nationwide data on a six-monthly basis for New Zealand yield a similar predominance of noise. We are reminded of the failure of attempts to link the stock market with underlying economic information flows, evidenced by some as a demonstration of the efficiency of that market.

We have found greater success (in relative terms) in explaining the volume of transactions in the market. One interpretation of this might remark on the divergence in expectations between buyers and sellers which is often a feature of a stationary market. Thus following the boom period of 1975-76 in the Perth urban area, sellers continued to place unrealistically high reservation prices on their houses. Rather than contemplate lower offers, they often preferred to withdraw from the market and let the house, until more favourable times. Such behaviour is self-reinforcing in the sense that with reduced supply in the market, prices at least remain firm. A similar mechanism may account for the near-significance of the credit-rationing variable in the transactions equation, but not in the price equation. If agreements collapse because of lack of finance, both vendor and buyer may leave the market. If tight finance becomes - as it usually does - a matter of public knowledge, this will likewise deter both buyers and sellers from entering the market. The net result is a shift downwards of both supply and demand schedules leading to a smaller volume of transactions, but prices which may remain unchanged.

The popular view of the transmission mechanism outlined in the introduction to this paper is very much oriented to the workings of the price mechanism. Thus the effect of, for instance, expansionary monetary policy is to raise the price of durable assets relative to their reproduction cost, thereby - again via the price mechanism - leading home-seekers to build rather than buy. Our results do not do a great deal to support such a view of the world. Prices in the existing market seem to react systematically only to changes in income, and the link between prices of new and used houses is weak. On the other hand, this study has found some support for the determination of transactions in durable goods, rather than their prices, by credit policy. In this sense it supports the "fix-price" view of the world, in which quantities adjust faster than prices, which has become the hallmark of recent reinterpretations of Keynesian economics.

Data Appendix : Chapter 7

(A.B.S. = Australian Bureau of Statistics; C.B.C.S. = Commonwealth Bureau of Census and Statistics (old name for A.B.S.))

P	Quarterly averages of monthly data kindly furnished by the Real Estate Institute of Western Australia. Coverage is confined to properties listed with the Institute's Multiple Listing Bureau. Since the M.L.B. was started in 1957, its penetration has increased as a proportion of all sales in the metropolitan area. This does mean that the sample may be small towards the beginning of the data series. Note also that M.L.B. results may not represent an unbiased sample, for very high-priced houses will not usually be multiply-listed. However since we use P in the form of % changes this will not unduly distort our results. Indeed the exclusion of very high-priced houses may be desirable in reducing the amount of noise in the data; one need only think of the effect on our quarterly averages of a single $500,000 sale. Up to and including October 1969, the index includes also sales of unimproved land in the urban area. Distortions from the effect of the small amount of unimproved land involved are again minimised by the use of % changes. Period of total availability was June 1957 - June 1976.
S	No. of sales, obtained and used on the above basis from R.E.I.W.A. Again used in the form of % changes. Sales fallen through were also employed, for the limited period available, namely March 1973 - June 1976.
N	Stock of houses in Perth metropolitan area September 1954 to March 1976. Calculated from number of completions (A.B.S. *Quarterly Statistical Abstract* (W.A.)) with benchmarks established from the A.B.S. *Census of Population and Housing*, various issues. Kindly supplied by J. Ellis.
BMR	Rates of the largest institution in the lending field, the Perth Building Society. By kind permission of the Society, and from R.M.C. Lourens, *The Perth Building Society: A Study in Institutional Growth*. Ph.D. Thesis, University of Western Australia, 1973.
DV	The demographic variable employed was the number of people in the 15-24 age group, or % changes therein. Correspondence from Perth office of A.B.S. to J. Ellis.
AWE	Average weekly earnings per employed male. From A.B.S. *Labour Reports* and *Quarterly Statistical Abstract* (W.A.) September 1954 - June 1976.

M3	A broad definition of deposits with trading banks, savings banks and building societies. C.B.C.S. *Finance, Part 1, Banking and Currency, Insurance and Other Private Finance*, and A.B.S. *Quarterly Statistical Abstract* (W.A.).
AP, COM	Approvals and Commencements. From A.B.S. *Building Statistics*.
PC	Wholesale price index of materials used in home building. A.B.S. *Quarterly Statistical Abstract* (W.A.) and C.B.C.S. *Labour Reports*.

Footnotes to Chapter 7

[1]Fair's original notation is RM. To avoid confusion with the (0,1)-ramp function we use the lower-case r.

[2]Recall that p enters in two ways; directly via equation (12), indirectly via the term $\Delta \log\left(\frac{R}{P}\right)$. The latter term contributes $(-\Delta \log P) = -p$, while the former term has a positive coefficient. The net result is hence *a-priori* of indeterminate sign.

[3]The list of exogenous or predetermined variables used in this stage-one regression is: $SMFA_{t-1}$, $M3_t$, AWE_t, DV_t, P_{t-1}, N_{t-1}, $S1_t$, $S2_t$, $S3_t$.

[4]In a standard demand-supply system the jointly-determined variables are P and Q, where Q is the quantity bought or sold on the market. Thus corresponding to $\Delta \log P$, the dependent variable in the price equations, we consider $\Delta \log Q$, the proportional (or percentage) change in sales.

CHAPTER EIGHT

MARKET DYNAMICS FOR A DURABLE GOOD[1]

The models discussed in previous chapters have presumed that pricing and quantity clearing can be cast in terms of flow demand and supply schedules. These schedules are presumed to be stable from period to period - in other words defined as a time-invariant function of p_t, or perhaps some distributed lag thereof. But while this be adequate for fish, it will not necessarily do for houses. Where the commodity involved is durable, if the market is supposed to be in disequilibrium for a finite length of time, we have to consider what happens to the unsatisfied demand or supply. Does it simply go away? If it does not, that is, if at least some of it is backlogged, then if price change is to be related to a discrepancy between demand and supply, these schedules can no longer be regarded as stable, in the sense that they are invariant to the recent history of the process. Backlogging can occur in a market for a nondurable good, particularly in respect of unsatisfied demand. However it is the existence of frustrated sellers of a commodity which can be carried forward to next market day, so to speak, that is responsible for the peculiar importance of the backlogging phenomenon for the dynamics of a durable good.

The difficulties associated with durable goods are not limited to the subject of backlogging. We have to consider also the relationship of the market for new goods with the market for existing goods - newly constructed houses versus older ones, for instance. We must achieve a proper integration of these two markets, which will involve consideration of both flow and stock dimensions. A proper theory of this kind will sooner or later have to come to grips with the awkward question of what constitutes a market. Consider for instance the buying or selling of existing houses. The circus within which ruling prices are determined is comprised of those actively wishing to buy and sell, and the arena concerned is the daily newspaper listings, the books of estate agents and similar if less tangible manifestations of buying and selling interest. At the same time, nonactive but potential participants will be observing this activity. They may do so only imperfectly, for ruling prices may be difficult to gage unless one is an active buyer or seller. Sooner or later, based on their observations, the spectators may themselves enter the pool of active agents. Now if prices respond directly to supply and demand pressures, these can only represent the preferences, backed by the available information, of those in the active arena. Under some circumstances these may not coincide with those of the spectators. The point is that it may not be correct to model a price dynamics in terms of the preferences and information of all agents, both players and spectators. This indeed is one of the less satisfactory features of the model constructed in chapter 7.2. The way out seems to be to expand the model by explicitly modelling decisions by the spectators to enter the arena as active agents, or again, decisions by the players to leave the active arena in favour of the public stand. Such decisions will be functions of - *inter alia* - perceptions as to the ruling price.

Even if we confine our attention to the pool of active agents, we need to specify the nature and origin of backlogging. We must therefore consider the problem of the determination of prices and quantities, that is to say market clearing, in more detail than the rather mechanistic and arbitrary processes of earlier chapters. It is necessary to specify how active agents go about seeking the other side of the bargain and how they react to possible failure to make contact or to consummate the exchange.

In the present chapter we attempt to model a complete price and quantity dynamics which is much influenced by recent ideas on market clearing under conditions of imperfect information. The model is not econometric. Rather it is an exercise in specification, to explore possible ways of handling some of the more difficult questions of disequilibrium analysis. We shall see in particular that specification of market dynamics in terms of stable flow demand and supply schedules may be misleading.

A model of this kind should be able to tell us what happens when a variation in one or more of the underlying assumptions occurs. One of the most interesting and important of these, both from the theoretical and practical point of view, is the case where buyers may be subject to a financing constraint. The role of financing constraints in general has received widespread attention as a result of the so-called "Keynesian reinterpretation". To financial economists, it appears as the phenomenon of credit rationing, which may have either a temporary aspect, or else be of more permanent duration ("equilibrium rationing" in the terminology of D.M. Jaffee and F. Modigliani [1969]; see chapter 1.3). Rationing of any kind has always been of interest in economic theory because of the implied contrast between two forms of stabilisation or control, the one based on a *diktat* of some kind, the other emerging out of the unencumbered operation of a pricing system. From the practical point of view this contrast is full of interest for those fortunate or unfortunate enough to live in a financial milieu of heavily regulated interest rates, particularly in respect of mortgage rates on real estate. Whether or not it is true that frustrated buyers succeed in obtaining finance from an uncontrolled fringe market, the question as to whether such direct controls would succeed of themselves in stabilising the housing market is obviously of interest. The model we establish appears to yield some useful insights into the effects of rationing of this kind.

The scheme of the chapter is as follows. In section 8.1 we establish the basic model. Its equilibrium properties and some dynamics are investigated in section 8.2. We investigate here a question of some importance, namely whether a market is more or less stable the more imperfect is the information acquisition and processing on the part of its agents. Does "friction" increase or decrease a market's rate of convergence to equilibrium? In section 8.3 we impose credit rationing constraints of two kinds and study equilibrium and disequilibrium properties of the resulting system. Finally (section 8.4) we consider some potential applications of the model. Application to the housing market is implicit throughout much of the chapter. By appropriately interpreting its basic equations, we show that the model can also be adapted to labour market dynamics. In particular we demonstrate that it is capable of yielding a rich variety of hypotheses about the determination of labour force participation rates.

8.1 The Basic Model

Although our model is influenced by recent ideas concerning the probabilistic character of the search, by both buyers and sellers, for suitable transactions partners, we have chosen not to attempt to model explicitly the determination of the distribution of sellers' asking prices or else the precise search characteristics of buyers. Rather, we have chosen to model the clearing process in terms of the distribution of prices at which contracts actually take place (the "transactions price distribution") and in particular some simple central measure thereof, such as the mean. For this distribution represents the basic observable data which motivate the entry, continuation or exit of buyers or sellers from an assumed pool of active agents. By combining the idea of a ruling transactions price with a model based on underlying search behaviour, we are able to graft ideas derived from the probabilistic character of the search process on to the immensely fruitful stock of Marshallian demand and supply analysis.

There is a flow of new entrants, both buyers and sellers, to the pool and for the sake of simplicity such flows will constitute our stable or invariant demand and supply schedules. There is a flow of agents out of the pool consisting (a) of those who have concluded agreements and (b) those who decided to exit for other reasons: either their costs of search (psychological or financial) may have mounted to the point where in the light of an unchanged subjective probability distribution of qualities or prices, they assess the probability of success in the coming period as not worthwhile. Or else their assessment of the distribution of prices may have changed so that they exit for the same kind of reason that they entered, namely their assessment of the ruling price. After each round of transactions, we imagine a new ruling price based on the discrepancy between the number wanting to buy and those wanting to sell at the previous price. Given this new price, unsatisfied buyers and sellers will consider whether or not they wish to remain in the pool. Their decisions will depend (i) on the new ruling price and (ii) on the length of time that they have already been in the pool, a quantity which we shall proxy by the expected "age" of buyers or sellers.

In defining the following functions and adjustment mechanisms we have chosen to remain quite general. (We have suppressed in particular a rate of interest variable, the effect of which will be given some attention in section 8.3. Depending on the market under consideration, many more variables might enter, and identical variables to those we do consider might enter in different ways - e.g. we could have a demand function depending also on $\frac{p}{p_e}$, where p_e was a perceived long-term or "permanent" price):

p_t = ruling purchase price, time t.

$n^d(p_t)$ = flow of new entrants[2] to the buyers pool during period t.

$n^s(p_t)$ = flow of new entrants[2] to the sellers pool during period t.

N_t^d = stock of potential buyers in the pool at time t.

N_t^s = stock of potential sellers in the pool at time t.

n_t = transactions (agreements) during time t.

$\bar{n}_t$ = successfully concluded agreements, with finance available, during time t (used only in section 8.3).

(1)[3] $$p_t - p_{t-1} = \theta(N_{t-1}^d - N_{t-1}^s), \qquad \theta \text{ a positive parameter.}$$

This expresses the change in ruling prices.

(2) $$N_t^d = \phi_{dt}(N_{t-1}^d - n_{t-1}) + n_t^d .$$

(3a) $$N_t^s = \phi_{st}(N_{t-1}^s - n_{t-1}) + n_t^s \ .$$

Equations (2) and (3a) need further explanation. Consider the demand version (2). The quantity $N_{t-1}^d(p_{t-1}) - n_{t-1}$ represents unsatisfied demand in t-1, i.e. the number of unsuccessful buyers in the pool. The new ruling price is p_t. A proportion ϕ_d, which (given p_{t-1}) will depend among other things on p_t, of the unsatisfied buyers then elect to stay in the pool. The number of searching buyers in period t is then given by (2). A similar interpretation holds for equation (3). We have not as yet specified in any detail the functions ϕ_d and ϕ_s; this is done below.

(4) $$n_t = h(|N_t^d - N_t^s|)\min.(N_t^d, N_t^s) \ , \qquad 0 \le h \le 1, \quad h' \ge 0 \ .$$

The number of successful contacts during period t is determined by the short side of the market; but is closer to the minimum according to a measure of the discrepancy between the forces of demand and supply. This expresses some of the probabilistic character of search. The greater the discrepancy between the two different types of searcher, the higher the probability that a given agent of the type in short supply will be successful. Note that without the existence of credit rationing, n_t denotes successful contacts, which thereby exit from the pool. In section 8.3 this will not be the case, and some redefinition will be necessary.

Let us now investigate the functions ϕ_d and ϕ_s, which reflect decisions by unsuccessful agents to try again. If his past search experiences were a matter of indifference to him, a decision to stay on would reflect only the agent's assessment of the new ruling price. In this respect, one could argue that he would then be on all fours with a new entrant, so that for example

$$\phi_d = \frac{n^d(p_t)}{n^d(p_{t-1})} \simeq 1 + (p_t - p_{t-1})\varepsilon_d \ ,$$

where $\varepsilon_d = \frac{n^{d'}}{n^d}$ is the elasticity of the flow demand schedule, evaluated at p_{t-1} .

Such an assumption, however, is not palatable. As any prospective housebuyer knows, the process of search is rarely pleasant, and the longer it goes on, the more discouraging it becomes, in the light of point (b) at the start of this section. We therefore suppose that the functions ϕ_d and ϕ_s depend also upon the average age of the buyer (μ_t^d) and seller (μ_t^s), in the sense of the average time for which they have been in the pool. It is shown in Appendix 8.1 that

(5) $$\mu_t^d = 1 + \left(\frac{N_t^d - n_t^d}{N_t^d}\right)\mu_{t-1}^d ,$$

(6) $$\mu_t^s = 1 + \left(\frac{N_t^s - n_t^s}{N_t^s}\right)\mu_{t-1}^s .$$

The time convention applied in (5) and (6) refers to the end, rather than the beginning, of the period. Thus at the end of period 1, all unsatisfied searchers are 1 period old. We can now write

(7) $$\phi_{dt} = \phi_d(p_t - p_{t-1}, \mu_{t-1}^d) \qquad \phi_{d,1} < 0, \quad \phi_{d,2} < 0 .$$

(8) $$\phi_{st} = \phi_s(p_t - p_{t-1}, \mu_{t-1}^s) \qquad \phi_{s,1} > 0, \quad \phi_{s,2} < 0 .$$

The specification of our underlying model is now complete. Although we have used arguments which have a probabilistic flavour, the model is nevertheless deterministic. We achieve this by use of the "ruling price", which we might identify with the mean of the distribution of prices at which agreements are actually completed. The ruling price change (1) is taken to be the outcome of a probabilistic process in which the ruling price and transacted quantities emerge jointly. The factors θ in (1) and h in (4) are therefore not independent, so that to assume θ constant is obviously only a first approximation. We have simply moved a little way from standard Marshallian supply and demand analysis towards a more realistic model of market clearing for a durable good, without wholly abandoning the great usefulness of the former.

Alternative specifications to equation (1) for price adjustment are available. A leading possibility is to make use of the PAMEQ specification. Given N^d_{t-1}, N^s_{t-1}, μ^d_{t-1}, μ^s_{t-1} and n_{t-1}, let us define a moving equilibrium price $\hat{p}_t$ by the relationship:

$$\hat{N}^d_t = \phi_d(\hat{p}_t - p_{t-1}, \mu^d_{t-1})(N^d_{t-1} - n_{t-1}) + n^d_t(\hat{p}_t)$$

$$= \phi_s(\hat{p}_t - p_{t-1}, \mu^s_{t-1})(N^s_{t-1} - n_{t-1}) + n^s_t(\hat{p}_t) = \hat{N}^s_t \ .$$

In place of equation (1) we might then write:

$$(1)' \qquad p_t = \lambda p_{t-1} + (1-\lambda)\hat{p}_t \ , \qquad 0 < \lambda < 1 \ .$$

This formulation has the advantage that the flow magnitudes n^d_t and n^s_t help to determine the current price, and are in turn determined by that price. The original formulation (1) does not allow this.

There is in fact quite a simple relationship between (1) and (1)' which will illustrate the simultaneity referred to. To anticipate subsequent discussion a little, let us suppose that a full-equilibrium, or long-run stationary point, exists. Consider the local dynamics about this point (denoted *). Linearising N^d_t and N^s_t about (*) we have:

$$N^d_t \simeq \hat{N}^d_t + \delta_d(p_t - \hat{p}_t)\frac{N^*}{p^*}$$

$$N^s_t \simeq \hat{N}^s_t + \delta_s(p_t - \hat{p}_t)\frac{N^*}{p^*}$$

Here $\delta_d = \phi^*_{d1}(1 - h(0)) + \varepsilon^*_d h(0)$

$\delta_s = \phi^*_{s1}(1 - h(0)) + \varepsilon^*_s h(0)$,

where ε^*_d and ε^*_s are the elasticity of the flow demand and supply schedules $n^d(p)$ and $n^s(p)$ evaluated at (*). The factors ϕ^*_{d1} and ϕ^*_{s1} are likewise the partial elasticities with respect to $p_t - p_{t-1}$ of the functions ϕ_d and ϕ_s, evaluated at the long-run equilibrium. Since $\hat{N}^d_t = \hat{N}^s_t$, it follows that

$$N_t^d - N_t^s \simeq \frac{N^*}{p^*}(\delta_d - \delta_s)(p_t - \hat{p}_t) .$$

Now from (1)' ,

$$p_t - p_{t-1} = \frac{1-\lambda}{\lambda}(\hat{p}_t - p_t)$$

$$= \frac{1-\lambda}{\lambda(\delta_d - \delta_s)} \frac{(N_t^d - N_t^s)}{N^*} p^* .$$

Hence (1)' is locally equivalent to:

$$\frac{p_t - p_{t-1}}{p^*} = \theta' \frac{(N_t^d - N_t^s)}{N^*} ,$$

where

$$\theta' = \frac{1-\lambda}{\lambda} \frac{1}{(\phi_{s1}^* - \phi_{d1}^*)(1 - h(0)) + (\varepsilon_s^* - \varepsilon_d^*)h(0)} .$$

This equation is of the same form as the original (1), except that price changes are related to discrepancies between demand and supply at the end of the period. Considered as a dynamic system the two will differ, but the stationary points of both will be the same. Consequently all the stationary theory of the next section will apply equally to specification (1) or (1)' for the price-adjustment equation. For the purposes of the simulation study of sections 8.2 and 8.3 we employed (1). The alternative specification would have involved solving at each time point a set of nonlinear simultaneous equations, making the exercise materially more difficult.

A final remark concerning the price adjustment parameter θ (or λ in equation (1)') is in order at this point. We have assumed that this adjustment parameter and the function $h(\cdot)$ of equation (4) can be independently specified. One relates to the speed of price adjustment in response to a disequilibrium position. The other relates to the "friction" in the clearing mechanism, in the sense that it measures the closeness of the clearing path to the short sides of the demand and supply schedules. As a convenient parameter summarising the latter we may consider the quantity $(1-h(0))$. This may be regarded (see section 8.2) as an equilibrium "friction" coefficient. Even at the equilibrium price there will still exist a certain number of unsatisfied participants, measured by the proportion $1-h(0)$.

Now we should expect that if this frictional component were small, it might signify a market where information was readily available to participants. In such a market, prices might move very quickly to adjust the forces of supply and demand. Conversely, in a market characterised by a poor flow of information, prices would not adjust quickly to a discrepancy between the number of demanders and the number of suppliers. Another manifestation of such a poor information structure would be a high degree of friction. In short, we might expect an inverse functional relationship between the parameters θ and $(1-h(0))$. In general, therefore, we may not be able to specify independently the price adjustment parameter and the clearing path. The point has some significance for the allowable perturbations of parameters in studying the comparative dynamics of the model, and we shall return to it later in the next section.

8.2 Behaviour of the Unconstrained Model

Equations (1) to (8) of section 8.1 constitute our model of market dynamics unhampered by the availability of finance. The first six equations comprise a nonlinear difference equation system in the variables p_t, N^d_t, N^s_t, n_t, μ^d_t and μ^s_t. A stationary point, if it exists, will satisfy the following equations

(9) (a) $N^{d*} = N^{s*} = N^*$

(b) $N^* = \phi_d(0,\mu^{d*})(N^*-n^*) + n^{d*}$

(c) $N^* = \phi_s(0,\mu^{s*})(N^*-n^*) + n^{s*}$

(d) $n^* = h(0)N^*$

(e) $\mu^{d*} = \frac{N^*}{n^{d*}}$

(f) $\mu^{s*} = \frac{N^*}{n^{s*}}$

where $n^{d*} = n^d(p^*)$ and $n^{s*} = n^s(p^*)$.

The above equations indicate that the flow demand and supply schedules may not necessarily yield the correct equilibrium price or transacted quantity. In other words, equilibrium p^* and n^* are not necessarily defined by the relations

(10) $n^d(p^*) = n^s(p^*) = n^*$.

Equations (10) define two independent conditions:
(i) that $n^d(p^*) = n^s(p^*)$ defines the equilibrium price, with their common value equal to η^*, say, and (ii) that the equilibrium transacted quantity $n^* = \eta^*$. Suppose that only (i) were to hold. From (9)(e) and (f) it follows that $\mu^{d*} = \mu^{s*} = \mu^*$, say. From (b) and (c) it will follow that either $N^* = n^*$ (which is of little interest to us, since it can hold only if $h(0) = 1$) or else $\phi_d(0,\mu^*) = \phi_s(0,\mu^*) = \phi^*$ say. Now in this

stationary state, new entrants into the pool must be equal to exits. Thus:[4]

$$\eta^* = n^* + (1-\phi^*)(N^*-n^*) \ ,$$

the first term on the RHS corresponding to completed contracts, the second to frustrated exits. Hence $\eta^* = n^*$ only if $\phi^* = 1$ (or else once again $N^* = n^*$). If $\eta^* = n^*$, we obtain $\mu^* = \frac{1}{h(0)}$. In summary, a necessary condition for a stationary state to be completely described (in the sense of equation (10) above) by flow functions is that

$$(11) \qquad \phi_d\left(0, \frac{1}{h(0)}\right) = \phi_s\left(0, \frac{1}{h(0)}\right) = 1 \ .$$

If condition (ii) does not hold, there are three other possibilities:

(a) Price can be obtained from the intersection of flow demand and flow supply schedules, but transacted quantities cannot.

(b) An equilibrium exists which cannot be predicted in any of its aspects from the flow schedules. Suppose, for instance that $n^d(p^*) > n^s(p^*)$. From (e) and (f), $\mu^{d*} < \mu^{s*}$ as we should expect. But from (b) and (c), we must have $\phi_d(0,\mu^{d*}) < \phi_s(0,\mu^{s*})$. Recalling that $\phi_{d2} < 0$, $\phi_{s2} < 0$, the requirement is evidently that in the neighbourhood of equilibrium, buyers become frustrated much more readily than sellers. Once again, the behaviour of the function ϕ is crucial.

(c) No stationary point may exist.

Finally, we have not considered the question of uniqueness of a proposed equilibrium, which turns out to be rather intractable in its full generality. We remark also that even if a stationary point exists, it may never be attained; indeed our simulation studies suggest that the model has a propensity to generate limit cycles rather readily.

This brings us to the question of disequilibrium dynamics. Since backlogging of demand and supply is permitted, we should expect our model to possess at least some of the dynamic features of such models (see e.g. P.A. Samuelson [1941]). Thus a monotonic divergence of price away from equilibrium is ruled out, for this would imply a backlog of ever-increasing size which, under any reasonable price adjustment mechanism, would altimately reverse the price movement. We should expect also that the model would overshoot the equilibrium position, leading to cyclical behaviour, for at the point p* where $n^d = n^s$, the existence of a backlog accumulated from past disequilibrium will nevertheless imply a non-zero price change. But apart from these intuitive impressions, the intrinsically nonlinear nature of the system renders a more precise dynamics hard to give.

We can, however, obtain a degree of insight into its local dynamic properties by linearising the system about its equilibrium position. We report here some features of the more extensive study of this question contained in a draft of the present study.[5] We found it convenient to work in terms of proportional deviations from the equilibrium position, e.g. $\tilde{N}_t = \frac{N_t}{N_t^*} - 1$, and accordingly defined elasticities such as $\varepsilon_d^* = \frac{1}{n^d} \frac{dn^d}{d(p/p^*)}$ evaluated at p = p*, with similar expressions for ε_s^* and the partial elasticities ϕ_{di}^*, ϕ_{si}^*, i = 1,2. We found that the system could be linearised into one of two distinct regimes, corresponding to excess supply or excess demand $(N_t^d - N_t^s)$ in the pool, with a different 5th-order characteristic function for each. However if we assumed that the stationary point in question could be described by the flow schedules in the sense of equations (10) and (11) above, and also that $\phi_{d2}^* = \phi_{s2}^* = \phi_2^*$ (buyers and sellers react equally to increasing age), matters become easier. Local price dynamics can now be expressed in terms of the differences $(\tilde{\mu}_t^d - \tilde{\mu}_t^s)$ in the ages of buyers and sellers rather than each age individually. The system reduces to 3rd-order, and the same characteristic equation prevails in each of the two regimes, excess demand and excess supply. We can write this as:

$$(12) \qquad F(\lambda) = \lambda^3 + a_2\lambda^2 + a_1\lambda + a_0 = 0 ,$$

where $a_2 = -(1-h)(1+\phi_2^*) + 1 + \gamma_1^d - \gamma_1^s + \theta(\varepsilon_d^*-\varepsilon_s^*)$

$$a_1 = (1-h)(1+\phi_2^*) + (2-h)(\gamma_1^d-\gamma_1^s) + \theta(1-h)(2+\phi_2^*)(\varepsilon_d-\varepsilon_s)$$

$$a_0 = -(1-h)(1+\theta(1-h)(\phi_{d1}^*-\phi_{s1}^*)) ,$$

with $h = h(0)$

$$\beta = N^*\frac{h'(0)}{h(0)}$$

$$\gamma_1^d = \gamma_2^d + (1-h) ,$$

$$\gamma_2^d = (1-\beta)h + \theta(1-h)(\phi_{d1}^*-\varepsilon_d^*)$$

$$\gamma_1^s = \gamma_2^s + (1-h)$$

$$\gamma_2^s = -\beta h + \theta(1-h)(\phi_{s1}^*-\varepsilon_s^*) .$$

For stability we require the roots of (12) to lie inside the unit circle. A convenient set of necessary and sufficient conditions for this to be so is given in E.I. Jury [1964] p.93.[6] In general, we found that for plausible combinations of parameter values, these conditions were not likely to be violated.

Possibly the most interesting dynamic study relates to the effect of the quantity h(0). The term (1-h(0)) can be interpreted as a stationary state "friction coefficient", in the sense that if $h(0) = 1$ we have $n^* = N^*$ and markets are fully cleared in each period. The question that immediately springs to mind (see also R.J. Bowden [1975]) is whether the stability of the market is related to this coefficient of friction, as a measure of the imperfections of information and organisation. As one measure of the (in)stability of the system we might take $|a_0|$, the product of its characteristic values. (Viewed as such an indication it is decidedly imperfect, the only perfect measure being the root with largest absolute value, which is not analytically available.) Now unless the elasticity parameters ϕ^*_{s1} and ϕ^*_{d1} are unrealistically large in absolute value, it will be the case that $\theta(1-h)(\phi^*_{d1}-\phi^*_{s1}) > -1$. Thus from (12) it will follow that $a_0 < 0$, so that $|a_0| = -a_0$. If we now plot against (1-h) the quantity

$$|a_0| = (1-h)(1+\theta(1-h)(\phi^*_{d1}-\phi^*_{s1}))$$

we find either an interior maximum between $1-h = 0$ and $1-h = 1$, or much more likely that $|a_0|$ increases monotonically at decreasing rate with (1-h). This suggests that for plausible elasticity parameters, increasing friction leads to decreasing stability.

Such a conclusion is clearly not a rigorous or even an intuitively satisfactory one, and it is useful to check it and other dynamic matters in a simulation study of the unconstrained model. In Bowden [1978] we carried out a simulation study of a simple model based on the specification (1)-(8) of section 8.1. We reported the interesting finding that there appeared to be an optimal value for the friction coefficient $(1-h(0))$. For very high values (close to unity) prices became caught in a limit cycle, failing to converge to a single equilibrium point. For very low values, the model did indeed converge, but a long time was required. In the model employed the optimal value for $(1-h(0))$ was in the vicinity of 0.35.

However these results, as well as the preceding theoretical discussion on the effect of friction on stability, may be vitiated by the failure to consider a point raised at the end of the previous section, namely the possibility of functional dependence between the price adjustment parameter θ and the friction coefficient $(1-h(0))$. The above experiments concerning the effects of friction varied the parameter $(1 - h(0))$ while holding θ constant. It may be more realistic to vary θ at the same time that variation in $(1 - h(0))$ is imposed. The difficulty here is that our model of market clearing is not detailed to the point of postulating a specific functional relationship between θ and $(1 - h(0))$. Such a relationship can only be manifest from the deeper treatment of the probabilistic structure of market clearing and price adjustment which must underlie a model like that outlined in section 8.1. Thus our present findings concerning the effect of "friction" on the stability of a system must be regarded as tantalisingly incomplete. We leave our discussion of this matter having pointed up a problem area and a possible formalisation for its study. We turn in the next section to the effect of a financing constraint.

8.3 Credit Rationing

Implicit in the foregoing treatment has been the idea that if finance is required to complete transaction, it is always available, so that if necessary interest rates rise in the derived market for funds. Our flow demand and supply schedules are assumed to reflect possible interest effects. But suppose now that there is some imperfection in the market for funds, so that the rate of interest cannot rise or fall to maintain equality of the derived demand and supply for funds. The number of transactions that can be successfully completed will then depend on the flow of finance during the period. We shall suppose[7] two cases

(a) A constant flow of funds (M) is available for financing each period. Or

(b) funds may be backlogged, so that if not all the available funds are required in a period, the excess may be transferred forward to finance transactions in the following period.

Since successful contacts will turn into completed contracts only if finance is available, we have now to distinguish n_t, the number of contacts as defined in Section 8.1, from $\bar{n}_t$, the number of consummated agreements. Thus in case (a) above,

(13) $$\bar{n}_t = \min(n_t, \frac{M}{ap_t}) ,$$

expressing the requirement that $a\bar{n}_t p_t \leq M$. Here a is a constant reflecting the financing requirement for each transaction. Henceforth we simply absorb it in the quantity M. In case (b) above,

(13b) $$\bar{n}_t = \min(n_t, \frac{M_t}{p_t}) , \text{ where}$$

(14) $$M_t = M + (M_{t-1} - \bar{n}_{t-1} p_{t-1})$$

expresses the backlogging of funds. We consider first case (a).

(a) No backlogging of funds

Suppose that the system is (as described in Section 8.1) initially in equilibrium at the point E in Figure 8.1, the intersection of the flow demand and supply schedules. For simplicity, we shall assume that the price and transaction quantity stationary states are determined by the intersection of flow demand and supply schedules in the sense of equation (10) of section 8.2. Imagine that there is now a sudden drop in the flow of available financing, so that new transactions are constrained to lie below or on the hyperbola np = M, as indicated. The immediate temptation is to imagine that this merely creates a new effective flow demand function CDE'FG, as distinct from the notional schedule n^d. The intersection E' of this effective demand schedule with the supply schedule n^s would then

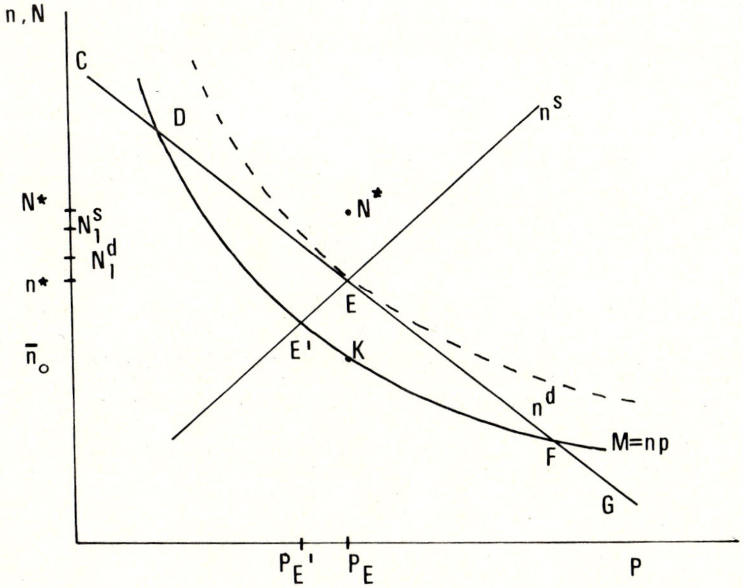

Figure 8.1

indicate the new constrained equilibrium. We shall shortly show that this is a temptation which must be resisted; E' is not a stationary point of the system.

Following the imposition of the finance constraint in period 0, $n^*-\bar{n}_0$ transactions cannot now be consummated for lack of finance. Let us consider the effect of this on decisions to remain in the pool. These will not be symmetric as between buyers and sellers. If a buyer is refused finance, this is likely to have a rather shattering effect on his decision to remain in the pool. He may judge it better to withdraw from the pool until such time as his prospects for obtaining finance appear to have improved. As a matter of contrast, we shall thus imagine that if a buyer is refused finance, he immediately exits from the pool of searchers. So far as buyers are concerned, equation (2) of section 8.1 remains unchanged as a description of total demand pressure. The exit of buyers from the pool comprises all those who have made contacts, n_t. Under the above discouragement assumption, it is immaterial whether or not all of the n_t pencilled agreements have been consummated with finance.

However, the effect of a buyer's failing to obtain finance on the seller, i.e. on the other half of such a pencilled agreement, is not as clear-cut. Failure to obtain finance is more often a reflection on the creditworthiness of the buyer, rather than on the quality of the good offered by the seller. The discouragement effect of the falling through of an agreement on the buyer's decisions is consequently not likely to be quite as dramatic. He may elect to remain in the pool of active sellers. Under these circumstances, equation (3a) of section 8.1 must be replaced with

$$N_t = \phi_{st}(N^s_{t-1}-\bar{n}_{t-1}) + n^s_t . \tag{3b}$$

Strictly speaking, the function ϕ_{st} should now be altered, to reflect the fact that the collective decision on the part of sellers to remain in the pool should now depend on the history of unconsummated contacts $(n_t-\bar{n}_t)$. That is, an additional argument, as well as the (unchanged) arguments p_t-p_{t-1}, and μ_t^s, should appear in ϕ_{st}. We will assume, however, to highlight the contrast with buyers, that sellers are indifferent to such failures in their decision to stay on the market.

Let us return then to Period 0, with the initial shock provided by the decrease in available finance. As of Period 0, there are no directly consequential pressures on price. However it follows from the arguments given above, that in the following period, there will be more sellers than buyers at the unchanged price p_E. That is $N_1^s > N_1^d$, as indicated on the vertical axis of Figure 8.1. In this sense, the initial gap EK between n^s and the "effective" demand curve DCE'KM provides a clue as to the depressant effect on price of our initial financial shock.

However, the interpretation of the latter curve as a new effective flow demand does not extend to consideration of new equilibrium positions. Note first that, if * denotes a presumed stationary solution, we cannot have $\bar{n}^* < \frac{M}{p^*}$. For this would correspond to an unconstrained system as in section 8.1. Assuming that the equilibrium is unique in the latter case, this rules out the above contingency. We must therefore have $\bar{n}^* = \frac{M}{p^*}$. Consider, then, the following equations, which will define any new stationary solution:

(15) (i) $N^{d*} = N^{s*}$,

(ii) $N^{d*} = \phi_d(0,\mu_d^*)(N^{d*}-n^*) + n^{d*}$,

(iii) $N^{s*} = \phi_s(0,\mu_s^*)(N^{s*}-\bar{n}^*) + n^{s*}$,

(iv) $\bar{n}^* p^* = M$,

(v) $n^* = h(0)N^*$,

(vi) $\mu_d^* = 1 + \left(\frac{N^{d*} - n^*}{N^{d*}}\right)\mu_d^*$,

(vii) $\mu_s^* = 1 + \left(\frac{N^{d*} - n^*}{N^{s*}}\right)\mu_s^*$.

Combining (ii) and (vi), it follows that $\mu_d^* = \frac{N^{d*}}{n^{d*}}$, and similarly $\mu_s^* = \frac{N^{s*}}{n^{s*}}$. We can now reduce 15(i) to (vii) to the two equations:

(16) $N^* = \phi_d\left(0, \frac{N^*}{n^{d*}}\right)(1-h(0))N^* + n^{d*}$

(17) $N^* = \phi_s\left(0, \frac{N^*}{n^{s*}}\right)\left(N^* - \frac{M}{p^*}\right) + n^{s*}$.

Bearing in mind that $n^{d*} = n^{d*}(p^*)$ and $n^{s*} = n^{s*}(p^*)$, these two equations define any equilibrium in terms of N^* and p^*. By considering the slope of (16) and (17) in the N-p plane, one can show that along (16), $\frac{dN^*}{dp^*} < 0$. And provided that $N^* \geq \frac{M}{p^*}$, which is certainly a sensible requirement for a stationary solution, $\frac{dN^*}{dp^*} > 0$ along (17) in such a region. It follows that if a stationary solution exists, it must be unique.

Particular interest attaches to the question of whether E' of Figure 8.1 can constitute a new equilibrium. This point is characterised by $n^s(p) = \frac{M}{p}$, defining $p_{E'}$. It accordingly satisfies equation (17) only if either (i) $\phi_s\left(0, \frac{N_{E'}}{n_{E'}^s}\right) = 1$ or (ii) $N_{E'} = n_{E'}^s$ and $\phi_s\left(0, \frac{N_{E'}}{n_{E'}^s}\right) = 0$. Only case (i) is sensible. The equation

$$\phi_s\left(0, \frac{N_{E'}}{n_{E'}^s}\right) = 1 \text{ , with the condition } n_{E'}^s = \frac{M}{p_{E'}} ,$$

defines $N_{E'} = N_{E'}(M)$, $p_{E'} = p_{E'}(M)$.

Substituting these values into equation (16) yields an <u>independent</u> condition that E' must satisfy if it is to constitute a stationary solution. Evidently there will in general be at most one value of M for which this condition is satisfied. Thus in general, i.e. for an arbitrary M, the point E' cannot be a stationary solution.

Let us now turn to the dynamics of disequilibrium adjustment. Even if $\phi_{d2} = \phi_{s2}$, as in section 8.2, it is no longer possible to cast our price dynamics in terms of the difference $N_t^d - N_t^s$, since the transactions quantity relevant for N_t^d, namely n_t, is different from that apposite to N_t^s, namely $\bar{n}_t$. In Bowden [1978] we resorted to a simulation study in the hope that this would yield some insight into possible dynamics. Given a constant flow of funds (contingency (a) above) we found that a well-defined limit cycle emerged after quite a short time. This limit cycle did not include the point E' of figure 8.1. One of the interesting features of the cycle was that the price fluctuations set up by credit rationing may depress supply to the point where not all of the available credit is needed. The system does not, therefore automatically move along the financing constraint or frontier M = np (see figure 8.1). The cyclical behaviour imposed by credit rationing contrasted with the unconstrained model which, for the chosen parameter combination, showed a steady convergence to the unique equilibrium point E. Thus the imposition of credit rationing, perhaps to control a situation where the equilibrium price is regarded as too high, can hardly be regarded as a stabilising device.

(b) <u>Backlogging of Funds</u>

Let us now substitute equation (13b) with (14) for equation (13a), to allow for the possibility that funds not used in any period may be backlogged. The comparative statics of stationary states are the same as those of case (a) above, where no backlogging occurs. For if a stationary state were to occur, it would follow from equation (14) above that $M^* = M$, the constant of the previous analysis.

A dynamic simulation on a similar basis for that in case (a) was reported in Bowden [1978]. Once again, price and transacted quantities oscillated, and the amplitude of oscillation in price, at least, was very little different from that where no backlogging is permitted. However, no limit cycle, in the exact sense, appeared to exist. Instead the dynamics consisted of a series of oscillations, each of which folded back on itself in the n-p plane, of roughly similar shape. It may be that a true limit cycle does exist, but if so would take a very long time indeed to emerge.

We have tried in this section to build a model of market dynamics under a finance constraint which while undoubtedly polar in nature and abstract in the sense that it might be applicable to a wide range of particular markets, is hopefully reasonably realistic in its description of the behaviour of participants. Naturally, there have been implicit comparisons and contrasts with existing models of market clearing. We single out two:

(a) The first is between our model of credit rationing and the case where interest rates rise quickly to preserve equality between the demand and supply for funds. The polar case is where interest rate adjustment is instantaneous, by a tatonnement process within one of our single periods. In this case we can write our flow demand function as $n^d = n^d(p,r)$, to reflect the fact that higher interest rates will affect decisions to enter the pool. Moreover ϕ_s and ϕ_d will also depend on r, in the sense that the interest-rate tatonnement is supposed to take place jointly with the formation of the ruling price. Assume now a lowering of the available funds for transactions. By replacing the rationing device by the rate of interest as a pricing device, the result is to create a stable equilibrium, in the sense that no limit cycle will in general emerge. This stable equilibrium will now coincide with the point E' of Figure 8.1, at which point $n^d(p,r)$, evaluated at the new equilibrium interest rate, will intersect the flow supply curve, $n^s(p)$, assumed unchanged. In this sense, interest rate flexibility, as a pricing device, can do what credit rationing cannot.

(b) Our second comparison is with the case where market behaviour is assumed to follow more standard concepts of demand and supply. Thus suppose $h(0) = 1$ and $\phi_s \equiv \phi_d \equiv 0$, so that pure flow concepts are applicable. The system (without backlogging of funds) is then

$$n_t = \min(n_t^d, n_t^s) ,$$

$$\bar{n}_t = \min(n_t, \frac{M}{p_t}) .$$

Suppose we start from the point E of full equilibrium in Figure 8.1. M is now lowered as in the previous experiment. The new quasi-equilibrium is now at point K. For in the absence of backlogging of any kind, there are no pressures on price. Moreover, if the system starts at any other point, price adjustment will follow classical rules and come to rest at p_E. Equilibrium transactions are solely determined by the rationing constraint and price gets stuck at p_E. Intuitively, such a separation of price and quantity adjustments seems a little implausible.

If we regard the matter as one of judging the relative efficacy of a price mechanism or a rationing mechanism for the use of funds, the conclusions of this section are fairly clear-cut. In the model we have used, rationing is responsible for providing a wrong signal to sellers as to the state of effective demand. If the cost of funds rises, the price which buyers are willing to bid falls, and sellers will be faced with longer periods without a contact, inducing them to lower their reservation prices directly. But if the price of funds is held constant, so that rationing becomes necessary, there is no such direct signal. The failure of a buyer to find the necessary finance may be seen by the seller only as a reflection on the buyer's credit-worthiness. So far as the seller is concerned, there is no direct incentive to lower his price, for the existing price has been seen to attract attention. Only when frustrated buyers exit, does the more indirect force of the growing relative number of sellers to buyers start to make itself felt.

8.4 Applications

The original motivation for the model of market clearing outlined in the preceding sections arose from observation of the market for existing houses. We have just remarked on one implication of the clearing model, that the proximal manifestation of tighter finance is a decline in transactions, while prices do not immediately fall. What happens to prices will depend upon the precise formulation of the exit functions (ϕ) and the entry functions (n^d and n^s) to the pool of those actively wishing to buy or sell houses. A leading possibility with respect to this market is that these crucial functions depend upon longer-term "expected prices" as well as those currently ruling. Faced with a shortage of effective offers, sellers may be reluctant to lower their prices to below these long-term impressions and may simply leave the market. Combining this with our previous observations about the impact of credit rationing, the model is clearly capable of explaining some of the phenomena observed in the empirical work of chapter 7, in particular the observed flexibility of transactions but the stickiness downward of prices, in times when finance becomes binding.

Although the clearing model was designed with goods or assets in mind, it was subsequently realised that the basic model of sections 8.1 and 8.2 might offer a convenient representation of the microdynamics of the labour market. The clue lies in the distinction made in the construction of the model between "spectators" and "active agents". In labour market terms this distinction is embodied in official unemployment statistics which typically define the unemployed as those actively seeking work during or just before the survey period. A great volume of recent empirical work is concerned with the problem of discouraged workers, defined as potential workers who are not looking for work because they think that jobs are not available. Such a "reserve army" constitute the so-called "hidden unemployed" and the numbers may according to some studies be substantial [for U.S. data see e.g. studies by A. Tella (1965), T. Dernburg and K. Strand (1966) and W.G. Bowen and T.A. Finegan (1969)].

Defining the active labour force L^f as those either employed or actively seeking work, estimates of the number of hidden unemployed of a given type of worker may be derived from equations explaining the participation rate $\frac{L^f}{P}$, where P is the total population of the workers in question. Such an equation may be derived by an appropriate reinterpretation of the clearing model discussed in this chapter. We redefine the active pool of sellers (hitherto N^s) as U the number of those actively seeking work, according to conventional statistical criteria. The average age of the pool (μ^s) can then be taken as a prime determinant of the participation rate, and one can build an explanatory equation for participation rates in the context of a complete model of labour market dynamics.

Let us be more specific. We start by reinterpreting equation (3a) of section 8.1. As indicated above we write U instead of N^s and to expedite discussion we shall now write the system in terms of continuous time. Accordingly, the analogy of equation (3a) is:

$$\dot{U} = \phi_s U - n + ne + q \ . \tag{18}$$

Here the dot denotes the time derivative. The transacted quantities are now defined as the engagement rate n, i.e. the rate of uptakes into the employed. Corresponding to the flow supply n^s we introduce ne, the flow of entrants to the unemployed pool who have not been in employment in the previous instant, and q, the flow of quits, sackings and retrenchments from existing employment. As before, the term $\phi_s U$ indicates those already in the pool searching for work who elect to remain inside the pool.[8]

Turning now to those actually employed (denoted E) we must have

(19) $\dot{E} = n - q - re$,

where now re is retirements from employment. We shall assume that $re = rE$, where r is a function of time and possibly other current variables. Thus engagements are n , separations are q + re . Combining (18) and (19), we have an equation for the time-derivative of the labour force L^f :

(20) $\dot{L}^f = \dot{U} + \dot{E} = \phi_s U + ne - re$.

To complete the model we need an equation for the demand for labour (corresponding to N^d), which in the present context will be cast in terms of vacancies. We need also a market clearing equation, which will specify uptakes n in terms of the pool of employed (U) and the pool of vacancies (V), the analogue of the clearing equation (4) of section 8.1. For our present task of deriving a participation rate equation we shall merely assume that these relationships have been postulated without actually specifying them.

We must now extend the model to take account of what happens outside the pool of active searchers or those employed, i.e. in respect of the "spectators". We may write

(21) $U + E + R = P$,

where P is the total population of the workers in question. The residual R is the number of "spectators", plus the number of those in permanent retirement. (We could break down R further into its constituent parts.) The rate of increase $\dot{P}$ of the population in question we shall take as exogenous to the model. So given $\dot{U}$, $\dot{E}$ and now $\dot{P}$, the growth of the residual $\dot{R}$ is specified in terms of the additive decomposition (21). We have

$$\dot{R} = \dot{P} - \dot{L}^f = \dot{P} - \phi_s U - ne + re \quad . \tag{22}$$

We assume that $ne = \varepsilon R$ determines entry from the inactive force R into the pool of those actively seeking work. The function ε will depend upon the age structure of the population as a whole. It will also depend upon the value of current variables such as the unemployment rate (negatively) and the number of vacancies (positively).

We are now in a position to obtain the desired participation rate equation. Define $\pi = \frac{\dot{P}}{P}$ as the growth rate for the population of workers in question. Then

$$\dot{\left(\frac{L^f}{P}\right)} = \frac{\dot{L}^f}{P} - \pi\frac{L^f}{P}$$

$$= \phi_s\frac{U}{P} + \varepsilon\frac{R}{P} - r\frac{E}{P} - \pi\frac{L^f}{P} \quad .$$

This can alternatively be expressed

$$\dot{\left(\frac{L^f}{P}\right)} = -(\pi + r + \varepsilon)\frac{L^f}{P} + \varepsilon + (\phi_s + r)\frac{U}{P} \quad , \tag{23}$$

i.e. as a first-order differential equation in the participation rate $\frac{L^f}{P}$. It will of course be nonlinear, since its coefficients are themselves functions of variables currently determined in conjunction with the rest of the model.

From equation (23) we can see that the determinants of the participation rate are likely to include:

(a) The unemployment rate $\frac{U}{P}$. This enters as such, and also via the entry schedule ε.

(b) The growth rate π of the population of workers in question.

(c) The average or expected duration of unemployment (μ^s) which enters via the function ϕ_s.

(d) The rate of change of wages (via ϕ_s).

(e) Time. Enters especially via the determinants of π and r.

(f) Lagged values of the participation rate (assuming that a discrete approximation of (23) is to be used for estimation).

In addition there will be factors specific to a particular group of workers. Thus the participation rate of so-called "secondary" workers, comprising mainly juveniles and women, will be affected by unemployment among primary workers (the breadwinners), as in the "encouraged worker" hypothesis. The arguments of the entry function ε for such a group would therefore include the unemployment rate for the primary group.

In summary, equation (24) embodies a rich variety of hypotheses about the determinants of the participation rate. As with the housing market, the deployment of an explicit model of market clearing seems a necessary first step in unravelling some of the subtleties of disequilibrium dynamics. As it stands of course the general clearing model is highly nonlinear and observable proxies must be found for some of its unobservable components (such as the "age" of participants in the pool of searchers). We are still therefore a step or two away from its econometric application.

Appendix 8.1

We prove equations (5) and (6) of section 8.1. We consider only buyers; the case of sellers is identical.

Leftovers from Period t-1 trading are $N^d_{t-1} - n_{t-1}$. Let $P^d_{t-1}(\tau)$ be the age distribution of these leftovers; $\tau = 1,2 \ldots$. The number of t-1 leftovers who decide to remain for Period t trading is $\phi_{dt}(N^d_{t-1} - n_{t-1})$. The number of new entrants is n^d_t. The total is N^d_t. Assume that the probability that a buyer is successful is independent of whether he is one of the new entrants or one of the old hands. Then

$$P^d_t(\tau) = \frac{n^d_t}{N^d_t} \qquad \tau = 1 ,$$

$$= \left(\frac{N^d_t - n^d_t}{N^d_t}\right) \times P^d_{t-1}(\tau - 1) \qquad \tau \geq 2 .$$

So

$$\mu_t = \sum_{\tau=1}^{\infty} \tau P^d_t(\tau) = \frac{n^d_t}{N^d_t} + \sum_{\tau=1}^{\infty} \left(\frac{N^d_t - n^d_t}{N^d_t}\right) \tau P^d_{t-1}(\tau - 1) .$$

Since $\mu_{t-1} = \sum_{\tau=1}^{\infty} \tau P^d_{t-1}(\tau)$, by writing $s = \tau - 1$ we obtain

$$\mu_t = \frac{n^d_t}{N^d_t} + \sum_{s=1}^{\infty} \left(\frac{N^d_t - n^d_t}{N^d_t}\right) (1 - s) P^d_{t-1}(s) ,$$

which reduces to equation (5) of the text.

Footnotes to Chapter 8

[1]This chapter draws heavily on Bowden [1978]. I am grateful to the editor of *Journal of Monetary Economics* for permission to reproduce material from this paper.

[2]Note that the assumption that this is stable may under many circumstances be questionable. For example, the world at large will include those who have just emerged from the pool of searchers, and their recent experience will affect their decision to re-enter. One would certainly require a large population of holders ("reservation stock demand") relative to the size of the pool for the presumption of stability. Section 8.4 may be useful here.

[3]This adjustment function might be taken to depend also upon the age difference between potential buyers and sellers (see below). Such a hypothesis could be justified from the probabilistic nature of price determination. First, it is true that for any given distribution of asking prices on the part of sellers, and reservation prices on the part of buyers, the transactions price distribution will move upwards if $N^d_{t-1} > N^s_{t-1}$, as (1) suggests, as a matter of the natural selection of successful agents. But secondly we have to consider the distance between the buyers' and sellers' distribution as another determinant of transacted prices. Presumably, the longer a seller has been in the market, the lower is his asking price; and for a buyer, the higher is his reservation price. We might therefore proxy the distance referred to by the difference between the average age of buyers and sellers. Thus a more general price adjustment mechanism might be:

$$p_t - p_{t-1} = g(N^d_{t-1} - N^s_{t-1}, \mu^d_{t-1} - \mu^s_{t-1}), \qquad g_1 > 0,\ g_2 > 0,$$

which could be appropriately linearised. I am grateful to Dwight Jaffee for pointing out a possible role for the age of participants in this respect.

[4]More precisely, consider the destinations of the N* currently in the pool. We can write

$$\underset{}{N^*} = \underset{\text{(contracts)}}{n^*} + \underset{\text{(frustrated exits)}}{(1-\phi^*)(N^*-n^*)} + \underset{\text{(spillovers to next period's trading)}}{\phi^*(N^*-n^*)} .$$

Likewise we can write the sources of N* as:

$$N^* = \underset{\text{(new entrants)}}{\eta^*} + \underset{\text{(last period's spillovers)}}{\phi^*(N^*-n^*)} .$$

Equation of sources and sinks yields the required relationship.

[5]Issued as Research Memorandum No. 96 [1975], Institute for Advanced Studies, Stumpergasse 56, A-1010 Vienna, Austria.

[6]In the present notation, the following four conditions are necessary and sufficient for stability:

(i) $F(1) > 0$

(ii) $F(-1) < 0$

(iii) $|a_0| < 1$

(iv) $a_0^2 - 1 < a_0 a_2 - a_1$.

[7]In assuming credit rationing to take this form, we are supposing that the probability of any particular buyer obtaining finance is independent of any of his other characteristics such as his search history. More generally the representation of credit rationing must depend on a specific theory of such, and we refer the reader on this question to D.M. Jaffee and F. Modigliani [1969] and the references cited therein. The approach of this paper does not appear to be incompatible with such previous work, although this is really a matter for substantive research. We note also that the effect of credit rationing in a dynamic context - specifically macrodynamics - has also been investigated by D. Tucker [1968].

[8]In continuous time it might be more transparent to write

$$\dot{U} = -\varphi U - n + ne + q ,$$

where $-\varphi$ denotes the propensity to exit from the pool of unemployed. That is, exits are comprised of discouraged workers and engagements while additions comprise new entrants (ne) to the labour force and quits, fires etc. from those previously employed. Define now $\phi_s = -\varphi$ and interpret ϕ_s as the propensity to remain. In continuous time it does not follow that $0 \leq \phi_s \leq 1$.

CONCLUSION

The progress of new areas in a discipline, like the development of towns, is typically concentrated along the lines representing its closest links with settled areas of thought. It seems natural as a first step in relaxing equilibrium models to employ Walrasian price dynamics; and to suppose that if transacted quantities are not to be identified with the intersection of Marshallian demand and supply curves, they may nevertheless be located along one of these schedules as in the "short-side" models. The PAMEQ specification employed in this study is in this tradition, unifying and extending the received Walrasian price dynamics. In particular it allows "equilibrium" to be represented as a testable hypothesis. The price adjustment specification bears a close relationship with existing econometric practice in respect of distributed lags. Use of an imputed equilibrium price simplifies the switch between regimes of excess demand and excess supply. This leads to a better understanding of the probabilistic structure of the "short-side" model, and the development of more efficient limited-information methods.

Undoubtedly, however, there is more work to be done along these lines. We have identified some of the outstanding matters of econometric technique at various points throughout the text. Thus it would be desirable to improve our understanding of the identification both of the excess demand model (where lagged prices occur among the predetermined variables) and in the short-side problem. The estimation theory of the PAMEQ specification for general distributed lag adjustment mechanisms remains to be developed.

In the context of the short-side model, the existence of a consistent estimator for the noisy-clearing case is still not fully resolved. Finally the effects of postulating serially-correlated residuals in both excess-demand and short-side models also warrants further investigation.

We believe, however, that the major tasks lie in other dimensions of the problem. Foremost among these must be the question of quantity dynamics. Especially in chapters 6 and 8 we have raised some of the problems involved; the definition of what constitutes a market, the representation of imperfect information, and in a multimarket context, the existence and effects of constraints in one market upon actions in another. What is needed is a reasonably simple and robust specification for the movements of transacted quantities, and the relationship of these to the behavioural schedules of the agents concerned. Preferably this should allow the "parametisation" of equilibrium, in the sense referred to in connection with the PAMEQ specification for prices. It may be, on the other hand, that no such general representation exists so that each particular application must be treated on its own merits. Or it may be that the Marshallian scissors have outlived their usefulness. Whatever the answer, the art of the econometrician will stand revealed in his approach to the problems of specification quite as much as in his solution to the resulting problems of estimation and inference.

REFERENCES

Aigner, D.J. and A.S. Goldberger (eds) *Latent Variables in Socio-Economic Models.* North-Holland, Amsterdam, 1977.

Allen, R.G.D. *Macroeconomic Theory: A Mathematical Treatment.* Macmillan, London, 1967.

Amemiya, T. "Regression Analysis when the Dependent Variable is Truncated Normal", *Econometrica* Vol. 41 No. 6 (November 1973), 997-1016.

________. "The Nonlinear Two-Stage Least-Squares Estimator", *Journal of Econometrics* Vol. 2 (1974), 105-110.

________. "A Note on a Fair and Jaffee Model", *Econometrica* Vol. 42 (1974), 759-762.

Anderson, T.W. *An Introduction to Multivariate Statistical Analysis.* John Wiley and Sons Inc., New York, 1958.

Ando, A. "Some Aspects of Stabilization Policies, the Monetarist Controversy and the MPS Model", *International Economic Review* Vol. 15 (1974), 541-571.

Basmann, R. "A Generalized Classical Method of Linear Estimation of Coefficients in a Structural Equation", *Econometrica* Vol. 25 (1957), 77-83.

________. "On the Asymptotic Distribution of Generalized Linear Estimators", *Econometrica* Vol. 28 (1960), 97-107.

Bergstrom, A.R. "A Model of Technical Progress, the Production Function and Cyclical Growth", *Economica* Vol. 29 (November 1962), 357-370.

________. (ed) *Statistical Inference in Continuous Time Econometric Models.* North-Holland (contributions to Economic Analysis series), Amsterdam-Oxford, 1976.

Bergstrom, A.R. and C.R. Wymer. "A Model of Disequilibrium Neo-classical Growth and its Application to the United Kingdom" in Bergstrom (ed) *Statistical Inference in Continuous Time Econometric Models* (q.v.).

Bowden, R.J. "The Theory of Parametric Identification", *Econometrica* Vol. 41 No. 6 (November 1973), 1069-1074.

________. "On Constrained and Unconstrained Models of the Investment Accelerator", *Economic Record* Vol. 50 (1974), 269-277.

________. "Disequilibrium and Speculation in the Housing Market", *Economic Record* Vol. 51 No. 136 (December 1975), 513-521.

________. "On Market Dynamics for a Durable Good, With and Without a Financing Constraint", *Journal of Monetary Economics*

________. "Specification, Estimation and Inference for Models of Markets in Disequilibrium", *International Economic Review*

Bowden, R.J. and D.A. Turkington. "A Comparative Study of Instrumental Variables Estimators for Nonlinear Simultaneous Models." Department of Economics, University of Western Australia, March 1978.

Bowen, W.G. and T.A. Finegan, *The Economics of Labour Force Participation.* Princeton University Press, Princeton N.J., 1969.

Brundy, J.M. and D.W. Jorgenson. "The Relative Efficiency of Instrumental Variables Estimators of Systems of Simultaneous Equations", *Annals of Economic and Social Measurement* Vol. 3 No. 4 (October 1974), 679-700.

Bury, K.V. *Statistical Models in Applied Science.* J. Wiley and Sons, New York, 1975.

Byron, R.P. "Efficient Estimation and Inference for Large Econometric Systems", *Econometrica* Vol. 45 No. 6 (September 1977), 1499-1515.

Cannon, M. *Who's Master? Who's Man? : Australia in the Victorian Age.* Thomas Nelson (Australia) Ltd, Melbourne, 1971.

Clower, R.W. "The Keynesian Counter-Revolution: A Theoretical Appraisal" in *The Theory of Interest Rates* (ed) F.H. Hahn and F. Brechling, IEA/Macmillan, London, 1965.

Cox, D.R. and H.D. Miller. *The Theory of Stochastic Processes.* Methuen and Co., London, 1965.

Davidon, W.C. "A Variable Metric Method for Minimization", A.E.C. Research and Development Report ANL-5990 (revised), 1959.

Dernburg, T. and K. Strand. "Hidden Unemployment 1953-62: A Quantitative Analysis by Age and Sex", *American Economic Review* Vol. 56 (March 1966), 71-95.

Dixon, L.C.W. *Nonlinear Optimisation.* E.U.P. London, 1972.

Dhrymes, P.J. *Econometrics: Statistical Foundations and Application.* Harper and Row, New York, 1970.

Edgerton, D.L. "Some Properties of Two Stage Least Squares as Applied to Nonlinear Models", *International Economic Review* Vol. 13 (1972), 26-32.

Eckstein, O. and G. Fromm. "The Price Equation", *American Economic Review* Vol. LVIII (1968), 1159-1183.

Fair, R.C. *A Short-Run Forecasting Model of the United States Economy.* D.C. Heath & Co., Lexington, Mass., 1971.

Fair, R.C. and D.M. Jaffee. "Methods of Estimation for Markets in Disequilibrium", *Econometrica* Vol. 40 (1972), 497-514.

Fair, R.C. and H.H. Kelejian. "Methods of Estimation for Markets in Disequilibrium - A Further Study", *Econometrica* Vol. 42 (1974), 177-190.

Fisher, F.M. *The Identification Problem in Econometrics.* McGraw-Hill, New York, 1966.

Fletcher, R. and M.J.D. Powell. "A Rapidly Convergent Descent Method for Minimization", *Computer Journal* Vol. 6 (1963), 163-168.

Fletcher, R. and C.M. Reeves. "Function Minimisation by Conjugate Gradients", *Computer Journal* Vol. 7 (1964), 149-154.

Friedman, M. "The Quantity Theory of Money - A Restatement", *Studies in the Quantity Theory of Money* (ed) M. Friedman, Chicago University Press, Chicago, 1956.

Friedman, M. and A. Schwartz. *A Monetary History of the United States 1867-1960.* Princeton University Press (for N.B.E.R.), Princeton N.J., 1963.

Gibson, W.E. "Demand and Supply Functions for Money in the United States: Theory and Measurement", *Econometrica* Vol. 40 No. 2 (March 1972), 361-369.

________. "Demand and Supply Functions for Money: A Comment", *Econometrica* Vol. 44 No. 2 (March 1976), 387-389.

Goldberger, A.S. *Econometric Theory.* J. Wiley, New York, 1964.

________. "Maximum-Likelihood Estimation of Regressions Containing Unobservable Independent Variables", *International Economic Review* Vol. 13 No. 1 (1972), 1-15. (Reprinted in D.J. Aigner and A.S. Goldberger (1977).)

Goldfeld, S.M., R.E. Quandt and H.F. Trotter. "Maximisation by Quadratic Hill Climbing", *Econometrica* Vol. 34 (1966), 541-551.

________. "Minimisation by Improved Quadratic Hill Climbing and Other Methods", Princeton University, E.R.P. Research Memo No. 95 (1968).

Goldfeld, S.M. and R.E. Quandt. "Nonlinear Simultaneous Equations" Estimation and Prediction", *International Economic Review* Vol. 9 (1968), 113-136.

________. *Nonlinear Methods in Econometrics.* North-Holland, Amsterdam, 1972.

________. "Estimation in a Disequilibrium Model and the Value of Information", *Journal of Econometrics* Vol. 3 (November 1975), 325-348.

Gramley, L. and S.B. Chase. "Time Deposits in Monetary Analysis", *Federal Reserve Bulletin*, October 1965, 1380-1406.

Grossman, H.I. "Money, Interest and Prices in Market Disequilibrium", *Journal of Political Economy*, Vol. 79 (1971), 943-961.

________. "A Choice-Theoretic Model of an Income-Investment Accelerator", *American Economic Review* Vol. LXII (1972), 630-641.

________. "The Nature of Quantities in Market Disequilibrium", *American Economic Review* Vol. LXIV (1974), 509-514.

Gurley, J.G. and E.S. Shaw. *Money in a Theory of Finance.* The Brookings Institution, Washington D.C., 1960.

Hartley, M.J. and P. Mallela. "The Asymptotic Properties of a Maximum-Likelihood Estimate for a Model of Markets in Disequilibrium", *Econometrica* Vol. 45 No. 5 (July 1977), 1205-1220.

Heathfield, D.F. and I.F. Pearce. "A View of the Southhampton Econometric Model of the U.K. and its Trading Partners" in *Modelling The Economy* (ed) G.A. Renton, Heinemann Educational Books for the (U.K.) S.S.R.C., London, 1975.

Hicks, J.R. "Mr. Keynes and the 'Classics': A Suggested Interpretation", *Econometrica* Vol. 5 (1937), 147-159.

Hines, A.G. "The Determinants of the Rate of Change of Money Wages and the Effectiveness of Incomes Policy" in *The Current Inflation* (ed) H.G. Johnson and A.R. Nobay, Macmillan: St. Martin's Press, London and Besingstoke, 1971.

Hosmer, D.W. Jr. "On M.L.E. of the Parameters of a Mixture of Two Normal Distributions When the Sample is Small", *Communications in Statistics* Vol. 1 (1973), 217-227.

Howard, D.H. "Rationing, Quantity Constraints and Consumption Theory", *Econometrica* Vol. 45 No. 2 (March 1977), 399-412.

Hunt, B.F. and M.R. Upcher. "Generalized Adjustment of Asset Equations." Working Paper No. 48, Faculty of Economics and Research School of Social Sciences, Australian National University, September 1977.

Jaffee, D.M. "An Econometric Model of the Mortgage Market", in *Savings Deposits, Mortgages and Housing: Studies for the Federal Reserve-MIT-Penn Economic Model* (ed) E.M. Gramlich and D.M. Jaffee. Lexington Books, D.C. Heath & Co., Lexington Mass., 1972.

Jaffee, D.M. *Credit Rationing and the Commercial Loan Market.* J. Wiley & Sons Inc., New York, 1971.

Jaffee, D.M. and F. Modigliani. "A Theory and Test of Credit Rationing", *American Economic Review* Vol. 59 No. 4 (December 1969), 850-872.

Jennrich, R.I. "Asymptotic Properties of Non-linear Least Squares Estimators", *Annals of Math. Statistics* Vol. 40 (1969), 633-643.

Johnston, J. *Econometric Methods.* 2nd edition, McGraw-Hill, N.J., 1972.

Jorgenson, D.W. "Anticipations and Investment Behaviour" in *The Brookings Quarterly Econometric Model of the United States* (ed) J.S. Duesenberry *et al*, Rand McNally & Co., Chicago, 1965.

Jorgenson, D.W. and J.J. Laffont. "Efficient Estimation of Nonlinear Simultaneous Equations with Additive Disturbances", *Annals of Economic and Social Measurement* Vol. 3 No. 4 (October 1974), 615-640.

Jury, E.I. *Theory and Application of the z-Transform Method.* J. Wiley & Sons Inc., New York, 1964.

Kalchbrenner, J.H. "A Model of the Housing Sector" in *Savings Deposits, Mortgages and Housing; Studies for the Federal Reserve - MIT - Penn Economic Model.* Lexington, D.C. Heath & Co., Lexington Mass., 1972.

Kaldor, N. "The New Monetarism", *Lloyd's Bank Review,* July 1970, 1-17.

Kalman, R.E. "A New Approach to Linear Filtering and Prediction Problems", *Journal of Basic Engineering* A.S.M.E., Vol. 82 (1960), 35-49.

Kalman, R.E. and A.S. Bucy, "New Results in Linear Filtering and Prediction Theory", *Journal of Basic Engineering* Vol. 83 (1961), 95-107.

Kaplan, A.D.N., J.B. Dirlam and R.F. Lanzilotti. *Pricing in Big Business - A Case Approach.* Brookings Institution, 1958.

Kelejian, H. "Two-stage Least Squares and Econometric Systems Linear in Parameters but Nonlinear in the Endogenous Variables", *Journal of the American Statistical Association* Vol. 66 No. 334 (June 1971), 373-374.

Kiefer, J. and J. Wolfowitz. "Consistency of the Maximum Likelihood Estimator in the Presence of Infinitely Many Incidental Parameters", *Annals of Math. Statistics* Vol. 27 (1956), 887-906.

Koopmans, T.C.(ed). *Statistical Inference in Dynamic Economic Models.* J. Wiley & Sons Inc., New York, 1950.

Kowalik, J. and M.R. Osborne. *Methods for Unconstrained Optimisation Problems.* American Elsevier, New York, 1968.

Kullback, S. *Information Theory and Statistics.* J. Wiley & Sons Inc., New York, 1959.

Laffont, J.J. and R. Garcia. "Disequilibrium Econometrics for Business Loans", *Econometrica* Vol. 45 No. 5 (July 1977), 1187-1204.

Laidler, D. and Parkin, M. "The Demand for Money in the U.K. 1956-1967: Preliminary Estimates", *Manchester School* Vol. 37 No. 3 (September 1970), 187-208.

Lee, Lung-Fei. "Identification and Estimation in Binary Choice Models with Limited Dependent Variables", Department of Economics, University of Minnesota, April 1977.

Leijonhufvud, A. *On Keynesian Economics and the Economics of Keynes.* Oxford University Press, New York, 1968.

Lipsey, R.G. "The Relation Between Unemployment and the Rate of Change of Money Wage Rates in the United Kingdom 1882-1957: A Further Study", *Econometrica,* Vol. 27 (1960),

Loève, M. *Probability Theory.* D. Van Nostrand, Princeton, 1955.

Maddala, G.S. and F.D. Nelson, "Maximum-likelihood Methods for Models of Markets in Disequilibrium", *Econometrica* Vol. 42 (1974), 1013-1030.

Malinvaud, E. *Statistical Methods of Econometrics.* 2nd ed, North Holland.

Patinkin, D. *Money, Interest and Prices.* 2nd ed, Harper and Row, New York, 1965.

Phelps, E. *Microeconomic Foundations of Employment and Inflation Theory.* Norton, New York, 1970.

Phillips, A.W. "A Simple Model of Employment, Money and Prices in a Growing Economy", *Econometrica* Vol. 28 (November 1961), 360-370.

Pollak, R. "Conditional Demand Functions and Consumption Theory", *Quarterly Journal of Economics* Vol. 83 (1969), 60-78.

Robinson, P.M. "Identification, Estimation and Large-Sample Theory for Regression Containing Unobservable Variables." *International Economic Review* Vol. 15 No. 3 (October 1974), 680-692. (Reprinted in D.J. Aigner and A.S. Goldberger (1977.)

Rothenburg, T.J. and C.T. Leenders. "Efficient Estimation of Simultaneous Equation Systems", *Econometrica* Vol. 32 (1974), 57-76.

Rothschild, M. "Models of Market Organisation with Imperfect Information: A Survey", *Journal of Political Economy* Vol. 81 No. 6 (November/December 1973), 1283-1308.

Samuelson, P. *Foundations of Economic Analysis.* Harvard University Press, 1947.

Smith, W.L. "A Neo-Keynesian View of Monetary Policy" in *Controlling Monetary Aggregates*, Federal Reserve Bank of Boston, Boston, 1969.

Stein, J.L. *Money and Capacity Growth.* Columbia University Press, New York, 1971.

Suits, D. "An Econometric Model of the Watermelon Market", *Journal of Farm Economics* Vol. 37 (1955), 237-251.

Swamy, P.A.V.B. and J.S. Mehta. "Bayesian and Non-Bayesian Analysis of Switching Regressions and of Random Coefficient Regression Models", *Journal of the American Statistical Association* Vol. 70 No. 351 (September 1975), 593-602.

Teicher, H. "Identifiability of Mixtures", *Annals of Math. Statistics* Vol. 32, 244-248.

________. "Identifiability of Finite Mixtures", *Annals of Math. Statistics* Vol. 34, 1265-1269.

Teigen, R.L. "Demand and Supply Functions for Money in the U.S." *Econometrica* Vol. 32 No. 4 (October 1964), 476-509.

________. "Demand and Supply Functions for Money: Another Look at Theory and Measurement", *Econometrica* Vol. 44 No. 2 (March 1976), 377-385.

Tella, A. "Labour Force Sensitivity to Employment by Age, Sex", *Industrial Relations* Vol. 4 No. 2 (February 1965), 69-83.

Theil, H. *Economic Forecasts and Policy*. 2nd ed, North-Holland, Amsterdam, 1961.

________. *Principles of Econometrics*. J. Wiley & Sons Inc., New York and North-Holland, Amsterdam-London, 1971.

Tinbergen, J. *Statistical Testing of Business Cycle Theories. Vol. 1: A Method and its Application to Investment Activity*. League of Nations, Geneva, 1939.

Tintner, G. *Econometrics*. J. Wiley & Sons Inc., New York and London, 1963.

Tobin, J. "Estimation of Relationships for Limited Dependent Variables", *Econometrica* Vol. 26 (1958), 24-36.

________. "Commercial Banks as Creators of 'Money'" in *Banking and Monetary Studies* (ed) D. Carson, R.D. Irwin, Homewood, Illinois, 1963.

Tucker, D. "Credit Rationing, Interest Rate Lags, and Monetary Policy Speed", *Quarterly Journal of Economics* Vol. LXXXII (1968), 54-84.

Valentine, T.J. "Adjustments in Employment, Overtime and Inventory Investment in the Australian Economy", *Economic Record* Vol. 51 No. 134 (June 1975), 232-241.

Van Doorn, J. *Disequilibrium Economics*. Macmillan, London, 1975.

Wald, A. "Note on the Consistency of the Maximum Likelihood Estimate", *Annals of Math. Statistics* Vol. 20 (1943), 595-601.

Whittle, P. *Probability*. Penguin Library of University Mathematics, Harmondsworth, Middlesex, 1970.

Yakowitz, S.J. and J.D. Spragin. "On the Identifiability of Finite Mixtures", *Annals of Math. Statistics* Vol. 39 (1968), 209-214.

Zellner, A. "Estimation of Regression Relationships Containing Unobservable Independent Variables", *International Economic Review* Vol. 11 (1970), 441-654. (Reprinted in D.J. Aigner and A.S. Goldberger (1977).)

INDEX